# The New Terrorism

Stefan Goertz • Alexander E. Streitparth

# The New Terrorism

Actors, Strategies and Tactics

 Springer

Stefan Goertz
Bundespolizei
Hochschule des Bundes
Lübeck, Germany

Alexander E. Streitparth
Bundeswehr
Zentrum Operative Kommunikation
Mayen, Germany

ISBN 978-3-030-14591-0          ISBN 978-3-030-14592-7    (eBook)
https://doi.org/10.1007/978-3-030-14592-7

Library of Congress Control Number: 2019934102

This Springer imprint is published by the registered company Springer Nature Switzerland AG
The registered company address is: Gewerbestrasse 11, 6330 Cham, Switzerland

# Contents

# Chapter 1
# Introduction

New terrorism is one of the most dangerous threats to security worldwide. In the last years and months, the interaction, cooperation and in some cases even fusion of Islamist terrorism (Jihadism) and transnational organised crime have reached a new threat, for states of the so-called First World as well as for states of the so-called Second World and Third World.

New terrorism, the international Jihadism of the twenty-first century, poses an asymmetric threat to Western democracies. It recognises neither national nor international boundaries and blurs the frontiers between offensive and defensive behaviour, war and peace, domestic security and foreign policy as well as criminal acts and political offences. This analysis will demonstrate that this new terrorism has taken on both local and international dimensions.

The following examples illustrate—on a qualitative and a quantitative level—what is new about new terrorism: a historically new level of intensity affecting the so-called First World as well as the so-called Second and Third World.

In the period from spring 2015 to 2017, Scotland Yard (the headquarters of the British police force) arrested on average one terrorist suspect every day. Temporarily Scotland Yard investigated more than 500 cases of Islamist terrorism at the same time (Buchsteiner, 2017). In 2016, the antiterror hotline of Scotland Yard received 22,000 calls with relevant information for preventing and investigating Jihadist crimes, twice as many as in 2014 (Buchsteiner, 2017). From 2013 to the Jihadist attack on 22 March 2017, Scotland Yard reportedly prevented no less than 13 Jihadist attacks in Great Britain (Buchsteiner, 2017). The German intelligence authorities for inner security have detected the highest number of Salafists so far: 10,000 reported cases of Salafist extremists in 2017 (Stürmer, 2017). In association with this high number of Salafist extremists is the number of 1600 potential Jihadist offenders (Bewarder & Flade, 2017). The implication of at least 1600 Jihadist potential offenders will be explained in Chap. 5 using selected examples of Islamist lone operators in the new analytical category of low-level terrorism.

In the period from 2014 to 2015, the "Islamic State" (IS) controlled territory the size of Great Britain and was influential in nine states, in Syria, Iraq, Libya,

© Springer Nature Switzerland AG 2019
S. Goertz, A. E. Streitparth, *The New Terrorism*,
https://doi.org/10.1007/978-3-030-14592-7_1

Afghanistan, Pakistan, Egypt, Yemen, Saudi Arabia and West Africa (Burke, 2015: 19). In just one country, Pakistan, 33 different Salafist-Jihadist organisations were detected in the year 2017 (SATP, 2017). Since the summer of 2011, more than 100 Salafist-Jihadist organisations, groups, brigades and units have been fighting in Syria (Lister, 2014). Much more quantitative circumstantial evidence will elaborate on what is new about new terrorism in Chaps. 2–6.

On a qualitative level, what is new about new terrorism will be explained on four levels, ideology (Chap. 2), cooperation of organised crime and terrorism (Chap. 3), the Internet and telecommunication media of the twenty-first century as a crucial means of new terrorism (Chap. 4) and the level strategy and tactics of new terrorism (Chap. 5).

## 1.1   Theory

The proclamation of the "Islamic State" on the territory of Syria and Iraq in June of 2014 led to a sudden awakening in the German scientific field of Islamic studies and partly also in the field of political science, to the fact that the threat of international Jihadism had reached an extraordinary level (Krause, 2017; Said, 2014; Steinberg, 2015). For the first time an Islamist organisation founded an "Islamic State" (Krause, 2017: 15).

Since the proclamation of a contemporary interpretation of a caliphate, political scientists described IS as a "new threat", as "a new terrorist group", but that "new" aspects only describe some levels of what is new about new terrorism (Burke, 2015; Cockburn, 2015; Stern & Berger, 2015; Weiss & Hassan, 2015). Quite appropriate, for example, is the question, whether the "Islamic State", which not only forced 30,000 Iraqi soldiers to a tactical about-turn but also thousands to desert, was still a "terrorist organisation" or already a state with its own armed forces.

Linked to the scientific analysis of the new player "Islamic State" is the search for "the correct" definition of terrorism. Jenkins compared the question of social sciences for the correct definition of terrorism with the Bermuda Triangle: "Definitional debates are the great Bermuda Triangle of terrorism research. I've seen entire conferences go off into definitional debates, never to be heard from again" (Jenkins, in Stampnitzky, 2011: 11). In passing, it can be said that terrorism research is a complex field, investigated from numerous angles: heuristically on a national or international level, from the political science perspective theoretically, in international relations from a sociological point of view, etc.[1]

International social science realised at the end of the twentieth century and at the beginning of the twenty-first century that it is impossible to find a definition of terrorism that meets with universal consensus (Schmid & Jongman, 2005). "The"

---

[1]Dealing with the "correct" definition of terrorism (Andersen, 2011: 259–270; Gärtner, 2008: 234–239; Schmid & Jongman, 2005).

generally accepted definition of terrorism does not exist, because terrorism is not a coherent phenomenon. Moreover, terrorism has to be understood as a strategy of very different players (Goertz, 2017; Tilly, 2004). Apart from that, this analysis understands terrorism as the strategic choice of players who act rationally. "Terrorism can be considered a reasonable way of pursuing extreme interests in the political arena. It is among the many alternatives open to radical organizations" (Crenshaw, 2010). A current diagnosis of the strategy of the "Islamic State" (IS) reveals that IS uses terrorism as one of many tactical means apart from regular military tactics like offensive and defensive actions of military or paramilitary units.

The empirical analysis of Chaps. 2–4 shows that the reflex of social sciences to create a definition with theoretical boundaries fails when dealing with new terrorism. "Old" criteria of social sciences[2] like state versus non-state, terrorism as tactics versus guerilla warfare or rather insurgency do not reflect that the IS as a player of new terrorism is a protostate player (with its own territory) and at the same time a non-state player. It uses the tactics of terrorism (e.g. suicide bombers in countries like Iraq and Syria and also in the Western world) as well as regular combat tactics such as attack and defence using more or less regular units.

To analyse hypotheses dealing with terrorism and Islamist terrorism or Jihadism, respectively, in this book, the terms Islamist terrorism and Jihadism are used synonymously.

Islamist terrorism/Jihadism exists and operates on the level strategy, doctrine and tactics. The non-state players of terrorism use terrorist strategies, doctrines and tactics as long as they are inferior in political, military, technological and financial terms. The players of Islamist terrorism/Jihadism use strategies, doctrines and tactics against the civilian population as well as against state players, to intimidate societies, force governments and rulers to apply political and military means, destabilise regions and states and finally to overthrow the existing political order and replace it by an Islamist caliphate system.

According to Schmid and Jongman (2005), in this analysis Islamist terrorism/Jihadism is based on the following factors:

- Spreading fear and terror
- Violence and force
- Religious-political ideology
- Threat
- Psychological effects and anticipated reactions
- Victim-target differentiation
- Purposeful, systematic, organised acting
- Strategy, tactics, means, method
- Operating outside the law of the land, violation of rules, without humanitarian consideration
- Coercion, extortion

---

[2]For example Andersen (2011: 260).

- Publicity
- Arbitrariness, non-combatants, neutrals as targets and victims
- Intimidation
- Group, movement, organisation as perpetrator
- Symbolic and demonstrative aspects
- Unpredictability, abruptness of violence
- Secrecy
- Repetition, campaigns of violence
- Crime
- Political, financial demands

Hoffman (2006) defines the aims, the logic of terrorism, as follows:

- Drawing public attention
- Forcing a broad audience to acknowledge the political agenda of a terrorist movement or group
- Claiming to be the legitimate representative of that political agenda
- Accumulating the necessary power to influence political, economic, social and religious processes and decisions
- Attaining a monopoly of power over a territory

Obviously Jihadism is linked to Salafism and Islamism which are described as: Islamism is a religious-cum-political ideology with the agenda to change the political system, the social order based on an extremist ideology and to only acknowledge its own interpretation of Islam.

Salafism is a category of Islamism, a particularly fundamentalist Islamist variety that strives for an idealised ancient version of Islam from the seventh and eighth century as an example for a reformation of state and society based on Salafist interpretations of Islamic values and rules. As a result, Salafism appears to be an extremist counterculture to modernity that uses this fencing-off from the majority of the society as a unique elitist stance strengthening its own identity.

The empirical analysis of Chaps. 2–5 shows that new terrorism, its actors, its strategies and tactics cannot be classified in established scientific categories like terrorism, guerilla, small war, insurgency, revolutionary warfare and hybrid warfare by operating in all these categories at the same time.[3] In these chapters analytical categories like insurgency and counterinsurgency will be analysed.

In this analysis organised crime is defined as follows: organised crime is the planned committing of crimes, motivated by profit or power aspirations which are significant when more than two participants collaborate over a longer period.

(a) Using commercial or businesslike structures
(b) With violence or other intimidating means

---

[3]More elaborations on guerilla, small wars, insurgency, revolutionary warfare and hybrid warfare (see Goertz, 2012; Marston & Malkasian, 2008; Moghadam, Berger, & Beliakova, 2014; Rid & Keaney, 2010; Shultz & Dew, 2006; Whiteside, 2016).

(c) Influencing politics, the media, public administration, legal authorities or the economy (Bundeskriminalamt, 2016).

To understand the attribute transnational, this analysis follows the description of the United Nations.

The United Nations Convention Against Transnational Organized Crime describes organised crime as (a) the offence which was committed in more than one state, (b) the offence which was committed in one state but planned in a different state, (c) when the offence was committed in one state but is connected to criminal organisation that is active in more than one state and (d) when the offence was committed in one state but has significant consequences for other states (UN, 2004).

## 1.2   The Empirical Method

The design of this analysis is interdisciplinary, comparative and focuses empirically on what is new about new terrorism. The analytical characteristics of new terrorism are investigated on the following levels:

- Players
- Strategy
- Tactics
- Doctrine
- Means, weapons, methods
- Interaction, cooperation and fusion of players and strategies of organised crime and Jihadism

International Jihadism as a form of new terrorism will be analysed in Chap. 2 with emphasis on its Jihadist ideology. The design of this analysis is mostly political science and depicts the concept of Jihad with reference to its political, strategic and operative consequences. Moreover, the question of the relationship of religion and terrorism, Islam and terrorism, is also covered, since Jihad is a theology (analytical level of religion) as well as a strategy and doctrine. All these parameters shape the centuries-old concept of Jihad. The analysis of the theology, strategy and doctrine of the Jihad of the twentieth and twenty-first century led to the categories "old" and "new" mullahs of Jihad, as expounded in Chap. 2, with reference to international Islamic studies. Empirically the principle mullahs of Jihad are investigated. The design of the new analytical category "the new preachers of Jihad" shows that Jihadist ideology has many more manifestations than Islamist theology. Specifically Jihadist strategy and doctrine lead to tactical results, for example, individual Jihad, which is a form of low-level terrorism for lone Jihadist operators.

The longest empirical chapter, Chap. 3, examines the cooperation, interaction and fusion of transnational organised crime and international Jihadism on various levels of analysis, for example, drug cultivation, transport of drugs and drug trafficking, kidnapping for ransom and other parameters and players. The empirical analysis of players of new terrorism, for example, Ansar Dine, Al-Mourabitoun and Al Qaida in the Islamic Maghreb, illustrates vividly that the parameters of new terrorism are spreading worldwide. These parameters include a decentralised network and cell structure, multiple and heterogeneous financing of organised crime, the political-cum-religious agendas of regionally and internationally operating players and structure of their members. This book uses interdisciplinary expertise from political science, international relations, African studies and area studies of the Middle East to analyse the interaction, cooperation and partial fusion of regional and international players, strategies and tactics of organised crime and international Jihadism. The analysis of chosen players, the Haqqani network, the D-Company and Lashkar-e-Tayyiba, indicates what is new about new terrorism in the form of strategic, tactical and personnel cooperation and hybrid tactics like kidnapping for ransom.

In Chap. 4 the new technological means of the Internet and the telecommunication media of the twenty-first century are analysed as indispensable means or game changers, using political science, sociology and media science. Sentence the fact that a terrorist organisation like Al Qaida has survived for longer than 20 years to the existence of the Internet, whereas terrorist groups generally exist on average for less than 1 year. What is also undisputed is that the "Islamic State" would not have recruited such an immense number of European foreign fighters and supporters for its Jihad in Syria and Iraq and for terrorist attacks in Western countries without the existence of the Internet and social media. The analysis in Chap. 4 starts with strategies and tactics of Jihadist organisations on the Internet and examines the Internet as a Jihadist instrument for propaganda, social networking, communication and tactical control of attacks. Chapter 4 identifies technical formats and medial resources as new means of Jihadism to spread the narrative of "true Muslims/true Islam" propagandistically to radicalise and indoctrinate Muslims worldwide. An additional subject of analysis is the worldwide dissemination of execution videos on websites and via social media in order to transport excessive, archaic violence as Jihadist psychological warfare.

On the level of political science as well as on the level of international relations, the strategies and tactics of the new terrorism will be examined in Chap. 5. This analysis has two levels, the level of international Jihadist organisations such as Al Qaida and the "Islamic State" and lone operators and cells as players of low-level terrorism. Selected Jihadist attacks carried out in Europe in recent years are examined tactically, illustrating a new operative intensity.

The result of this theoretical and empirical research of numerous players of international Jihadism and (regional and transnational) organised crime as well as their strategies and tactics is the new terrorism. New terrorism is significantly more than a mere terrorist organisation. It is new on the levels of ideology, cooperation and even fusion with other players, the use of technological means of the Internet and the levels of strategy and tactics. Both the scientific analysis (political science, international relations, law, regional studies of Africa and the Middle East and economics) and the analysis by security authorities have to identify and examine these levels of new terrorism, above all their interaction and interconnectivity. This book is intended to serve the identification and examination process of the various levels of new terrorism.

# References

Andersen, U. (2011). Internationaler Terrorismus. In W. Woyke (Ed.), *Handwörterbuch Internationale Politik* (12th ed.). Opladen: Barbara Budrich.

Bewarder, M., & Flade, F. (2017, March 8). Terrorgefahr IS nimmt Deutschland noch stärker ins Visier. *Die Welt*. Retrieved January 15, 2019, from https://www.welt.de/politik/deutschland/article162687417/IS-nimmt-Deutschland-noch-staerker-ins-Visier.html

Buchsteiner, J. (2017, March 23). Terror in Großbritannien Ein schwarzer Tag für Londons "Antiterror-Chef". *Frankfurter Allgemeine Zeitung*. Retrieved January 15, 2019, from http://www.faz.net/aktuell/politik/ausland/antiterror-chef-mark-rowley-war-erfolgreich-bis-zu-dem-attentat-14939090.html

Bundeskriminalamt. (2016). *Bundeslagebild Organisierte Kriminalität 2015*. Wiesbaden.

Burke, J. (2015). *The new threat: The past, present, and future of Islamic militancy*. London: Vintage.

Cockburn, P. (2015). *The rise of the Islamic state: ISIS and the new Sunni revolution*. London: Verso.

Crenshaw, M. (2010). *Explaining terrorism: Causes, processes and consequences*. New York: Routledge.

Gärtner, H. (2008). *Internationale Sicherheit*. Baden-Baden: Nomos.

Goertz, S. (2012). *Die Streitkräfte demokratischer Staaten in den Kleinen Kriegen des 21. Jahrhunderts*. Berlin: Wissenschaftlicher Verlag.

Goertz, S. (2017). *Islamistischer Terrorismus: Analyse – Definitionen – Taktik*. Heidelberg: C.F. Müller.

Hoffman, B. (2006). *Inside terrorism*. New York: Columbia University Press.

Krause, J. (2017). Terrorismus im Wandel. In S. Hansen & J. Krause (Eds.), *Jahrbuch Terrorismus 2015/2016* (pp. 15–22). Opladen: Barbara Budrich.

Lister, C. (May 2014). *Dynamic stalemate: Surveying Syria's military landscape*. Washington, DC: Brookings Institute.

Marston, D., & Malkasian, C. (2008). *Counterinsurgency in modern warfare*. Oxford: Osprey.

Moghadam, A., Berger, R., & Beliakova, P. (2014). Say terrorist, think insurgent: Labeling and analyzing contemporary terrorist actors. *Perspectives on Terrorism, 8*(5), 2–17.

Rid, T., & Keaney, T. (2010). *Understanding counterinsurgency: Doctrine, operations, and challenges*. London: Routledge.

Said, B. (2014). *Islamischer Staat: IS-Miliz, al-Qaida und die deutschen Brigaden*. Munich: C.H. Beck.

Schmid, A., & Jongman, A. (2005). *Political terrorism: A new guide to actors, authors, concepts, data bases, theories and literature*. New Brunswick, CA: Transaction.

Shultz, R., & Dew, A. (2006). *Insurgents, terrorists and militias*. New York: Columbia University Press.

South Asia Terrorism Portal. (2017). *Terrorist and extremist groups of Pakistan*. Retrieved January 15, 2019, from http://www.satp.org/satporgtp/countries/pakistan/terroristoutfits/group_list.htm

Stampnitzky, L. (2011). Disciplining an unruly field: Terrorism experts and theories of scientific/intellectual production. *Qualitative Sociology, 34*(1), 1–19.

Steinberg, G. (2015). *Kalifat des Schreckens: IS und die Bedrohung durch den Islamistischen Terror*. Munich: Knaur.

Stern, J., & Berger, J. (2015). *ISIS. The state of terror*. New York: Harper Collins.

Stürmer, M. (2017, April 1). 10.000 Salafisten in Deutschland. Das ist ein Alarmzeichen. *Die Welt*. Retrieved January 15, 2019, from https://www.welt.de/debatte/kommentare/article163319198/10-000-Salafisten-in-Deutschland-Das-ist-ein-Alarmzeichen.html

Tilly, C. (2004). Terror, terrorism, terrorists. *Sociological Theory, 22*(1), 5–13.

United Nations. (2004). *United Nations Convention against transnational organized crime and the protocols thereto*. Vienna. https://www.unodc.org/documents/treaties/UNTOC/Publications/TOC%20Convention/TOCebook-e.pdf

Weiss, M., & Hassan, H. (2015). *ISIS: Inside the army of terror*. New York: Regan Arts.

Whiteside, C. (2016). New masters of revolutionary warfare: The Islamic State Movement (2002–2016). *Perspectives on Terrorism, 10*(4), 2–17.

# Chapter 2
# Jihadism of the Twenty-First Century as Worldwide Religious/Political Ideology: The New Jihad as Theology and Strategy

## 2.1 Religions and Their Affinity to Violence, Fundamentalism and Totalitarianism

Every religion, consequently also Islam, can influence the individual, a group and entire societies through five features. In order to help understand the features of religion for fundamentalism and totalitarianism, in this book religion is considered as a category of the social sciences. Fox and Sandler identify five features that religions use to influence individuals, groups and societies:

1. They form identities.
2. They are systems of belief that influence the behaviour of individuals and groups.
3. They devise doctrines, all-embracing points of view.
4. They engender legitimacy.
5. They create institutions.

From an anthropological perspective, it can be argued that religious interpretations—when used as a cultural precept legitimising violence—are particularly likely to trigger and encourage the readiness to use violence.

From a socio-scientific perspective, religions can increase the propensity for violence because they have the ability to inspire ultimate commitment from their followers. This is done by creating a spiritual/religious language that shows violence in a different light, serving a higher purpose, controlling violence in the form of rituals and sacrifice. Thus a kind of monopoly on the use of force evolves, resembling that of modern states (Rapoport, 1992). In addition, in certain psychological and societal crises or wars, religions can fall back on their own violent, militant genesis and trigger violence (Rapoport, 1992).

The following phenomenological types of violence are all related to religion: ritual and symbolical violence (sacrifice victims); physical violence against "the others"; religiously justified theft, murder, persecution or punishment based on dualist stereotypes (friend or foe); religiously motivated social violence

© Springer Nature Switzerland AG 2019
S. Goertz, A. E. Streitparth, *The New Terrorism*,
https://doi.org/10.1007/978-3-030-14592-7_2

(on account of sex); and organised revenge as religiously motivated terrorism, a so-called sacred struggle or a holy war. On the one hand, religious fundamentalism creates doctrines and strategies to preserve group identity by accentuating selected dogmas, norms and customs. On the other hand, religious fundamentalism also strives for a religious, spiritual reformation. At the same time it is always derivative, because it is rooted in the past in the origins of its religion (Pfürtner, 1991). By presenting its followers with absolute and exclusive dichotomies and truths, religious fundamentalism creates an ontological certainty (Pfürtner, 1991).

Through their earthly pretension to order and interpretation, religions develop the potential to create order out of the (earthly) chaos in accordance with the principles of their own religion. This process is described as a "cosmic battle", which in the end prevails over chaos. Cosmic battle because it is centred on the metaphysical conflict between good and evil, "us versus them". Religions derive a moral legitimacy for violence from this "us versus them" dichotomy. Fundamentalism—or in the case of Islamism, Salafism and Jihadism—also literalism and (Salafist) neo-fundamentalism are the determining factors of the militant ideology and theology of Jihadism.

## 2.2  Jihad and Islam

Jihad is more than just a "holy struggle" or "holy war"—expressions that were used in mediaeval times in connection with the crusades by the Christians. A "holy struggle" is a neutral generic term for the Arabic *harb* and *quital* and many more terms related to struggle, fight, attack and battle—all mentioned in the primary source Quran and numerous secondary sources of Islam. The religious/political concept of Jihad is more comprehensive than just warfare; it is also a death cult, a cult of the apocalypse. The expression Jihad is more than 1400 years old and is mentioned numerous times in the Quran together with related terms such as battle, struggle, attack and military campaign and has been interpreted in many ways.

The internationally acknowledged *Encyclopedia of Islam* defines Jihad as *warfare with spiritual significance* and *in law, according to general doctrine and in historical tradition, the Jihad consists of military action with the object of expansion of Islam and, if need be, of its defense* (Bearman, Binquis, & Bosworth, 2004).

Early Islam of the seventh century is described by international Islamic studies as being dominated by Jihad (Cook, 2015; Firestone, 1999; Johnson, 1997; Jones, 1957; Kelsay & Johnson, 1991; Morabia, 1993; Noth, 1966). The last 10 years of Muhammad's life are unanimously described as *al maghazi*, the attack (Al Waqidi, 1984; Cook, 2015; Johnson, 1997). Muhammad led at least 27 military campaigns personally and ordered at least 59 military campaigns (Al Waqidi, 1984; Cook, 2015; Johnson, 1997).

As far as the relationship between religion and violence, religion and terrorism and Islam and Jihad are concerned, it can be said that the Islamist/Jihadist declaration of Jihad as the religious obligation of "all Muslims" derives from theological origins.

The theology of Jihad in the Quran can be traced back to the third and fourth phase of Muhammad that began with the Battle of Badr in the year 624, when Muhammad followed the divine command to fight against the "polytheists" (sura 2, verses 192–194 and sura 47, verse 4–5)[1]. Between the seventh and ninth century, Islam and the suras and verses of the Quran in this period are dominated by divine revelations to Muhammad relating to the capitulation of the Meccans and the conquest of Mecca in the year 629.

To answer the question of the political content of Jihad and its consequences, the so-called verses of the sword in sura 9 are of vital importance. For example, in verse 5, sura 9, the Muslims are ordered to fight against the infidels. Moreover, in verse 29 of sura 9 Muslims are called upon to attack the monotheists (Jews and Christians) until they surrender.[2] Verse 40 of sura 9 orders the Muslims to wage war until Islam prevails.[3]

The four theological Sunni schools reflect on situations where Allah orders Muslims to conduct Jihad as a violent struggle. It is therefore the duty of every able-bodied Muslim to engage in Jihad when in a "state of defence", or in other situations it may suffice if only "some Muslims" fight on behalf of others.

In answer to the question of what function an Islamist/Jihadist understanding of Islam and the Quran has for the development of Jihadism, the majority of international English-speaking scholars is of the opinion that the religion of Islam is fundamental in the development of Jihadist violence.

## 2.3   Jihad and the Quran

Muhammad received his divine revelations, which were written down in the Quran, in a decade of wars and military actions. Sura 8, verses 16–18 say:

> And you did not kill them, but it was Allah who killed them. And you threw not, (O Muhammad), when you threw, but it was Allah who threw that He might test the believers with a good test. Indeed, Allah is Hearing and Knowing. That [is so] and [also] that Allah will weaken the plot of the infidels.

Numerous suras deal with Jihad, for example, suras 8, 9, 33 and 48. According to the international majority of scholars of Islamic studies, sura 9, verse 5, is pivotal for Jihad in the Quran:

> And when the sacred months have passed, then kill the polytheists wherever you find them and capture them and besiege them and sit in wait for them at every place of ambush [...].

---

[1]The holy Quran, Arabic and German. Ahmadiyya Muslim Jamaat in the FRG 2016.
[2]The holy Quran, Arabic and German. Ahmadiyya Muslim Jamaat in the FRG 2016.
[3]The holy Quran, Arabic and German. Ahmadiyya Muslim Jamaat in the FRG 2016.

In sura 9 of the Quran, Jihad focuses on the dualist relationship of believers (Muslims) and infidels (non-believers):

> Fight those who do not believe in Allah or in the Last Day and who do not consider unlawful what Allah and His Messenger have made unlawful and who do not adopt the religion of truth from those who were given the Scripture—[fight] until they give the *jizyah* willingly while they are humbled.

An Islamist/Jihadist interpretation of the Quran takes the above-mentioned suras and verses literally and refers to the internationally important Muslim school of Wahhabism, which has the status of a state religion in Saudi Arabia. The concept and interpretation of the "great Jihad" as personal struggle of each individual believer against his own inner weaknesses is controversial in Islamic law because the concept of "great Jihad" is based on a *hadith* whose authenticity is highly disputed.

To summarise, a link between the primary source Quran and Jihadist, terrorist violence can be detected in the Quran as well as in secondary documents of Sunni law. The Jihadist interpretation of the Quran uses the Quran literally (see the above-mentioned suras and verses) and cites the most important Muslim schools of law, as, for example, Wahhabism, Hanbalism and the old and new mullahs of Jihad.

## 2.4 Jihad and Its Old Mullahs: The Jihad of the Twentieth Century

Together with the Quran as primary source, the religious/political ideology of the Jihad is based on old and new mullahs of Jihad and the dogmatic Sunni schools of Hanbalism[4] and Wahhabism.[5]

### 2.4.1 Hanbalism as Islamic/Theological Source of Islamism

Abu Abdallah Ahmad Ibn Hanbal (780–855 AD) was the youngest of the four founders of Sunni theological schools of Islam and is described as an Islamic traditionalist. Within the four theological schools of Sunni Islam, the school of the Hanbalites was named after him. His most well-known work—his life's work—is *Al-Musnad*, a collection of more than 29,000 hadiths of the prophet Muhammad. Hanbal tried to collect every piece of information about the early phase of Islam, about Muhammad and his early followers, and make its reading binding for all Muslims (Steinberg, 2014: 269). Hanbal's goal was to trace back all laws and rules

---

[4]Dating back to its founder Imam Ahmad Ibn Hanbal who preached at the beginning of the ninth century.

[5]Muhammad Ibn Al Wahhab is the founder of the Sunni school of Wahhabism. Thanks to a long life, he was quite influential in the eighteenth century.

to the Quran and the sunnah. He and his followers were intolerant towards all those who did not treat the sunnah as binding (Steinberg, 2014: 269). Consequently, the Islamic/theological analogy lost its relevance with Hanbal. On the basis of the dogma that all Islamic laws and rules dealing with political systems, society's constitution and individual lives should derive exclusively from the Quran and the sunnah, Hanbalism can be said to be the earliest Islamic/theological source of Islamism. Hanbal initiated an open hostility towards the Shiites, so that he can be held responsible for the epic violence between Sunnis and Shiites which has endured for the past 12 years.

### 2.4.2   Wahhabism as Islamic/Theological Source of Islamism: Reading the Quran Literally

Wahhabism[6] is described as a purist/traditionalist movement of Sunni Islam, which also follows the school of Hanbalism. The Wahhabis refer to the teaching of Muhammad Ibn Abd Al Wahhab and strictly reject Sufism and Shia. In his youth, Al Wahhab severely criticised the discrepancy between the contemporary practice of Islam and the ideal Quran and sunnah (Steinberg, 2014: 266). In contrast to other Islamic teachers of law, Al Wahhab strictly refused to develop Islamic law and to use analogies to deal with contemporary questions (De Long-Bas, 2009). Like Al Hanbal, Al Wahhab also taught a literal interpretation of the legitimate Islamic sources of law derived from the Quran and sunnah. Al Wahhab created the dogma that a "true Muslim" had to follow the example of the righteous predecessors (*Al Salaf Al Salih*), exclusively based on the Quran and *sunna* (Steinberg, 2014: 267). On an Islamic/theological level, Al Wahhab was innovative and influential through a new interpretation of the monotheistic principle of tawhid. Al Wahhab named that principle *tawhid al uluhiyya* ("practical tawhid") (Steinberg, 2014: 268).

To summarise, Wahhabism is deeply fundamentalist and political at the same time (Khosrokhavaer, 2009). Its antimodernist religious/political agenda includes the prohibition of alcohol, drugs, gambling and homosexuality, combined with brutal penalties, and the repudiation of the public and private spheres. Sovereignty of the people and consequently laws of democratic parliaments are entirely inacceptable. In other words, Wahhabism and Jihadism have the same Islamic/theological origins (Khosrokhavaer, 2009), and Wahhabism was basically the precursor of the Jihadism we see in the twentieth and twenty-first century. The logical consequence of the strict Wahhabi distinction between Wahhabi Muslims and non-Wahhabi infidels was the religious justification of a Jihad against the neighbouring territories of the Saud family in the eighteenth century, although they were also Muslims (Steinberg, 2014: 270). Consequently, since the eighteenth century, theological opponents of Wahhabism have criticised the fact that Wahhabism is overhasty in condemning

---

[6]Wahhābīya.

fellow Muslims as infidels for profane or political reasons and excommunicating them (takfir) (Steinberg, 2014: 270).

### 2.4.3   Hassan Al Banna: His Muslim Brotherhood as Mass Movement with Parallel State Structures and Jihad as Theological and Military Means

Allah is our objective; the Prophet is our leader; the Koran is our law; Jihad is our way; dying in the way of Allah is our highest hope, slogan of the Muslim Brotherhood.

Hassan Ahman Al Banna (1906–1949) was the founder and leader of the Egyptian Muslim Brotherhood, one of the most important and influential Islamist movements of the twentieth century. Al Banna's Islamist ideology can be traced back to his early writings, for example, *Ilā aiyi šai' nad ū n-nās* and *Da watu-nā*, in which he formulated religious/spiritual and strategic goals of the *dawa*, which aims to bring back Muslims to the "real Islam" (Gershoni & Jankowski, 1995: 235). Shortly thereafter he glorified the death of Muslims as a means for accomplishing political aims, which can be classified as Islamist extremist (Brynjar, 1998; Gershoni & Jankowski, 1995; Krämer, 2010; Moser, 2012). The Muslim Brotherhood reached its peak in the year 1948, with 500,000 members and many more sympathisers in Egypt. It had a state-like structure, with its own mosques, companies, factories, hospitals and schools. It also had close ties to the Egyptian armed forces and unions.

In his book *Naḥwa Al-nūr* (*Towards the Light*), Al Banna advocated the return to the "original Islam", which can be seen as an Islamist reaction to the political situation in Egypt in the first half of the twentieth century. Al Banna demanded political, legal and administrative reforms for Egypt:

• Elimination of the party system
• Reform of legislation in agreement with the Islamic Sharia
• Consolidation of the armed forces, development of Islamic youth organisations and triggering of their fighting spirit on the basis of the Islamic Jihad
• Strengthening of relations between Islamic countries, especially Arab countries, to promote thought processes about the lost caliphate
• Spreading of the Islamic spirit in government authorities
• Supervision of the personal conduct of civil servants because no difference is allowed between private and professional life in the Islamic world
• Organising working hours so as to guarantee fulfilment of Islamic religious duties
• Elimination of corruption and favouritism
• Alignment of all governmental order according to Islamic rules (public holidays, working hours, etc.)
• Preferential employment of graduates from the Islamic university of Azhar in military and administrative posts (Al Banna, 1995: 109)

Al Banna (1947) declared Jihad to be a decisive duty of Islam and made it clear that there is an inseparable relationship between Jihad and martyrdom:

> Jihad is an obligation from Allah on every Muslim and cannot be ignored or evaded. Allah has ascribed great importance to Jihad and has made the reward of the martyrs and the fighters in his path a splendid one. Only those who have acted similarly and who have modelled themselves upon the martyrs in their performance of Jihad can join the others in this reward. Furthermore, Allah has specifically honoured the Mujahideen [those who wage Jihad] with certain exceptional qualities, both spiritual and practical, to benefit them in this world and the other. Their pure blood is a symbol of victory in the world and the mark of success and felicity in the world to come. Those who can only find excuses, however, have been warned of extremely dreadful punishments, and Allah has described them with the most unfortunate of names. He has reprimanded them for their cowardice and lack of spirit, and castigated them for their weakness and truancy. In this world, dishonour will befall them and in the next world a fire from which they shall not escape will engulf them although they may possess much wealth. The weakness of abstention and evasion of Jihad are regarded by Allah as one of the major sins, and one of the sins that guarantee failure.

### 2.4.4   Sayyid Qutb and His Brother Muhammad Qutb as Connecting Link of the Muslim Brotherhood to Wahhabism in Saudi Arabia

Sayyid Qutb is known as one of the authors of Islamism in Egypt in the second half of the twentieth century. His book *Milestones* is still available in its millions in the bookshops of many mosques in London, free of charge as a PDF file on thousands of Islamist websites, in libraries of Quran schools in Pakistan and Afghanistan, in the Syrian and Iraqi accommodation of IS fighters and—obviously—in his native country, Egypt. Here, there is a similar situation to that experienced at the peak of Sayyid Qutb's popularity: thousands of Muslim brothers, followers of Mursi, who was elected president of Egypt in 2012 as leader of the "Freedom and Justice Party" in the so-called Arabellion against the Egyptian president Mubarak, were sentenced to prison sentences and are currently undergoing radicalisation processes that can make Egypt the new hotspot of Islamist/Jihadist attacks and a possible Salafist revolution (Burke, 2015: 34–35).

Explaining his Islamist ideology, Qutb (2006) says:

> Muslims at war had only one concern, and it was to make the name of Allah supreme; there was no room at all for any other objective. The wish for glory and reputation was forbidden to Muslims. Love of wealth, misappropriation of the benefits of war, and striving to conquer through unjust methods were all forbidden to the Muslim. Only one intention was possible, and that was the offering of sacrifice and the taking of pains for the guidance of mankind.[7]

---

[7]Banna, Jihad, www.youngMuslims.ca/online_library/books/Jihad/

And:

> Islam is not only faith, Islam is the public declaration for the liberation of the people from the worship of human-beings and its aim was from the beginning to wipe out the systems and the political powers that act on the basis of the domination of man over man and the worship of man by man. It frees people to choose the faith they want, after having removed the political pressures on them, attempting at talking to their soul and their reason. (Qutb, 2006)

Furthermore, Qutb (2006) talks of "total war" and the impossibility of coexistence between "right" and "wrong".

> Total war against a world that is ruled by the domination of one people over another instead of Allah's, a world where the wrong dominates the right: This is a permanent situation, not an incidental one because Right and Wrong cannot coexist on this earth until Islam succeeds in its declaration of Allah's rule in the two worlds [this world and the world of the afterlife] and emancipates man from the worship of people. Usurpers fight against the rule of Allah on earth and do never make peace with it and therefore, they defend the rule of man on earth, this usurper of power. This situation is permanent and the emancipating movement of Jihad does not stop until religion is only Allah's on earth.

As a consequence of this statement by Qutb, a spiritus rector of Islamism, Muslims worldwide (the *Umma*) live in a constant state of Jihad because there can be no peace with other earthly powers. According to Qutb, those who reject "Allah's reign on earth" are the enemies of Islam. Khosrokhavar identifies the roots of this interpretation of Jihad in the early Islam of the seventh and eighth centuries. At the same time he sees similarities with totalitarian ideologies of the twentieth century. In Qutb's Jihad interpretation, Khosrokhavar sees "Islam as the liberator of mankind from the yoke of other humans", showing parallels to Marxism. Qutb's interpretation is global, universal and theological/political.

> After annihilating the tyrannical force, whether political or a racial tyranny, or domination of one class over the other within the same race, Islam established a new social and economic political system, in which all men enjoy real freedom.

As co-originator of Islamism as a religious/political ideology with concrete aims, Qutb divides the world into belief and disbelief, light and darkness, good and evil and justice and injustice. He uses a very simple, extremely direct language, which means that his books are easily comprehensible to millions of people with different educational backgrounds. Qutb focused on the fight against idolatry, against the "infidels"; to his mind "modernity" and "the west" were based on the worship of "the false gods" of Western democracies. According to his logic, Islam is always at war with infidels, and peaceful coexistence with "the infidels" is impossible. In this way, Qutb created a dualism with "true Muslims" in total opposition to "the infidels".

Qutb coined the expression *ḥākimiyyat Allāh* which outlines the absolute sovereignty of Allah, opposing any form of secular nation-state, democracy or sovereignty of the people (Carré, 1984). His book *Milestones*[8] was of vital importance for Islamist/Jihadist groups. Furthermore, the expression *Qutbiyyūn* is used to describe his followers and his dogmas. Theologically and as a doctrine, the expression

---

[8] معالم فى الطريق, *maʿālim fī ṭ-ṭarīq*.

*Jahiliya/ǧāhilīya*[9] describes the "era of ignorance" before Muhammad and the advent of Islam on the Arabian Peninsula. Qutb revitalised this theology in the twentieth century and proclaimed that the Muslim *Umma*, all the Muslim societies of his time, had reverted to the state of *Jahiliya*. According to Qutb, the *Umma* no longer followed the laws and rules of Islam and consequently was in a pre-Islamic State of "ignorance" (Kepel, 1985: 46).

Qutb's logic of the dichotomy of "good" versus "evil" concluded that when assessing whether a society was Islamic or anti-Islamic, only one criterion should be decisive: the complete implementation of the *Sharia*. In order to escape from the social state of *Jahiliya*, Qutb propagated a distinct disassociation from all anti-Islamic influences and ideas. Every Muslim should live according to the Sharia, which would have a domino effect and stimulate the healing process of the Muslim community (Moser, 2012: 96–99).

For Qutb, Allah's reign is the reign of Islamic law and an Islamic lifestyle. This reign has to follow *Dawa* and Jihad. Various Islamist/Jihadist groups of the 1970s in Egypt, Syria and Saudi Arabia followed Qutb's theology and ideology of *Jahiliya* and Jihad.

When an assassination attempt on Egypt's President Nasser—supposedly carried out by members of the Muslim Brotherhood—failed in 1954, the Egyptian government dissolved the Muslim Brotherhood. Various members were imprisoned and tortured; Qutb was one of them. He was sentenced to 25 years in prison, part of which he spent in a prison hospital where he was allowed to write. Thus his two books, *Fī zilāl al-Qur'ān (In the Shadow of the Quran)* and *Ma'ālim fī t-tarīq (Milestones)* came into being. On the intervention of the Iraqi president, Qutb was released from prison in 1964, having served 10 years of his sentence, and published his book *Milestones*. After a second charge, Qutb was sentenced to death in 1966 and executed.

After the temporary dissolution of the Muslim Brotherhood in Egypt, numerous members migrated to Saudi Arabia, where many of them found employment in the religious education system. The list of educated Egyptian Muslim brothers who emigrated at the end of the 1960s/beginning of the 1970s reads like a who's who of the Muslim Brotherhood, for example, Sayyid Qutb's brother Muhammad Qutb (1919–2014) (Steinberg, 2014: 282). Shortly after his release from an Egyptian prison, Muhammad Qutb became professor at the Sharia faculty of the university in Mecca. Muhammad Qutb added his own interpretation to the teaching of his brother, and they fitted into the religious/political environment of contemporary Saudi Arabia by adapting the concept of radicalist Wahhabi monotheism (Lacroix, 2011; Steinberg, 2014: 282).

---

[9] جاهلية

## 2.4.5  *Mustafa Shukri*

Mustafa Shukri—who strangely enough is barely mentioned in German literature—can be described as one of the first Salafists of modern times. Being a member of the Egyptian Muslim Brotherhood, a spiritual follower of the Islamist ideology of Sayyid Qutb, a charismatic mullah and a leader of Jama'at al-Muslimin, he gathered up to 5000 active members and followed the shining example of the Salafist followers of Muhammad (Kepel, 2002: 73–78, 87). Born in 1942, Shukri went to a Quran school and later studied agriculture at Assiut University, where he made contact with the Islamist Muslim Brotherhood.

After various prison sentences for Islamist activities, in the 1970s, Shukri led his followers into the Salafist opposite of modernity: in 1971, he described his followers as prone to the "sins of modernity" and chose the tactics of a strict separation from modernity (Burke, 2015). In his opinion, his religious/political teaching was portrayed incorrectly by the "Westernised" Egyptian government and the media, so he took the former Egyptian minister and moderate Muslim scholar Muhammad al-Dhababi—who had previously criticised Shukri in public—as hostage in July of 1977. Shukri demanded the release of his followers from prison, public apologies from both the Egyptian government and the media and permission to publish his writings. Since the Egyptian government turned these demands down, Shukri killed Muhammad al-Dhababi. Consequently hundreds of his followers were arrested and condemned to long prison sentences. Shukri and five of his inner circle of followers were executed by order of a military tribunal in March 1978.

In a nutshell, Shukri's teaching can be labelled as an extremist, purist version of Islamist theology, as he declared all four Islamic schools as superfluous and attributed every individual Muslim the right to live as "true Muslim" according to the Quran and the Sunnah (Kepel, 1985: 79–80).

## 2.5  Jihad and Its New Mullahs: Towards the Jihad of the Twenty-First Century

> Jihad is, without doubt, the pride of Islam and the basis of Islam, and the verses and hadiths regarding this are known to everybody inshallah.[10] Muhammad Al-Albani

A description of the Islamist/Jihadist mullahs of the new international Jihad of the twenty-first century, as well as their teaching, doctrines and dogmas, will follow below. Since the 1990s, these new mullahs of Jihad have been propagating a shift of the focus, away from the so-called close enemy (governments of the Muslim world) and towards the "far enemy" (Western states). In the logic of these new mullahs of Jihad, attacking the "far enemy" would lead to a loss of power of the "close enemy",

---

[10]Muhammad Al-Albani.

enabling them to be toppled and paving the way for a new caliphate and the foundation of Muslim states governed by the Sharia.


### 2.5.1 Abdullah Yusuf Azzam: The Internationalisation of Jihad

Azzam was born in a village in the West Bank in 1941 and studied Islamic theology until 1966 in Damascus, Syria. After the Six-Day War in 1967, Azzam and his family moved to Jordan, where he fought against Israeli troops in the West Bank for 18 years. Afterwards, in 1968, he immatriculated in Al-Azhar University in Cairo and graduated in Islamic theology and law (Hegghammer, 2006: 164–170). At the beginning of 1970, he started teaching at the University of Jordan in Amman, only to return to Al-Azhar University with a doctoral fellowship and be awarded a PhD in Islamic theology in 1973. In 1975 he became one of five members of the council of the Jordanian Muslim Brotherhood which led to a clash with the Jordanian government. As a consequence, he had to leave the University of Jordan and moved to the King Abdullah Aziz University in Jeddah, Saudi Arabia, where he made contact with Muhammad Qutb, the brother of Sayyid Qutb (Hegghammer, 2006: 164–170). In 1981 Azzam decided to support the Afghan resistance against the Soviet troops as one of the first Arabs and moved to Islamabad, Pakistan, together with his family. From 1982 on, he published articles in the Kuwaiti journal *Al-Mujama*, in which he wrote about heavenly rewards awaiting Afghan Jihadists and requested young Arabs to join the Afghan Jihad against the Soviet troops (Lacroix, 2011: 110).

In 1984 Azzam moved to Peshawar to head—together with Osama bin Laden—the Office of Services for the Mujahideen (Maktab Khadamat Al Mujahideen, MAK) that was primarily responsible for supplying and recruiting international Jihadists for the Jihad in Afghanistan (Maliach, 2010: 80). Since then Azzam was called the "spiritual mentor" of Osama bin Laden, which rather implies "religious/political leader" (Maliach, 2010: 80). At the end of 1989, Osama bin Laden founded—based on the idea of Al Qaida Al Sulbah, the "solid base"—Al Qaida.[11] Azzam had already explained in the 1980s that a theological, doctrinal and strategic division in a lesser versus a greater Jihad was irrelevant because all four normative law schools linked Jihad with *al qital*, militant, active fighting. His book *The Defence of the Muslim Lands: the First Obligation after Iman*, published in 1984, developed to become a theological doctrine of Jihad by extending the "fight against inner enemies" (one's own government) to the "fight against outer enemies" (Lacroix, 2011: 111). In this way Azzam

---

[11]Every principle must have its vanguard that will carry it forth. The vanguard will pay a steep price and suffer many losses while paving the road for the Islamic society. There is no belief, either earthly or heavenly, that does not need such a vanguard, one that will give all it has for its belief to be victorious. This vanguard is the solid base ('Al Qaida Al Sulbah') of the society we are awaiting (Osama Bin Laden in Peshawar 1989; Maliach 2010: 80).

internationalised the concept of Jihad (Lacroix, 2011: 111). Azzam labelled the Jihad in Afghanistan in the 1980s as Jihad against the "near enemy", the "infidel Afghan government" that made a pact with the Soviet Union and then moved on to the far enemy, the Soviet troops.[12]

Azzam renewed the idea of Jihad, developed it and globalised it by aiming at the conscience of Muslims worldwide. The Jihad interpretation of "defending or liberating Muslim territory as the duty of every Muslim" can be traced back to Azzam (Maliach, 2010: 82). Together with Osama bin Laden, Azzam can be described as pioneer of the first wave of Jihadism (in Afghanistan of the 1980s). This observation is reflected in the following statement by Azzam:

> Whoever thinks that Jihad in Afghanistan means the abandonment of the Islamic problem in Palestine is delusional [...] The blood story of Kabul is the story of the war of a wounded Palestine [...]. We hereby declare to the Jews and their satellites and the Americans and Communists: We will not rest until we return to the Jihad in Palestine.[13]

From December 1984 on, Azzam published a journal, named *Al Jihad*, which was published over the course of many years from Peshawar. It came out on a monthly basis and contained reports from the Jihad territories of Afghanistan and religious/political texts which were afterwards translated into English. In the course of his international doctrine of Jihad, Azzam travelled all over the world in order to recruit material and personnel support for the Afghan Jihad within the *Umma*. Consequently, he founded a branch office of his Jihadist recruiting organisation in the USA.

The estimated number of international Jihadists who fought against Soviet troops in Afghanistan between 1982 and 1989 varies between 16,000 and 30,000 (Atkins, 2004; Commins, 2006; Rashid, 2000). Based in Peshawar, Azzam organised material and personnel supplies for this first internationally waged Jihad.

Moreover, Azzam took part in the foundation of the Palestinian Hamas, and in his publications, Azzam listed Afghanistan, Palestine, Eritrea, Chad, Somalia, the Philippines, Burma and Yemen as theatres of Jihad. Accordingly, Azzam stated at a conference of the *Islamic Association of Palestine* (IAP) in Oklahoma City, USA, in December 1988 with reference to the *Intifada* of the Palestinians against Israel:

> Sons of Palestine, the time has come for you to swear allegiance to death. It is good to die with honor. Sons of Palestine, there is no turning back after today. Follow death, the path has been opened for you, the time has come to step up to the stage of preparation and death for the sake of God (istishab)...Sons of Palestine, you have an opportunity to train on every type of weapon in Afghanistan, this is a golden opportunity, do not miss it.[14]

---

[12]Azzam, A. (1989). In the Sea of Battle. Peshawar: The Office of Services for the Mujahideen.

[13]Azzam, A. (1989). Palestine Memories. Peshawar: The Office of Services for the Mujahideen.

[14]Azzam, Abdullah, in Maliach (2010: 84).

Azzam's Jihad doctrine was of paramount importance and had a huge influence in his native country, Palestine. Consequently, his publications are said to have led the way to a new definition of the Middle East conflict, because the struggle of the Palestinians against Israel was—according to Azzam—no longer a national struggle for an independent state but "a struggle for Muslim territory" (Hegghammer, 2006: 167).

Azzam followed the traditionalist Islamic Quran doctrine of dividing Jihad into an "offensive" and a "defensive" Jihad. The "offensive Jihad" (*Jihad talab*) attacks the "infidels" in their home countries. The "defensive Jihad" (*Jihad al daf*) is the defence of a Muslim country against foreigners and/or "infidels" who occupy Muslim territory. Azzam believed that "the defensive Jihad" is the absolute duty of every Muslim.

According to Azzam, Jihad is the highest form of Islam, and every "true Muslim" has to emigrate into Jihad (*hijra*), to prepare militarily (*idad*) and protect the borders of the Muslim country (*ribat*), and finally has to wage war (*qital*).

Additionally, Azzam is seen as propagandist of suicide bombers (*shahid* for "martyrs"):

> The shahids (martyrs) are those who write the history of nations, because the history of nations is written only in sweat and blood. They are the ones who build the palace of glory, because palaces of glory are built only of skulls and limbs severed from the body. They are the ones who keep the tree of this religion from wilting and drying up, because the tree of this religion is watered only with blood. They are the wise ones, because they found their way to Allah, while the others either mourn them or mock their thinking. They are the ones who love death so that they will earn life (after death).[15]

## 2.5.2  The Salafist-Jihadist Abu Muhammad Al Maqdisi as Link Between Saudi Arabian Legal Scholars and Jihadist Mullahs and Doctrines: Constructing Democracies as Dualist Opponents of Islam

Muhammad Al Maqdisi (Isam al-Barqawi) was born in 1959 in a village close to Nablus and is a Palestinian/Jordanian mullah of Salafist Jihadism. From 1992 on, he worked together with Abu Musab Al-Zarqawi, the later leader of the Jihadist organisation Al Qaida in Iraq (Wagemakers, 2008: 8–10). On various occasions, he was sceptical about the IS. Since the beginning of 2014, he has called on Jihadists worldwide to be loyal towards the leader of Al Qaida, Aiman Al Zawahiri.

Already as a student, he joined an Islamist group that was inspired by Juhayman Al Utaybi who had occupied the great mosque in 1979 (Lav, 2012). Maqdisi studied Sharia sciences at the Islamic University of Medina. During his studies in the beginning of the 1980s, he focused on the Islamic topic *takfir*, the practice of Islamic

---

[15] Azzam, Abdullah (1990). Who are the Shahids? In: Lahib Al Maraah, Peshawar, 13.1.1990.

law of accusing one Muslim or a group of Muslims of apostasy (*ridda*) and of then declaring him/them of being infidels (*kafir, kuffar*) (Wagemakers, 2009a, 2009b: 285).

Operating from Saudi Arabia, Al Maqdisi moved to Pakistan and Afghanistan in the mid-1980s to participate in the Jihad of the international Jihadists against the Soviet troops. In fact, Al Maqdisi did not participate in the active, military Jihad but acted as a mullah promoting his Jihad doctrine and his book *Millat Ibrahim* (Wagemakers, 2009a, 2009b: 284–286). In the meantime, he frequently travelled to Kuwait and Saudi Arabia, where he wrote more books on his Jihadist theology.

His book *Millat Ibrahim* (translated from Arabic *The Community of Abraham and the Dawa of the Prophets*) published in 1984 developed the idea of al-Otaybi and transported the crucial Islamic/theological demand that all Muslims had to implement the principle *Al Wala' Wa-l-bara'* ("loyalty and renunciation") to be "true Muslims". In his publications Al Maqdisi preaches absolute, rigid obedience and total loyalty towards Allah in every possible aspect, which had a critical influence for the Muslim *Umma* of the late twentieth century, in everyday life as well as on a political level (Wagemakers 2008). On a political level, Al Maqdisi derived from *Al Wala' wa-l-bara'* that Muslims worldwide should topple governments which do not adopt the rule of *Sharia* (Wagemakers, 2009a, 2009b). Consequently, Al Maqdisi's interpretation of *Al Wala' wa-l-bara'* forces Muslims to renounce democratic systems and to fight militarily against those Islamic systems and leaders that rule in a non-Islamic way, using man-made laws and making pacts with non-Islamic States, thereby becoming guilty of apostasy (*ridda*) (Farschid, 2014: 176). With reference to the originally "near enemy", for example, governments of various Islamic countries, militant Jihad becomes the highest form of *bara* (disavowal) (Farschid, 2014: 176).

At the beginning of the 1990s, Al Maqdisi met Abu Musab Al-Zarqawi in Pakistan, the later leader of Al Qaida in Iraq (Wagemakers, 2012: 40). In 1992 Al Maqdisi moved to Jordan where he was in close cooperation with Al-Zarqawi and was gradually recognised as the most important contemporary mullah of Jihadism (Lav, 2012). While Al-Zarqawi helped Al Maqdisi to spread his publications and doctrines in the Middle East, another Palestinian ideologist, Abu Qatada al-Filastini, moved to Great Britain to promote Al Maqdisi's Jihad doctrine (Wagemakers, 2012: 202).

Al Maqdisi sees every democratic political participation as a form of a forbidden religious renewal (*bida*), which was unknown to the followers (*salaf*) of Muhammad (Nedza, 2014: 84). Thus Al Maqdisi considered democratic participation to be a form of disbelief (*kufr*) because parliamentarism and a representative body of the people in his eyes are a deviation from Islamic monotheism (*tauhid*) and therefore are an apostasy (*ridda*). Al Maqdisi propagated his fear that political participation would lead to a fragmentation of the Muslim community (*Umma*) worldwide.

The innovative doctrine of Maqdisi can be found in his book *Al Dimuqratiyya Din*—"Democracy Is a Religion" (Al Maqdisi). In this book Al Maqdisi creates a dichotomy between the "real Islam" and democracies as opposing religions

(Moussalli, 2009: 8). According to Al Maqdisi, in Islam only God can be worshipped, so those Muslims who accept the rule of democracy violate Islam (Farschid, 2014: 178). Furthermore, Al Maqdisi condemned parliaments as places of polytheism where anti-religious ideas were propagated (Al Maqdisi: 8, 83). Consequently, Al Maqdisi depicts the introduction of parliaments and principles of democracies in the "Islamic world" as a means of weakening the Muslim *Umma* and of controlling it politically (Farschid, 2014: 179). An example for this is Article 21 of the *Universal Declaration of Human Rights*. This highlights the sovereign will of the people as a basis for public order, which is the complete opposite of Al Maqdisi's interpretation of Islam and his Jihad doctrine.

In 2009, Al Maqdisi created a Sharia committee of like-minded Islamic mullahs on his website who answered questions related to everyday, political matters and aspects of Jihad (Zelin, 2014: 335). On that website Al Maqdisi also differentiates between *qital al nikaya* (fight to harm the enemy) and *qital al tamkin* (fight to consolidate power) on which he had already elaborated in his book *waqafat maa thamrat al Jihad* (*Stances on the Fruit of Jihad*) in 2004 (Zelin, 2014: 335). Al Maqdisi explained that *qital al nikaya* would mean tactical, military success, while *qital al tamkin* would guarantee the prerequisites for an Islamic State of a long-term nature if there were coordinated implementation of planning, organisation, education and *dawa* activities (Zelin, 2014: 335). To put it briefly, it was not just his publications and his web presence that made Al Maqdisi a mullah of the new Jihad but his desire to establish a true and long-standing Islamic State governed by the Sharia (Wagemakers, 2010).

A social network analysis of the US Combating Terrorism Center analysed the degree of networking processes of the contemporary mullahs of Jihad. Degree centrality shows how many relationships a node (person) has to other nodes in a given network. The social network analysis of contemporary Jihadist mullahs revealed that Al Maqdisi has the highest density, the highest number of contacts. As a consequence, Al Maqdisi has the highest number of connections to conservative Wahhabi religious scholars of the Saudi Arabian establishment as well as to contemporary Jihadist mullahs.

### 2.5.3   Abu Musab Al Suri (Mustafa Setmariam Nasar): The Call for Global Islamic Resistance

Al Suri is one of the most prominent ideologists and mullahs of the new Jihad who has acted on behalf of Islamist/Salafist organisations such as the Syrian Muslim Brotherhood, the Algerian *Groupe Islamique Armé* (GIA), the Taliban and Al Qaida since the 1980s (Stalinski, 2011).

In the 1990s, Al Suri encouraged the Algerian *Groupe Islamique Armé* (GIA) to attack France using the tactical means of Islamist terrorism:

I recommended to the GIA amir [Emir] at the time, Abu Abdallal Ahmad [Ghousmi] and his leadership that they strike deeply in France in order to deter and punish her for her war against the GIA and for the French support for the dictatorial military regime in Algeria . . .to strike against France is our right. We are at war, and we do not play games, and our enemies should know that. (Al Suri, Lia, 2009: 156)

Al Suri is considered to be one of the most important theoreticians of the new global Jihad (Khosrokhavaer, 2009; Zelin, 2014). Like Al Maqdisi and Al Zawahiri, Al Suri is also a mullah of the Jihadist interpretation of *Al Wala' wa-l-bara'* (Farschid, 2014). Al Suri stands for a realpolitik Jihad that aims for the highest political and military efficiency. Moreover, Al Suri can be described as the Jihad strategist of lone-wolf terrorism (Berger, 2011; Lia, 2009).

Al Suri viewed the Taliban emirate in Afghanistan before the Western intervention in 2001 as a reflection, a reproduction of Medina, and described his move from London to Afghanistan as *hijrah* (Lia, 2009: 234). Al Suri's book *The Global Islamic Resistance Call* (*Da'wat al-muqawamah al-islamiyyah al-'alamiyyah*), published in 2005, extols the decentralised, individual Jihad of Islamist lone operators or of very small cells as innovative strategy and doctrine of new Jihad. In the chapters "military theories" and "organisational theories", Al Suri elaborates on the strategic/tactical basics of the new Jihad. Al Suri benefitted from his own paramilitary education which he had received in camps of the Syrian Muslim Brotherhood in the early 1980s. Additionally, his university studies in engineering at the University of Aleppo and his paramilitary skills were incorporated into a handbook about making improvised explosive devices (IED). This book was called *The Syrian Memorandum* and became popular in the camps of international Jihadists in Afghanistan. In July 1987, Al Suri met Abdullah Azzam in Afghanistan and rapidly became a tactics instructor. Unlike other mullahs of the old and the new Jihad, Al Suri was also active on the operational level. "Individual terrorism", the "individual Jihad", is the doctrinal message of his book *The Global Islamic Resistance Call* and can be found in his prominent phrase "nizam, la tanzim" (system, not organisation) (chapter 8.4. and 8.5).

In a nutshell, Al Suri propagates a Jihad strategy of an operative system and not a strategy of an "organisation for operations". Consequently, he is against hierarchical centralisation where an operative Jihadist cell or group receives orders for a terrorist attack and carries it out but prefers "general guidance" in the form of a doctrine of the individual Jihad: "a common aim, a common doctrinal program and a comprehensive (self-) educational program" (Al Suri, 2005: 1407).

With reference to tactical/operational education, Al Suri's idea "training should be moved to every house, every quarter and every village of the Muslim countries" follows his doctrine of a decentralised Jihad for everyone (Al Suri, 2005, chapter 8.6: 1414–1428). As a consequence, Al Suri rejects the centralisation of Jihadist training camps, and *Umma* is supposed to "strive to plant training camps across the Islamic nation, in all her houses and quarters" (Al Suri, 2005, chapter 8.6: 1425).

On a logistical level of space for the operative-tactical education, Al Suri also is quite concrete and consequently identifies five variables or tools for the operational/ tactical education of Jihadists:

- Secret training in safe houses. Al Suri talks of numbers of 5–12 forming a training group. Logistically this is possible in almost every country worldwide, even in Western democracies.
- Training in hidden camps that are quite small. Current examples are Somalia, Syria, Iraq and Mali.
- Overt training in countries that tolerate Jihadist training or even support it. But Al Suri is sceptical of this format because the reconnaissance success of Western armed forces and intelligence services is high.
- Overt training in the camps of fighting units. Currently that is possible in the camps of fighting units in Somalia, Syria, Iraq and Mali.
- Partly overt training on territories of failing states and/or failed states, for example, in Mali, Libya and Somalia, and in the border areas of Afghanistan and Pakistan, in Yemen and in other states (Al Suri, 2005: 1414–1419).

**Abu Musab Al Suri's Call for Global Islamic Resistance Is a Call for Global Insurgency**
In the year 2005, when he published *The Call to Global Islamic Resistance*, the above-mentioned options three to five were hardly possible because of the reconnaissance pressure of Western armed forces and intelligence services. Consequently, only options one and two were possible. Since the withdrawal of the US troops from Iraq and the drastic reduction of Western troops in Afghanistan and because of the "Arab Spring" in North Africa and Syria and the proclamation of the "Islamic State", all five training options above are far more feasible now and in the future than they have ever been before.

Unlike other Salafist-Jihadist mullahs and/or strategists, Al Suri does not reject military doctrines and terms of Western armed forces but uses them on a regular basis:

> All military schools agree that a will to fight and moral strength of the fighter is the basis for victory and good performance. While this determination to fight is important in regular armies, it is the fundament for the guerrilla fighter in general and the Jihadi resistance fighter in particular.

Al Suri reached an even wider target group through the publication of extracts from his book *The Call to Global Islamic Resistance* in the following articles of *Inspire*, the online magazine of Al Qaida:

- INSPIRE Issue No. 1 "The Schools of Jihad"
- INSPIRE Issue No. 2 "The Open Fronts & The Individual Initiative"
- INSPIRE Issue No. 4 "The Military Theory of Open Fronts"
- INSPIRE Issue No. 5 "Individual Terrorism Jihad and the Global Islamic Resistance Units"
- INSPIRE Issue No. 6 "Practical Steps for Partaking in Individual Jihad"

On the tactical-operative level, Al Suri propagates a decentralisation and individualisation of Jihad as the new Jihad. On a strategic doctrinal level, he promotes Jihad as a mass phenomenon: "the resistance is the Islamic nation's struggle and not a struggle by the elite" (Al Suri, 2005: 1425). Al Suri can be described as one of the most important mullahs of Jihad. Thanks to the close proximity of his doctrines to operational thinking, his works (and, above all, *The Call to Global Islamic Resistance*) have made their mark on the new Jihad doctrine: the new Jihad of a worldwide insurgency.

The theory of insurgency can be traced back to security and military studies about counterinsurgency. Counterinsurgency describes political, economic and military means of the regular state actor versus irregular non-state actors in asymmetric small wars (Goertz, 2012). The term insurgency is the military term for "revolt, rebellion, uprising and insurrection. Counterinsurgency is consequently the antonym of insurgency, thus all military, economic and political means against an insurgency. The theory, strategy and doctrine of counterinsurgency were coined by the classical French, British and US schools of counterinsurgency in and after the small wars in Indochina, Algeria, Vietnam and Malaysia".[16]

The theory, strategy and doctrine of counterinsurgency have developed since 9/11 and turned the small wars in Afghanistan and Iraq into the direction of coordinated civil/military means like nation-building and peacekeeping. In addition, neo-classical[17] and modern[18] counterinsurgency theories moved away from a regionally or nationally restricted analysis of insurgency to various factors like religion and society.

An insurgency can be analysed on a phenomenological, a theoretical and a strategic level. Consequently, insurgency is a phenomenon of small wars, involving irregular non-state actors who use asymmetric, unconventional strategies and tactics against regular state actors.

The US State Department defines insurgency as "protracted political-military activity conducted by an organized movement seeking to subvert or displace the government and completely or partially control the resources and/or population of a country through the use of force and alternative political organizations"[19] and as "the combination of propaganda and subversion, terrorism and/or guerrilla warfare, funded through illicit economic activity, undermines an affected nation's governing apparatus. When able to separate a population from the authority and services of the state, the insurgents may seek to fill the vacuum with a counter-government or parallel administrative structures to control, intimidate, or mobilize the population to their ends".[20]

In a nutshell, insurgency is part of the complex small wars, asymmetric warfare, multidimensional warfare, complex irregular warfare, wars of the third kind and

---

[16]Clutterbuck (1966), Clutterbuck (1977), Trinquier (1968), Blaufarb (1977), Horne (1977), Taber (1965).

[17]Beckett (2005), Mockaitis (1995), Nagl (2002), Sepp (2005).

[18]Aylwin-Foster (2005), Barno (2006), Cassidy (2006), Kilcullen (2005), Petraeus (2006).

[19]United States Department of State (2007: 7).

[20]United States Department of State (2007: 10).

360 degree warfare.[21] The theory of global insurgency defines a new category of insurgency with "utopian aims, intense motivation, global connectivity and mobility, extreme violence and constant adaptation".[22]

Currently the Jihadist organisations "Islamic State" and Al Qaida fulfil these criteria. From a religious, political, strategic, tactical and geographic point of view, the global insurgency of "Islamic State" and Al Qaida is by far the most hybrid and complex form of insurgency to date and—thanks to the totalitarian, theocratic Jihadist strategy for a caliphate—a worldwide insurgency of historic significance.

The religious/political ideology of a new Jihad propagates the fight for a caliphate in contemporary times, the "ideal Islamic State". This new Jihad is combined with an unprecedented religious/political sense of mission that is characterised by a degree of violence that goes beyond the limits of international laws of war and democratic principles such as the rule of law and human rights. By striving for caliphate interpretations in the twenty-first century, Jihadist organisations like the IS and Al Qaida have reached a new strategic and operative-tactical level of global insurgency.

### 2.5.4 Ayman Al Zawahiri: From a Mullah and Ideologist of the New Jihad to the Leader of Al Qaida

This decay of Muslim community's history witnesses a huge conflict between the forces of Heresy and Revolt against Allah and domination and arrogance (istikbar) on the one hand, and Muslim communities and their Jihadist vanguard, on the other. This conflict reaches its apogee in the fortunate attacks against New York and Washington [September 11] and as a consequence, the declaration by Bush of a new Crusader's war against Islam and what he called the war on Terror. (Al Zawahiri, in Khosrokhavaer, 2009: 165)

It is clear from the calamities of this war against the American crusaders and its consequences that there is a dire emergency to understand the significance of the principles *Al Wala' wa-l-bara'* in Islam and the extent of the neglect and carelessness for preserving this fundamental principle of the Islamic faith. Consequently one should grasp the imposture of enemies of the Islam and their followers and supporters, even among the people of the Islamic community who aim at disfiguring the features of this essential foundation, express their adversity in the guise of Custodians [of the two Holy Mosques, that is, the Saudi regime] and condemn innocent people by accusing them of being bombers. (Al Zawahiri, in Khosrokhavaer, 2009: 26)

It [the Jihad in Afghanistan] also gave young Muslim mujahidin—Arabs, Pakistanis, Turks, and Muslims from Central and East Asia—a great opportunity to get acquainted with each other on the land of Afghan Jihad through their comradeship-at-arms against the enemies of Islam. (Al Zawahiri in Knights under the Prophet's Banner: Meditations on the Jihadist Movement, in Devji, 2005: 64)

As a son of a respected family—his great uncle was imam at the Al-Azhar University in Cairo and his father professor of medicine–Al Zawahiri was born on

---

[21] See Goertz (2012: 41–89), Shultz and Dew (2006), Zahab and Roy (2004).

[22] Gompert (2007: ix), Wiktorowicz (2005), Kilcullen (2005).

19 June 1952, in Maadi, Egypt. Already in his youth, he became a member of Islamist groups and joined the Muslim Brotherhood. The capture and execution of Sayyid Qutb in 1966 was an important event in his radicalisation to Jihad (Ibrahim, 2007; Kepel & Milelli, 2010). Al Zawahiri finished his medical studies in 1974 and worked for 3 years as a surgeon for the Egyptian armed forces. Simultaneously he took part in Islamic-Jihadist activities, and by the beginning of the 1970s, he commanded a group of 40 Jihadists.

After the assassination of the Egyptian President Sadat, Al Zawahiri was imprisoned together with over 1000 other suspects. After his release in 1985, he travelled to Pakistan via Saudi Arabia and finally to Afghanistan, to join the Jihad against Soviet troops, cooperating with Osama bin Laden and Abdullah Azzam. In the 1990s he supposedly travelled to Pakistan, Malaysia, Taiwan, Singapore and Hong Kong. In December 1996, Al Zawahiri tried to travel to Chechnya, using a false identity, but he was arrested after a few hours. His companions and he himself managed to uphold their fake identities and were released after 3 days (Gebara, 2005).

On an international scale, little notice was taken of the fusion of the greatest Egyptian Islamic-Jihadist organisation, Gamaat Al Islamiyya, commanded by Al Zawahiri, with the internationally operating Al Qaida in 1998. This was an important step in developing a new internationally, globalised Jihad. Evolving from the Egyptian struggle against the Mubarak system, Gamaat Al Islamiyya transformed itself into a Jihadist group that merged with Al Qaida (Cook, 2015: 131–133). The foiled assassination of the Egyptian President Mubarak in June 1995, the assassination of 30 Greek tourists in Egypt in April 1996 and the assassination of 58 Western tourists (most of whom were Swiss) in Luxor in November 1997 show the tactical strength and terrorist power of Gamaat Al Islamiyya at the end of the 1990s. Before the assassination of the 58 tourists at the end of 1997, Gamaat Al Islamiyya had publicly threatened to fight tourism in Egypt with terrorist means (Cook, 2015: 133). Although scholarly literature gives the founding date of Al Qaida as the year 1988, the loose grouping did not acquire a tighter structure until 1996/1997 after Bin Laden and Al Zawahiri had begun to develop a common Jihad ideology and strategy (Steinberg, 2014: 291).

Since 9/11 and the subsequent military intervention of the USA and NATO in Afghanistan, the whereabouts of Al Zawahiri was unknown, although he was supposedly hiding in West Pakistan (BBC, 2006). Since then he has published more than 60 video messages (ABC News, 2008; BBC, 2003, 2011, 2014, 2015; CNN, 2006). At the beginning of 2006, US armed forces executed an air strike on Al Zawahiri's presumed whereabouts in a Pakistani village, close to the Afghan border (BBC, 2006). In the aftermath there were nationwide protests against the USA in Pakistan. At the end of January, Al Zawahiri referred to the US air raid in a video message (BBC, 2006). In September 2015 he commented publicly on the attacks of the IS against Al-Nusra Front (a branch of Al Qaida) in Syria and called upon the IS to form a coalition with all international Jihadists to fight against the alliance of USA, Russia, Europe, Shiites, Iran and Assad's Syrian regime (Joscelyn, 2015). As of 2007, the Rewards for Justice Program of the US Department of Justice offered a reward of 25 million US dollars for information leading to the arrest of Al Zawahiri (US Department of Justice, 2007).

In 2006, Al Zawahiri issued a warning to the Palestinian Hamas that possible peace talks with Israel and the recognition of Israel would violate the Sharia and the Islamist doctrine of tawhid.[23] To summarise, Al Zawahiri is one of the advocates of a strategic shift of Jihad, away from the "near enemy" towards the "far enemy". Up until the mid-1990s, Al Zawahiri had fought against the Mubarak regime as the "near enemy". His strategic shift can be traced back to his document Al-Nass al-Kamil li-muqtarah al-wasat bain al-haraka al islamiyya wa-al-gharb[24] (Steinberg, 2014: 292).

### 2.5.5   Al Wala' wa-l-bara' as Salafist-Jihadist Doctrine of "Us Versus Them", "Friend Versus Foe", "Good Versus Evil"

Al Wala' wa-l-bara',[25] "loyalty and rejection" is an Islamist concept which is hundreds of years old and which has diverse interpretations (Wagemakers, 2014). On the one hand, the idea of being "loyal and rejecting" has developed into quite an important doctrine of contemporary Wahhabi and Salafist Islam with specific relevance for the everyday life of Muslims worldwide. According to Al Wala' wa-l-bara', friendship and loyalty (wala) should only be shown towards "true Muslims". On the other hand, all other people, "non-true Muslims", should be rejected and avoided" (bara) (Kepel & Milelli, 2005; McCants & Brachman, 2007). Bara is derived from the Arabic word barā'a that expressed expulsion of a member of the tribe in the time before Muhammad. Bara is also used in the Quran, in sura 9, verse 1.

Interpretations of the Wahhabi and the Salafist doctrine Al Wala' wa-l-bara' can be traced back to Hanbali scholar Ibn Taimiya in the fourteenth century, who wrote Iqtida Al Sirat Al Mustaqim fi Muḥālafat Aṣḥab Al jaḥim. In that document he listed many Jewish, Christian and other non-Islamic religious celebrations that Muslims should not attend under any circumstances (Wagemakers, 2009a, 2009b). Ibn Taimiya's call to Muslims to keep "infidels" at bay was further developed by his student Qaiyim Al Jauziya in the fourteenth century (Wagemakers, 2014). The latter's theology of the segregation from non-Muslims was based on various Quran verses (Wagemakers, 2014). Furthermore, Al Jawziyya used the Sunna and writings of the caliphs of the Umayyad and Abbasid dynasties (Al Jauziya, 1997: 448–491).

Both Ibn Taimiya's and Ibn Al Jauziya's theologies are supposed to have been the decisive inspiration for the reformist Muhammad Ibn Abd Al Wahhab on the

---

[23]Video messages of Al Zawahiri from 6 January 2006 and 4 March 2006, Farschid (2014: 169).
[24]Internet publication, see Said (2013).
[25]الولاء والبراء.

Arabian peninsula (Wagemakers, 2014). In view of the absolutely strict individual piety and the rejection of *bida* (forbidden reforms), *Al Wala' wa-l-bara'* embodies the Salafist search for purity and serves contemporary Salafists as an ideal instrument to repel threats to Islam (Wagemakers, 2014).

In the 1980s, the Egyptian Islamic scholar Abd Al Rahman Abd Al Khaliq Al Yusuf and the Saudi scholar Muhammad Said Al Qahtani made their impact on *Al Wala' wa-l-bara'* (Ali, 2012). Said Al Qahtani's teacher at the Umm al Qura University in Mecca was Muhammad Qutb, the brother of Sayyid Qutb. The spreading of *Al Wala' wa-l-bara'* was even more enhanced when Wahhabi teachers started interpreting it and using it as a social doctrine forbidding Muslims to copy non-Muslims or imitate their way of life (Wagemakers, 2014). A second doctrine focuses on the commitment not to enter into political or military alliances with "the infidels". Finally, the third and last doctrine stipulates that besides Sharia any additional "man-made laws" are forbidden (Wagemakers, 2014). In a Salafist inter-pretation, the third doctrine should be implemented by all means, in this context with the militant means of Jihad (Wagemakers, 2014).

All key contemporary international Jihadist leaders use *Al Wala' wa-l-bara'* as a constituent principle of their Jihadist recruitment strategy. Already in December 2002, Aiman Al Zawāhirī, the current leader of Al Qaida, used *Al Wala' wa-l-bara'* in his book *Knights Under the White Banner: Meditations on the Jihadist Movement* to create dichotomies and "concepts of the enemy" (Devji, 2005). Khamatovich Umarov, who was the leader of Jihadist groups in Chechnya until 2013, considered *Al Wala' wa-l-bara'* as one of the most important duties of Islam (Lohlker, 2009: 63). And also the leader of the Islamist/Jihadist organisation "Laskar Jihad" in Indonesia, Jafar Umar Thalib, interprets *Al Wala' wa-l-bara'* the same way, so that the devout Muslim should love and defend his fellow Muslims and Islam as a whole, while it is his duty to keep away and protect himself and his community from influences of the "infidels" (Noorhaidi, 2006: 138). Together with *Tauhid*, *Aqida* and *Takfir*, Brachman considers *Al Wala' wa-l-bara'* as a determining principle of the contemporary doctrine of Jihad.

The new mullahs of Jihad, the Salafist-Jihadists of the twenty-first century, use *Al Wala' wa-l-bara'* on a theologically personal as well as on a political and social level. The Jihadist interpretation of *Al Wala' wa-l-bara'* is based on the first pillar of Islam and derives from it that *Tawhid* is compulsory for every male Muslim capable of waging war against the "infidels" (Kepel & Milelli, 2005; McCants & Brachman, 2007).

## 2.5.6  The New Jihad as Theology and Doctrine

The above-mentioned new mullahs of Jihad have been propagating a shift of focus, away from the "near enemy" (authoritarian regimes in the Near and Middle East) towards the "far enemy" (Western democracies) since the 1990s and on an even higher level since 9/11. According to their logic, to attack the "far enemy" with terrorist means leads to a loss of power for the "near enemy" who can eventually be toppled and gradually replaced state by state with a caliphate governed by the Sharia.

Abdullah Azzam transformed the theology of Jihad from the twentieth to the twenty-first century, developing and globalising it. He did this by recruiting for the Jihad against Soviet troops in Afghanistan and by linking this first international Jihad with Palestine. Azzam created and developed the Jihad interpretation that the defence and/or conquest of (Muslim) territories is the duty of every Muslim world-wide (Maliach, 2010: 82). Azzam interpreted the Jihad as the "most important deed for Islam", as every true Muslim has the duty to pursue Jihad (*hijra*), to prepare militarily (*idad*) and to protect the boundaries of his Muslim country and territories and—at the highest level—to wage war (*qital*). Together with Osama bin Laden, Abdullah Azzam can be described as a pioneer of the first wave of the international Jihad (in Afghanistan of the 1980s).

Abu Muhammad Al Maqdisi is the connecting link between the Saudi Arab Sunni/Wahhabi legal scholars and Jihadist mullahs and doctrines. His theology of Jihad rates democracy as counter-religion to Islam. As explained above, in his publications Al Maqdisi preaches total obedience and total loyalty towards Allah in every possible aspect (Wagemakers, 2008). On a political level, Al Maqdisi derives from the principle *Al Wala' wa-l-bara'* that Muslims worldwide have to overthrow political systems in which the Sharia is not established as legal system (Wagemakers, 2009a, 2009b). In classing democracies as counter-religions, Al Maqdisi committed true Muslims to renounce democracy and to fight those Muslim countries and rulers who used man-made laws and formed alliances with non-Muslim states (Farschid, 2014: 176). In the theology of Al Maqdisi, democratic participation is an expression of disbelief (*kufr*), because parliamentarism is a deviation from Islamic monotheism (*tauhid*).

Abu Musab Al Suri followed the Jihadist theology and strategy of Abdullah Azzam and Abu Muhammad Al Maqdisi and can be described as one the most important mullahs and theoreticians and moreover as strategist of the global Jihad, the new Jihad. Al Suri propagates a realpolitik Jihad of the twenty-first century that aims politically and tactically at the highest efficiency in a means/ends relationship. Moreover, Al Suri is also a strategist of "lone wolf Jihad", the Jihad of Islamist lone operators (Berger, 2011; Lia, 2009). His book *The Global Islamic Resistance Call* published in 2005 elaborates on strategic as well as on operative-tactical principles of "lone wolf Jihad", the decentralised, individualised Jihad of Islamist lone operators or very small autonomous cells.

He propagates Jihad as a mass phenomenon both on a strategical and tactical level, "the resistance is the Islamic nation's struggle and not a struggle by the elite", a global Jihad, the new Jihad of a worldwide insurgency (Al Suri, 2005: 1425). Al Suri's theology and strategy of the new Jihad propagates the fight for a caliphate in the contemporary world of the twenty-first century, the "ideal Islamic State". The caliphate interpretations of Jihadist organisations like the "Islamic State" and Al Qaida reach a new strategic and operative-tactical level of a global insurgency.

The theology and strategy of the new Jihad of the twenty-first century derives from a dualist concept of the world in which Islam either dominates or is dominated.

On an operative-tactical level, the individual Jihad derives from the dualist principle of *Al Wala' wa-l-bara'* and is supposed to be carried out worldwide either by Islamist single operators or cells or hit teams of Jihadist organisations. The decentralised, individualised contemporary Jihad of today (e.g. in Brussels, Nice, Ansbach, Würzburg, Berlin, London and Stockholm in the years 2016 and 2017) is the operative implementation of the theology and doctrine of the new Jihad.

## 2.6    Jihad and the Muslim "Martyr", the *Shahid*

In the course of the last decades, the *shahid*, the Jihadist "martyr", developed into an Islamist terrorist as a tactical game changer in small wars like in Afghanistan and in Iraq. Contrary to non-religious terrorists, the Jihadi *shahid* accepts that he may be caught, injured or killed. Usually non-religious terrorists do not consider that they may become "martyrs" (Khosrokhavaer, 2009). Khosrokhavar distinguishes between Christian and Jewish martyrs on the one hand and Muslim martyrs on the other: "Jewish and Christian martyrs accepted death without killing their enemies, unlike Muslims, who right from the beginning, defined martyrdom as dying in the path of Allah by actively fighting the enemy in order to neutralize it" (Khosrokhavaer, 2009: 41). The history of Muslim martyrs dates back to the early beginnings of Islam which were dominated by battles and conflicts, at first on the Arab peninsular and later when attacking the Persian Empire and parts of the Christian world. From the beginning Jihadi warriors accepted the possibility of dying or sacrificing themselves in battle. Khalid bin Walid, for example, a Muslim general, who conquered Persia and Roman Syria between 633 and 636, stated: "Accept our religion, or pay a tribute or prepare for war. Because the men who are with me like war and death as much as you like pleasures and life" (after Khosrokhavaer, 2009: 41).

The most common expression for martyrdom in the Quran is "dying for the sake of Allah". The following quotes from Quran are used by the new mullahs of Jihad to theologically explain the *shahid* concept:

Al Imran sura 3, verse 170 und 171

> Rejoicing in what Allah has bestowed upon them of his bounty, and they receive good tidings about those [to be martyred] after them who have not yet joined them—that there will be no fear concerning them, nor will they grieve.
> They receive good tidings of favor from Allah and bounty and [of the fact] that Allah does not allow the reward of believers to be lost.

Al Taubah sura 9, verse 111

> Indeed, Allah has purchased from the believers their lives and their properties [in exchange] for that they will have Paradise. They fight in the cause of Allah, so they kill and are killed. [It is] a true promise [binding] upon Him in (...) the Qur'an. And who is truer to his covenant than Allah? So rejoice in your transaction which you have contracted. And it is that which is the great attainment.

Al Hadj, sura 22, verse 59

He will surely cause them to enter an entrance with which they will be pleased, and indeed, Allah is Knowing and Forbearing.

Al Nisa, sura 4, verse 75

And what is [the matter] with you that you fight not in the cause of Allah and [for] the oppressed among men, women, and children who say, "Our Lord, take us out of this city of oppressive people and appoint for us from Yourself a protector and appoint for us from Yourself a helper?

Al Imran, sura 158

And whether you die or are killed, unto Allah you will be gathered.

According to prevailing opinion, the Muslim concept of a martyr, a *shahid*, is far more active than the martyr concepts of the other monotheist religions of Judaism and Christianity (Ayoub, 1987; Cook, 2015; Kohlberg, 1998). It was only for a short time in history before Muhammad's *hijra* that some Muslims became martyrs because they were persecuted by Meccans. After Muhammad's *hijra*, there were very few Muslim martyrs because Islam—compared with other religions—rapidly gained extensive power (Ayoub, 1987; Cook, 2015). The concept of Muslim *shahid* is illustrated in the *hadith* literature of Abdallah Al Mubarak's "Kitab Al Jihad": "O, God! Make my wife a widow, make my child an orphan, and ennoble Nawf with martyrdom!" (after Cook, 2015: 26). Islam of the seventh to ninth century understood Muslim martyrdom to be almost synonymous with "death in military battle" (Ayoub, 1987; Cook, 2015; Kohlberg, 1998). The unanimously acknowledged definition of a "martyr" or *shahid* is based on Quranic sura 9, verse 41, and describes "death in the fight for Allah": "A Bedouin came to the Messenger of Allah and said: 'A man can fight for fame, another can fight in order to receive praise, yet another to receive spoils, and another in order to show off'". The Messenger of Allah said: "Whoever fights in order to make the word of Allah the highest [see Qur'an 9:41], that person is fighting in the way of Allah" (Abu Daud, Sunan III, after Cook, 2015: 27).

For the Muslim martyrs, the Quran offers the reward of paradise in verses 13–15 of sura 13. In verses 54–58 of the suras 44, 21, 51, 23 and 56, paradise is described as a sensual place of temptations where the *hur al'in*, or *huris*,[26] the paradise virgins, are waiting.

In their "spiritual guidance", a religious/political manifest, the Jihadist assassins of 9/11 repeatedly mentioned the *huris*. In the "spiritual guidance" it says that "afterwards the day will come when God will allow you to spend your time in paradise with these *huris*". The idea of the paradise virgins, the *huris*, is a vital part of the Islamic concept of paradise, and it is not only present in the Quran but also in the *hadith* literature (Goertz, 2017; Lohlker, 2009). According to this concept and sura

---

[26]The paradise virgins who supposedly are waiting for the shahids, the Muslim "martyrs".

38, verse 52, of the Quran, the *huris* are a prized reward waiting for the Muslim *shahids* (Lohlker, 2009). Khalfaoui even states that "paradise turns into a virgin".

### 2.6.1  The New Cult of Martyrs: Jihadist Suicide Attackers as a Tactical-Operative Means of the Twenty-First Century

The analysis of the worldwide acknowledged "Suicide Attack Database" which was set up by the University of Chicago[27] took all suicide attacks in the period between 1974 and June 2016 into consideration. From this synopsis the conclusion was drawn that Jihadist suicide attacks have increased significantly since 9/11, while they have also become a regularly used means of Islamist terrorism. From the total of 5439 listed suicide attacks between 1974 and 2016, nearly 1000 have been committed in the 12 months between 2015 and 2016 within 8 Muslim countries: in Iraq (360), Afghanistan (130), Nigeria (120), Syria (120), Yemen (50), Pakistan (50), Libya (50) and Egypt (50).[28]

While there were "only" 35 Jihadist suicide attacks with 254 people killed in Israel in the 8 years between 1993 and 9/11, numbers almost doubled in the following 8 years between 2002 and 2010 with 77 suicide attacks killing 465 people.[29]

According to the *Suicide Attack Database*, between 2003 and June 2016 more than 3700 suicide attacks were committed in Iraq, Syria and Afghanistan (2200 in Iraq, 1200 in Afghanistan and 300 in Syria).[30] The even more intense suicide attacks conducted by the "Islamic State" since 2014 have not yet been statistically included in the *Suicide Attack Database*, but it is already apparent that the numbers increased again dramatically from June 2016 to May 2017.

As of 2002 in Afghanistan and 2004 in Iraq, with the beginning of the small war against Western and Iraqi coalition troops, Jihadist suicide attacks became a special tactical means against Iraqi police stations, military facilities and other government targets (Shultz & Dew, 2006). An analysis of Jihadists who were killed in the small war in Iraq 2005 has shown that every fourth one of them died as a suicide attacker. Seventy percent of these suicide attackers were Saudi Arabs (Paz, 2005). The analysis of the Jihadist insurgency in Iraq from 2003 to 2006 shows that the Jihadi suicide attacks did not exclude women or children from their operative logic and target selection (Shultz & Dew, 2006: 255). According to EUROPOL, until the Jihadist attacks in Paris on 13 November 2015, neither suicide attacks nor suicide

---

[27]CPOST Chicago Project on Security and Terrorism. The University of Chicago. http://cpostdata.uchicago.edu/search_new.php

[28]http://cpostdata.uchicago.edu/search_results_new.php

[29]http://cpostdata.uchicago.edu/search_results_new.php

[30]http://cpostdata.uchicago.edu/search_results_new.php

vests had been used in Europe, but since then EUROPOL describes suicide attacks as "possible tactical means of the future".[31] Questions of motivation, causality, reasons, effects and triggers for individual processes of radicalisation for conducting terrorist and suicide attacks are discussed quite controversially.[32]

In the course of an empirical study, 46 Pakistani Islamists from the Swat valley were asked why and how they had radicalised themselves. Over 90% of the interviewees answered that US drone attacks set the process of radicalisation in motion. But a closer analysis showed that of the 46 Pakistani Islamists questioned, not one had suffered losses in his family—because there had been no US drone attacks. In their subjective "parallel reality", the 46 Islamists questioned replied in collectively identifying themselves with the supposed victims that did not exist in reality. From this it can be concluded that supposed singular catalytic events are quite often overestimated in their function for individual radicalisation processes. This exaggeration of singular events seems to be a human reflex to make outside factors responsible for personal decisions and actions. In a nutshell the projection of causality and guilt on to "the enemy" is a reflex action as well as a serious mistake of attribution, the legitimacy for militant or even terrorist activity. Post and Denny established that the influence of the peer group on individual radicalisation processes is crucial. In their analysis of radicalisation processes of Islamists from Palestinian milieus, all families were rated as exclusively supportive of the terrorist actions of their sons. This finding is highlighted by the following quotations:

> Perpetrators of armed attacks were seen as heroes, their families got a great deal of material assistance including the construction of new homes [. . .].
> Recruits were treated with great respect. A youngster who belonged to Hamas or Fatah was regarded more highly than one who didn't belong to a group and got better treatment than unaffiliated kids.

This process of producing martyrs and heroes, combined with an enormous increase in social prestige and/or financial and social support for the families of Jihadist suicide attackers, has a vast influence on radicalisation processes in Arab and African countries.

In contrast to what is quite often stated, a suicide bomber is not a cheap weapon that is used arbitrarily. Especially in the twenty-first century, in the century of the media, the identities of suicide bombers hardly remain secret. Groups that use suicide bombers as tactical means—like Hamas, Hizbullah, Al Qaida and IS—are aware of the fact that the peer group of the bomber and his/her family require a good explanation why their son, brother, father or husband sacrificed himself as *shahid*. In the 1990s, Hamas and Hizbullah came to the conclusion that if they wanted to establish suicide attacks nationwide, a cult of martyrdom required systematic financial and propagandistic backing (Burke, 2015). Since 9/11 Hamas and Hizbullah

---

[31]Changes in Modus Operandi of Islamic State Terrorist Attacks. Europol. https://www.europol.europa.eu/content/changes-modus-operandi-islamic-state-terrorist-attacks

[32]Khosrokhavar (2006).

have systematically initiated statements by parents of killed suicide bombers, like "I am sad that my son has gone, but I am happy because of his sacrifice" (Burke, 2015: 99). Such statements have increased exponentially.

## 2.7  Summary

Socio-scientifically speaking, religions such as Islam are able to kindle violence because they have the ability to form a binding commitment with their followers. By creating a spiritual/religious language which makes it appear that violence serves a higher purpose, religions can generate violence or even worse. By invoking their often violent and militant origins, religions can trigger the impulse for violence or war in their followers in certain psychological, individual and social crisis situations.

Religions are able to create phenomenological violence like ritual and symbolic violence, physical violence against "the others", religiously justified persecution or punishment related to fundamentalist, dualist stereotypes. Besides religiously legitimised and organised social violence based on gender or "revenge", religiously motivated terrorism can also propagate a "sacred struggle", "holy conflict" or a "holy war".

Stressing dogmas, doctrines, norms and practices can create religious fundamentalism and strategies, protecting the group's identity from "outside". Religious fundamentalism usually strives for a religious, spiritual and social renewal. By presenting its followers with presumed absolute dichotomies and "truths", religious fundamentalism fabricates an ontological certainty.

Due to their interpretation of political and social processes and conditions, religions can offer reference systems for a "cosmic fight" for "good" prevailing over "evil". From a dualist perspective of "good and evil" and "us versus them", religions have the power to develop a moral justification for violence. Consequently, Islamist, Salafist and also Literalist fundamentalism is a main factor for the terrorist ideology and theology of Jihadism.

As analysed above in Sects. 2.2 and 2.3, the religious/political concept of Jihad is wider and more complex than war on a military-operative level on its own. Jihad is a religious/political theology, culture and strategy of war, a culture of death and of the apocalypse. The last chapter analysed how the Quran—as the primary source of Islam—relates to Jihadist violence. It further highlighted that this relationship can be also found literally in secondary sources of the Sunni school and in the expert assessments of various Islamic scholars. As mentioned above, Wahhabism, Salafism and Jihadism have the same Islamic/theological roots and resemble each other in their anti-modernism and in their demand to end the distinction between public and private life.

Furthermore, they all reject the sovereignty of the people and consequently man-made laws. Hassan Al Banna and Sayyid Qutb, the spiritual fathers of Islamism in Egypt in the second half of the twentieth century, based their theology and doctrine on a fundamentalist Wahhabism. The above-mentioned new mullahs of

Jihad have continued where the old mullahs—Al Banna, Sayyid Qutb and Mustafa Shukri—left off, but at the same time, they adapted their theology and doctrines in a progressive way to take the modern questions of internationalisation and globalisation in the twenty-first century into account. Since the 1990s, especially after 9/11 and the subsequent global war on terror waged by the Western coalition, the new mullahs even increased their propaganda efforts in order to broaden the strategic and tactical targeting of Jihad. Targets are not only the "near enemies" (non-Islamic regimes in the Middle East) but also the "far enemies" (Western countries). According to the logic of the mullahs of the new Jihad, fighting the "far enemy" would also lead to a loss of power of the "near enemy" and finally to its defeat. The final step of this new strategic approach is the establishment of a caliphate in the Muslim states which function under the rule of Sharia law.

Abdullah Azzam was the first of the new mullahs of Jihad who established the internationalised Jihad as a common principle for the worldwide *Umma*. In addition, in 2009 Al Maqdisi installed a "Sharia committee" with Islamic legal scholars on his website, who applied his Jihad doctrine to all aspects of a Muslim's everyday life—the more questions and participants, the better.

Like Al Maqdisi and Al Zawahiri, Al Suri also represents and preaches the Jihadist interpretation of *Al Wala' wa-l-bara'*. But in contrast to the more intellectual approaches of Jihad of Al Maqdisi and Al Zawahiri, Al Suri concentrates on the political and military aspects according to a goal/means perspective. Consequently, Al Suri is considered the Jihad strategist of a lone wolf terrorism for lone operators. On a strategic doctrinal level, Al Suri propagates Jihad as a mass phenomenon, as an insurgency on a global scale.

As mentioned above, both the theology and the strategy and tactics of the new Jihad of the twenty-first century have their roots in the *Al Wala' wa-l-bara'* principle that creates a dualist world view of "good versus evil", "friend versus foe". The Jihadist interpretation of *Al Wala' wa-l-bara'* propagates the individual Jihad, carried out by lone operators or small cells or hit teams of Jihadist organisations like Al Qaida or IS. This kind of a global decentralised and individualised Jihad (e.g. in Brussels, Nice, Ansbach, Würzburg, Berlin, London, Stockholm, Manchester, Hamburg, Carcassonne and Strasbourg in 2016, 2017 and 2018) is the operative realisation of the theology and doctrine of the new Jihad.

New Jihad as low-level terrorism is closely linked to the ideology of the *shahid*, the Jihadist "martyr" concept of "dying for Allah". The analysis of the above-mentioned *Suicide Attack Database* shows that Jihadist suicide attacks have increased exorbitantly since 9/11 and that they have become a persistent operative means that has the value of a tactical game changer.

# References

ABC News. (2008, August 10). *New Zawahiri Tape; He speaks English*. Retrieved January 15, 2019, from http://abcnews.go.com/Blotter/story?id=5552090&page=1

Al Banna, H. (1947). *Towards the light*. Retrieved January 15, 2019, from http://www.ikhwanweb.com/article.php?id=802

Al Banna, H. (1995). *Naḥwa n-nūr*, German text only: *Aufbruch zum Licht*. In A. Meier (Ed.), *Politische Strömungen im modernen Islam: Quellen und Kommentare*. Bundeszentrale für politische Bildung: Bonn.

Al Jauziya, I. (1997). Aḥkām ahl ad_-d_imma. *Beirut, 1*, 448–491.

Al Suri. (2005). *The global resistance call*. Retrieved January 15, 2019, from https://archive.org/stream/TheGlobalIslamicResistanceCall/The_Global_Islamic_Resistance_Call_-_Chapter_8_sections_5_to_7_LIST_OF_TARGETS_djvu.txt

Al Waqidi, M. (1984). *Kitab Al-Maghazi*. Beirut: Alam Al-Kutub.

Ali, B. (2012). *The Islamic Doctrine of Al-Wala' wa-l-Bara' (Loyalty and Disavowal) in modern Salafism*. University of Exeter. PhD Dissertation.

Atkins, S. (2004). *Encyclopedia of modern worldwide extremists and extremist groups*. Santa Barbara, CA: Greenwood Publishing.

Aylwin-Foster, N. (2005). Changing the army for counterinsurgency operations. *Military Review, 85*(6), 1–15.

Ayoub, M. (1987). Martyrdom in Christianity and Islam. In R. Antoun & M. Hegland (Eds.), *Religious resurgence: Contemporary cases in Islam, Christianity and Judaism* (pp. 67–77). Syracuse, NY: Syracuse University Press.

Barno, D. (2006, Summer). Challenges in fighting a global insurgency. *Parameters*, 15–29.

BBC. (2003, May 21). *'Al-Qaeda' statement: Full text*. Retrieved January 15, 2019, from http://news.bbc.co.uk/2/hi/middle_east/3047903.stm

BBC. (2006, January 15). *Pakistan rally against US strike*. Retrieved January 15, 2019, from http://news.bbc.co.uk/2/hi/south_asia/4614486.stm

BBC. (2011, June 8). *Al-Qaeda posts fresh warning from al-Zawahiri to US*. Retrieved January 15, 2019, from http://www.bbc.com/news/world-13696051

BBC. (2014, September 4). *Al-Qaeda chief Zawahiri launches al-Qaeda in South Asia*. Retrieved January 15, 2019, from http://www.bbc.com/news/world-asia-29056668

BBC. (2015, August 13). *Al-Qaeda's Zawahiri pledges loyalty to new Taliban chief*. Retrieved January 15, 2019, from http://www.bbc.com/news/world-asia-33907666

Bearman, P., Binquis, T., & Bosworth, C. (Eds.). (2004). *Encyclopedia of Islam*. Leiden: E.J. Brill.

Beckett, I. (2005). The future of insurgency. *Small Wars & Insurgencies, 16*, 22–36.

Berger, J. (2011). *Americans who go to war in the name of Islam*. Washington, DC: Potomac Books.

Blaufarb, D. (1977). *The counterinsurgency era: US doctrine and performance*. New York: Free Press.

Brynjar, L. (1998). *The society of the muslim brothers in Egypt: The rise of an Islamic mass movement*. Reading: Garnet Publishing and Ithaca Press.

Burke, J. (2015). *The new threat from Islamic militancy*. London: Penguin-Bodley Head.

Carré, O. (1984). *Mystique et Politique: Lecture révolutionnaire du Coran par Sayyid Qutb, Frère Musulman radical*. Paris: Presses de la Fondation nationale des sciences politiques.

Cassidy, R. (2006, Summer). The long small war. *Parameters, 36*, 47–62.

Clutterbuck, R. (1966). *The long war: The emergency in Malaya 1948–1960*. London: Cassell.

Clutterbuck, R. (1977). *Guerillas and terrorists*. London: Faber and Faber.

CNN. (2006, January 30). *Al Zawahiri: Bush the butcher of Washington*. Retrieved January 15, 2019, from http://edition.cnn.com/2006/WORLD/asiapcf/01/30/zawahiri.transcript/

Commins, D. (2006). *The Wahhabi mission and Saudi Arabia*. London: I.B.Tauris & Co.

Cook, D. (2015). *Understanding Jihad*. Oakland, CA: University of California Press.

De Long-Bas, N. (2009). Wahhābīya. In J. Esposito (Ed.), *The Oxford encyclopedia of the Islamic world* (Vol. 5, 511b–514a). Oxford: Oxford University Press.

Devji, F. (2005). *Landscapes of the Jihad: Militancy, morality, modernity*. Ithaca, NY: Cornell University Press.

Farschid, O. (2014). Salafismus als politische Ideologie. In B. Said & H. Fouad (Eds.), *Salafismus: Auf der Suche nach dem wahren Islam* (pp. 160–192). Freiburg: Herder.

Firestone, R. (1999). *Jihad: The origin of holy war in Islam*. New York: Oxford University Press.

Gebara, K. (2005, February 10). The end of Egyptian Islamic Jihad? *Terrorism Monitor, 3*(3) (The Jamestown Foundation). Retrieved from https://jamestown.org/program/the-end-of-egyptian-islamic-jihad-2/

Gershoni, I., & Jankowski, J. (1995). *Redefining the Egyptian Nation, 1930–1945*. Cambridge: Cambridge University Press.

Goertz, S. (2012). *Die Streitkräfte demokratischer Staaten in den Kleinen Kriegen des 21. Jahrhunderts. Analyse der doktrinären und organisationsstrukturellen Eignung der U.S.-Streitkräfte für die Counterinsurgency-Aufgaben Kleiner Kriege*. Berlin: Wissenschaftlicher Verlag.

Goertz, S. (2017). Zum Verhältnis von Islam und Terrorismus: Jihadismus als religiös-politische Ideologie und Strategie. *Die Polizei, 9*, 253–261.

Gompert, D. (2007). *Heads we win: The cognitive side of counterinsurgency*. Santa Monica, CA: RAND.

Hegghammer, T. (2006). Einführung: Abdullah Azzam, der Imam des Dschihads. In G. Kepel & J.-P. Milelli (Eds.), *Al-Qaida: Texte des Terrors* (pp. 145–173). Munich: Piper.

Horne, A. (1977). *A savage war of peace*. London: NYRB.

Ibrahim, R. (2007). *The Al Qaeda reader*. New York: Broadway Books.

Johnson, J. (1997). *The holy war idea in Western and Islamic traditions*. University Park, PA: Pennsylvania State University Press.

Jones, J. M. B. (1957). The chronology of the Maghazi: A textual survey. *Bulletin of the School of Oriental and African Studies, 19*, 245–280.

Joscelyn, T. (2015, September 13). Zawahiri calls for Jihadist unity, encourages attacks in West. *Long War Journal*. Retrieved January 15, 2019, from http://www.longwarjournal.org/archives/2015/09/zawahiri-calls-for-Jihadist-unity-encourages-attacks-in-west.php

Kelsay, J., & Johnson, J. (1991). *Just war and Jihad: Historical and theoretical perspectives on war and peace in Western and Islamic traditions*. Westport, CT: Praeger.

Kepel, G. (1985). *The prophet and pharaoh: Muslim extremism in Egypt*. London: Al Zaki Books.

Kepel, G. (2002). *Jihad: The trail of political Islam*. Cambridge: Belknap Press of Harvard University Press.

Kepel, G., & Milelli, J. (2005). *Al Qaeda dans le Texte*. Paris: PUF.

Kepel, G., & Milelli, J. (2010). *Al Qaeda in its own words*. London: Harvard University Press.

Khosrokhavaer, F. (2009). *Inside Jihadism. Understanding Jihadi movements worldwide*. London: Routledge.

Khosrokhavar, F. (2006). *Quand Al Qaeda parle: Témoignage derrière les barreaux*. Paris: Grasset.

Kilcullen, D. (2005). Countering global insurgency. *The Journal of Strategic Studies, 28*(4), 597–617.

Kohlberg, E. (1998). Martyrdom and self-sacrifice in classical Islam. *Peemim, 75*, 5–26.

Krämer, G. (2010). *Hasan al-Banna*. Oxford: Oneworld.

Lacroix, S. (2011). *Awakening Islam: The politics of religious dissent in contemporary Saudi Arabia*. Cambridge, MA: Harvard University Press.

Lav, D. (2012). *Radical Islam and the revival of medieval theology*. Cambridge: Cambridge University Press Press.

Lia, B. (2009). *Architect of global Jihad: The life of Al Qaeda Strategist Abu Musab Al Suri*. London: Hurst.

Lohlker, R. (2009). *Dschihadismus: Materialien*. Cologne: UTB.

Maliach, A. (2010, October). Abdullah Sazzam, Al Qaeda and Hamas: Concepts of Jihad and Istishhad. *Military and Strategic Affairs, 2*(2). Retrieved from http://www.inss.org.il/publication/abdullah-azzam-al-qaeda-and-hamas-concepts-of-jihad-and-istishhad/

McCants, W., & Brachman, J. (2007). *Militant ideology Atlas: Executive report*. West Point, NY: Combating Terrorism Center (CTC).

Mockaitis, T. (1995). *British counterinsurgency in the post-imperial era*. Manchester: Manchester University Press.

Morabia, A. (1993). *Le gihad dans l'Islam médiéval*. Paris: Bibliothèque Albin Michel Histoire.

Moser, T. (2012). *Politik auf dem Pfad Gottes, Zur Genese und Transformation des militanten sunnitischen Islamismus*. Innsbruck: Innsbruck University Press.

Moussalli, A. (2009). *Wahhabism, Salafism and Islamism: Who is the enemy?* Beirut: American University of Beirut.

Nagl, J. (2002). *COIN lessons from Malaya and Vietnam: Learning to eat soup with a knife.* Chicago, IL: University of Chicago Press.

Nedza, J. (2014). Überlegungen zur Schärfung einer Analysekategorie. In B. Said & H. Fouad (Eds.), *Salafismus: Auf der Suche nach dem wahren Islam* (pp. 80–105). Freiburg: Herder.

Noorhaidi, H. (2006). *Laskar Jihad: Islam, militancy and the quest for religious identity in post-new order Indonesia*. Ithaca, NY: Cornell Press.

Noth, A. (1966). *Heiliger Krieg und heiliger Kampf in Islam und Christentum*. Bonn: Röhrscheid.

Paz, R. (2005, March). Arab volunteers killed in Iraq: An analysis. The Project for the Research of Islamist Movements (Prism) Occasional Papers. *Global Jihad, 1*(3).

Petraeus, D. (2006, January/February). Learning counterinsurgency: Observations from soldiering in Iraq. *Military Review*, 1–12.

Pfürtner, S. (1991). *Fundamentalismus: Die Flucht ins Radikale*. Freiburg: Herder.

Qutb, S. (2006). *Milestones*. London: Islamic Book Service.

Rapoport, D. (1992). Some general observations on religion and violence. In M. Juergensmeyer (Ed.), *Violence and the sacred in the modern world*. London: Cass.

Rashid, A. (2000). *Taliban: Militant Islam, oil and fundamentalism in Central Asia*. New Haven, CT: Yale University Press.

Said, B. (2013). Djihadismus nach dem Arabischen Frühling und das Vermittlungsangebot Muhammad Al Zawahiris. *Zeitschrift für Außen- und Sicherheitspolitik, 6*(3), 429–452.

Sepp, K. (2005, May/June). Best practices in counterinsurgency. *Military Review*, 8–12.

Shultz, R., & Dew, A. (2006). *Insurgents, terrorists and militias: The warriors of contemporary combat*. New York: Columbia University Press.

Stalinski, S. (2011). *Al-Qaeda military strategist Abu Mus'ab Al-Suri's teachings on fourth-generation warfare (4GW), Individual Jihad and the future of Al-Qaeda*. Inquiry & Analysis Series No. 698, MEMRI.

Steinberg, G. (2014). Saudi-Arabien: Der Salafismus in seinem Mutterland. In T. Said & H. Fouad (Eds.), *Salafismus: Auf der Suche nach dem wahren Islam*. Freiberg: Herder.

Taber, R. (1965). *War of the flea: The classic study of guerilla warfare*. New York: Potomac Books.

Trinquier, R. (1968). *Guerre, Subversion, Révolution*. Paris: R. Laffont.

United States Department of State. (2007). *Counterinsurgency for U.S. Government Policy Makers*. Washington, DC

US Department of Justice. (2007, December 24). *Most wanted terrorists: Ayman Al-Zawahiri*. FBI, US Department of Justice.

Wagemakers, J. (2008). Abu Muhammad al-Maqdisi: A counter-terrorism asset? *CTC Sentinel, 6,* 8–10.

Wagemakers, J. (2009a). A Purist Jihadi-Salafi: The ideology of Abu Muhammad al-Maqdisi. *British Journal of Middle Eastern Studies, 36,* 281–297.

Wagemakers, J. (2009b). The transformation of a radical concept: al-wala' wa-l-bara' in the ideology of Abu Muhammad al-Maqdisi. In R. Meijer (Ed.), *Global Salafism. Islam's new religious movement* (pp. 81–106). London: Hurst & Company.

Wagemakers, J. (2010, Summer). Protecting Jihad: The Sharia Council of the Minbar Al Tawhid Wa Al Jihad. *Middle East Policy, 18*(2). Retrieved from https://www.mepc.org/protecting-jihad-sharia-council-minbar-al-tawhid-wa-l-jihad

Wagemakers, J. (2012). *A Quietist Jihad: The ideology and influence of Abu Muhammad al-Maqdisi*. New York: Cambridge University Press.

Wagemakers, J. (2014). Salafistische Strömungen und ihre Sicht auf al-wala wa-l bara (Loyalität und Lossagung). In T. Said & H. Fouad (Eds.), *Salafismus: Auf der Suche nach dem wahren Islam* (pp. 55–79). Freiberg: Herder.

Wiktorowicz, Q. (2005). A genelogy of radical Islam. *Studies in Conflict & Terrorism, 28*, 75–97.
Zahab, M., & Roy, O. (2004). *Islamic networks*. New York: Columbia University Press.
Zelin, A. (2014). Missionare des Jihad in Libyen und Tunesien. In B. Said & H. Fouad (Eds.), *Salafismus: Auf der Suche nach dem wahren Islam* (pp. 320–349). Freiburg: Herder.

# Chapter 3
# Cooperation, Interaction and Fusion of Transnational Organised Crime and Transnational Jihadism: The New Terrorism

## 3.1 A Scientific Analysis of Transnational Organised Crime and Transnational Jihadism

During the last two decades, the interest of political science in transnational non-state actors has increased. At the end of the Cold War, political science did not credit non-state actors with "playing a significant role" in international politics (Halliday, 1991: 197), but this changed significantly after 9/11 (Nölke, 2010: 395). Unlike ethno-national terrorism, Islamist terrorism (Jihadism) is internationally oriented due to its religious/political agenda. Since 9/11 a vast number of books and articles dealing with Jihadism have been published, focusing on various different analytical levels such as ideology, recruitment, organisation or strategic selection of targets.[1]

Before 9/11, analysis of the relationship between terrorism and organised crime had focused on narco-terrorism in South America (the Medellin Cartel in cooperation with the ELN in Columbia and FARC with Mexican groups and drug trafficking), but not on the field of Islamist terrorism (Esparza, 2003; US Department of State, 2000). On an international scale, political science has only recently started analysing the relationship between transnational organised crime and transnational Islamist terrorism, and until now there has not been much related research at all (Shelley, 2014). Since the end of the Cold War and the collapse of the Soviet Union, the boundaries between war, terrorism and organised crime have become blurred, and the phenomena are becoming more and more interdependent and interconnected (Wilkinson, 2003). Transnational crime of the twenty-first century no longer benefits from the existence of states—as it did until the end of the Cold War in the system of a bipolar world; it is no longer dependent on being tolerated by states. On the contrary, the new transnational organised crime seems to benefit from ongoing conflicts and wars within or between states or particularly in failing states (Briscoe & Dari, 2012; Patrick, 2011).

---

[1] Maher (2016), Horgan (2009), Bloom (2005), Heymann (2003).

© Springer Nature Switzerland AG 2019
S. Goertz, A. E. Streitparth, *The New Terrorism*,
https://doi.org/10.1007/978-3-030-14592-7_3

All over the world, organised crime has greatly benefitted from the process of transnationalisation and globalisation: it now has a worldwide network using the most up-to-date means of communication and is flexible to operate illegally, be it in Western, European states or *failing*, *weak* and *failed states*. Drug trafficking is one of the most profitable and fastest-growing illegal forms of worldwide "trading". After an introduction to the characteristics of organised crime and how it has changed over the last decades, the following chapter mainly analyses current data dealing with drug trafficking. It focuses on the question of how much of this international drug trafficking may be dominated by transnational organised crime related to new terrorism. This also includes taking a look at the organisational principles of the respective actors involved and their methods, like kidnapping for ransom, for example. Furthermore, this chapter will examine the ethnical, cultural or religious diaspora groups' function for the networks of various organisations, groups and cells of transnational organised crime at the interface of the so-called Second or Third World and Western industrial nations.

### 3.1.1 Characteristics of Contemporary Organised Crime

Symbiosis between organised crime and terrorism: The border between organised crime and terrorism will become more and more blurred. Funding through organised crime activities will become common, and it is still not known whether some terrorist actors will change their motives to those of more personal interest. Organised crime groups might also use terrorist tactics. (EUROPOL, 2011)

The characteristics of organised crime have been transformed by social, political, economic and technological developments. Nowadays the analysis of organised crime has become highly complex with several different sciences like legal studies, political science and economical studies involved. Consequently, scientific concepts and definitions of organised crimes have changed over the last decades, as have the differences in its regional and cultural forms and structures. Since the beginning of the twenty-first century, organised crime has become more international as far as human or drug trafficking and kidnapping for ransom are concerned. This process is also characterised by increased ethnic and religious influences.

Transnationalisation can be described as a process in which groups of people maintain stable relations with each other over a longer period of time in various societies or continents—without the involvement of state actors (Jäger, 2013). The transnationalisation process and globalisation are said to have a vital and rapidly evolving character inasmuch as they affect the phenomenon of organised crime (Allum & Gilmour, 2012). The specific profile of transnationally organised crime develops in differing circumstances, governed by the social and state environment. In the big picture, transnational organised crime is characterised by multiple cultural and regional influences, which is why there is a growing number of analytical categories like criminal law, psychology, sociology or economy. Today, organised crime appears in multiple forms and is more and more innovative. Besides their hierarchically structured organisations—very often based on a common ethnical, linguistic or partly even family background—organised crime networks are usually characterised by the personal and "business" ties of their members.

The European Union assumes that it is almost impossible to find a common definition of organised crime (EU, 2005). Consequently, EUROPOL describes transnational organised crime as a phenomenon which is poly-criminal and hard to define, developing with increasing diversity as far as its methods, group structures and impacts on different societies are concerned (EUROPOL, 2011). Already in 2011, the first European Police Chiefs Convention of EUROPOL issued a statement that was identical to that of the US strategy for combatting transnational organised crime, emphasising the significant future threat potential posed by the symbiosis of organised crime networks and terrorism (EUROPOL, 2011).

The "United Nations Convention against Transnational Organised Crime" set up four possible criteria according to which a crime is transnationally organised when it is committed:

(a) In more than one country
(b) In one state but the majority of the crime was committed in another state
(c) In one state but is connected to another criminal group that is active in more than one state
(d) In one state but has significant consequences for other states (UN, Jäger, 2013)

Finally, it can be concluded that a single international scientific definition of transnational organised crime does not exist. Nevertheless, the above-mentioned approaches are far-reaching.

## 3.2   *Weak* and *Failed States* as Crucial Factors for Transnational Organised Crime and Jihadism

Organised crime is an indicator for the stability of a country's political and legal system that is measured in the "Fragile States Index" (FSI). Organisations and groups of organised crime and of Jihadism aim for rational economic objectives in order to maximise their profit. Crimes range from drug and human trafficking, child pornography, identity theft, copyright piracy, cybercrime and—in the Middle East—looting of historical artefacts. At the same time, organised crime networks strive for a profitable and risk-minimising spread of their financial resources, also including legal transactions and investments.

An empirical analysis of the interaction of transnational organised crime and transnational Jihadism has shown that their combination and cooperation thrive most in conflict regions like northern and western Africa, the Middle East, the Balkans, the Caucasus and others. Both transnational organised crime and transnational Jihadism rely on the following decisive factors:

- Weak authorities, prone to corruption (and their shortage or lack of capabilities)
- Inadequate cooperation between state security agencies
- Underdeveloped economic structures
- Lack of adaptation of the legal system to the needs of globalisation
- Insufficient monitoring and control of national boundaries
- Border police that are prone to corruption
- Arbitrarily set national borders from colonial times (e.g. "Sykes-Picot Agreement")
- Cross-border relationships and connections of ethnically, religiously and/or culturally homogeneous groups

In the above-mentioned regions of the world, the direct interlinkage of state failure, organised crime and Islamist terrorism is evident. Under the conditions of weak and failing states, single actors, groups or organisations of organised crime are able to take over positions of (formerly governmental) power. Territory beyond governmental control offers space for retreat, financial resources, training camps, recruitment and transit areas for people and goods (Hirschmann, 2016: 229).

Both organised crime and transnational Jihadism are closely linked to domestic conflicts and disintegration of governmental structures while playing a major role in disintegrative circles that enhance fragility by creating parallel structures. These parallel structures can also derive from transnational organised crime and transnational Jihadism or a fusion of both. On the economic level, fragile states create opportunities especially for non-state actors (Hirschmann, 2016: 229), while vacuums of governmental power offer them a platform for their political and/or religious agenda on the political level. The so-called warlords, single leaders of hierarchically organised groups, used to be included in the so-called magic square (Hirschmann, 2016: 229).

But the current empirical examples of Afghanistan, Pakistan, Syria, Iraq and others show that the former "warlord" is prevalent both in transnational Jihadism and transnational organised crime. In addition to drug trafficking, terrorist organisations have been using means like fraud, extortion and human trafficking for years. Over a long period of time, Al Qaida's financial network in Europe was supposedly based on credit card fraud. Another tactical means of new terrorism is the segmentation of operations and optimised forms of money laundering, for example, the Hawala system (Bowers, 2009; Faith, 2011). An interaction and cooperation with Islamist terrorism is a perfect match for transnational organised crime because terrorist groups disrupt the political structure, the governance capabilities, the rule of law and internal state security. The empirical analysis of the cooperation and interaction of transnational organised crime and transnational Jihadism shows that both phenomena need conflict regions like North and West Africa, the Balkans, Palestine, Afghanistan, Syria and Iraq, from a logistics perspective, as far as personnel and also weak state structures are concerned, because space for retreating is seldom controlled by weak states. All of the above-mentioned conflict regions were and are influenced by the cooperation and interaction of various actors of transnational Jihadism and transnational organised crime, linked to the illegal trade of drugs, oil, diamonds and weapons (Collier & Hoeffler, 1998).

## 3.3   New Forms of Interaction, Cooperation and Fusion: Characteristics

> Terrorists and insurgents increasingly will turn to crime to generate funding and will acquire logistical support from criminals, in part because of successes by U.S. agencies and partner nations in attacking other sources of their funding. In some instances, terrorists and insurgents prefer to conduct criminal activities themselves; when they cannot do so, they turn to outside individuals and facilitators. Proceeds from the drug trade are critical to the continued funding of such terrorist groups as the Taliban, Al-Shabaab and drug trafficking organizations [. . .] are turning to criminal activities such as kidnapping for ransom to generate funding to continue their operations. Some criminals could have the capability to provide weapons of mass destruction (WMD) material to other terrorist groups, such as Hizballah and al-Qaida in the Islamic Maghreb, though the strength of these drug links and support remain unclear. U.S. intelligence, law enforcement, and military services have reported that more than 40 foreign terrorist organizations have links to the drug trade. Some criminal organizations have adopted extreme and widespread violence in an overt effort to intimidate governments at various levels. (DNI US Government, 2012)

Since the beginning of the twenty-first century, different studies find circumstantial evidence that indicates the existence of the development of a new phase of organised crime and new terrorism (Bybee, 2012; Duyvesteyn, 2004; Farah, 2013; Shelley, 2014; Wilkinson, 2003). With the end of the Cold War, hundreds of terrorist groups in Africa and in the Middle East lost their state sponsors (*proxy war*) (Bynum, 2005). This led to the dissolution of many terrorist organisations in the 1990s, while others discovered new financial sources. Because of this organised crime became a new and vital element for terrorist organisations (Shelley, 2014).

According to the US Country Reports on Terrorism for 2015, nowadays three state sponsors still exist: Iran, Sudan and Syria (US Department of State, 2015). In 2011, the same report had also mentioned Cuba as state sponsor for FARC (US State Department, 2011). For example, Iran supports the Lebanese Hizbullah, various Palestinian Jihadist groups in Gaza and various Shiite groups in Iraq including the Kata'ib Hizbullah. Moreover, Iran uses the Islamic Revolutionary Guard Corps-Quds Force (IRGC-QF) to support terrorist organisations and groups in the regional sphere of influence of Iran (US Department of State, 2015).

Before the separation of Sudan, the North was a safe haven for international Jihadist organisations like Al Qaida. Since 2015, North Sudan has been tolerating cells and groups that are affiliated with the "Islamic State" (US Department of State, 2015). In 2014, members of Hamas cooperated with North Sudanese actors and used North Sudan logistically for planning attacks and operations against Israel (US Department of State, 2015).

Until the Arabellion in Syria in 2011, the Assad system let international Jihadist organisations pass its territory on their way to Iraq, and some of the organisations were supplied by Syria (US Department of State, 2015). The cooperation with Hizbullah that existed before 2011 was even intensified during the war against IS and secular Syrian opposition groups (US Department of State, 2015).

On a political and religious level, various groups and cells of transnational organised crime have gradually altered over the last few years and so abandoned their originally apolitical, economically illegal character and come closer to adopting the inherent characteristics of terrorist organisations. In 2012, the US Director of National Intelligence found that the organisations, networks, groups and cells of transnational organised crime had intensified dramatically since the 1990s and spoke of a "threatening crime-terror nexus" as being one of the major threats to the internal security of the USA (DNI US Government, 2012).

Examples of groups that were originally based on purely political and/or ideological-religious agendas but which have gradually adopted strategies and tactics used by transnational organised crime are Abu Sayyaf, Al Qaida and its regional branches, the PKK, the Revolutionary Armed Forces of Colombia (FARC), the Haqqani network and Hizbullah.

The diaspora groups of Somali refugees all over the world are known for their support of piracy around the Horn of Africa, financed by monetary transactions in the state where they have found asylum (Shelley, 2014). Within ethnical and religious diaspora groups in Western, democratic states, enforced payments through extortion are common. For example, the PKK—which operates in a grey area between organised crime and terrorism—frequently extorts money from Kurds in Belgium, the Netherlands, Germany and other Western states (Roth & Sever, 2007). The turnover of extortion by the PKK alone is estimated to be hundreds of millions of Euros (Roth & Sever, 2007). Unfortunately, the Dutch International Centre for Counter-terrorism states that the Dutch police have neither the capacity nor the capability to institute legal proceedings against the extortion of the PKK (Fijnaut & Paoli, 2004).

The organisations, groups and cells of new terrorism are no longer secular with purely political agendas that focus exclusively on single states and their territories. Like the new forms, organisations, groups and cells of transnational organised crime, it is dependent—especially in the vulnerable phase of initial growth—on the territories of failing and failed states. These are states and territories of the so-called Second and Third World, for example, states in the Balkans, the Caucasus, Central Asia, Pakistan, West and North Africa, the Middle East and in Somalia. Empirically noticeable is that all these states, regions and societies have an Islamic background (Shelley, 2014).

Both transnational organised crime and Jihadism reflect current trends by using tactics and organising principles of network structures, outsourcing and autonomous cells which maintain limited contact with their leaders, which makes it all the more difficult to detect them. Moreover, it has been established that the support networks of both organised crime and Islamist terrorism have similar structures, and in many cases, they are headed by the same people (Keefe, 2013).

Jihadist actors and actors of organised crime both recruit from an almost identical personnel pool (Gallagher, 2016). When studying the effects of globalisation it can be said that transnational terrorism and transnational organised crime have benefitted from developments of globalisation, from open borders or borders that are hardly controlled (Shelley, 2014). Thus both phenomena are globally connected, and both use modern means of communication (Grabosky & Stohl, 2010). Groups and cells of Jihadism and of organised crime benefit from weak and failed states in the so-called Second and Third World that neither react to requests for judicial assistance from other states nor abide by extradition treaties. Moreover, both phenomena benefit from Western states with strict banking confidentiality, for example, Switzerland and Luxembourg (Thompson, 2011; Naylor, 2002).

One example for the development away from cooperation towards the fusion of organised crime and Islamist terrorism is the interaction between the Islamic Jihad Union of Uzbekistan and the Taliban, which both have members and operations involved in drug trafficking. A similar cooperation—likewise based on religion and ideology—has supposedly been in existence for years between Al Qaida and groups of organised crime in Bosnia, i.e. in close proximity to Western Europe. The cooperation covers personnel resources, training camps and smuggling routes from Afghanistan to the Balkans and Western Europe (Makarenko, 2004: 132). Transnational Jihadist organisations possess cells in ethnical and religious milieus in the USA, Canada, Australia, Europe and other democratic countries and have networks in conflict regions like Africa, the Middle East and the Caucasus.

### 3.3.1  Interaction, Cooperation and Fusion in Drug Trafficking

Whether it is by opium or by shooting, it is our common goal to harm all infidels as part of Jihad. (Court statement of a Taliban, US Department of Justice, 2008a, 2008b)

Coca cultivation is a political act in a much fuller sense than is conventional criminal behaviour. By cultivating coca, one is not only enhancing one's own income, one is also contributing—intentionally or unintentionally, directly or indirectly to Sendero Luminoso's effort to depose the government. (Shelley, 2014)

Currently the cultivation, transport and trafficking of drugs are mainly dominated by hybrid actors of organised crime and new terrorism (Reuter, 2016). Generally, the actors have a national or regional character; however, in Africa and the Middle East, their transnational network is often ethnically and religiously based.

The structure and organisation of drug trafficking varies from continent to continent, country to country, region to region, but groups and networks of transnational organised crime overcome these distinctions.

Drug trafficking is one of the most profitable and fastest-growing forms of trade worldwide. The value of annual drug trafficking from Afghanistan over the northern route through Central Asia to Russia is estimated at 13 billion US dollars by the *United Nations Office on Drugs and Crime.* The value of the heroin that is transported via the south route through Turkey to Western Europe can be estimated at over US$20 billion (UNODC, 2016a, 2016b, 2016c). In addition, the annual value of cocaine and synthetic drugs like marihuana accounts for the highest sum of illegal trade by far. Groups of transnational organised crime have benefitted significantly from the cultivation of drugs and drug trafficking over the last years, which has led to huge resources being invested in personnel and financing of infrastructure.

According to the US Drug Enforcement Administration, over 40% of transnational terrorist organisations have proven cooperation with the cultivation of drugs and drug trafficking carried out by organised crime (DEA, 2011). Vice versa, approximately 50% of international drug syndicates cooperate with international terrorist organisations (US White House, 2011). The US Ministry of Justice alleges that the vast majority of nationally and internationally operating groups of organised crime cooperate with international terrorist groups (US DOJ, 2008a, 2008b). According to the Country Reports on Terrorism 2015 published by the US State Department, more than 25 international terrorist organisations cooperate with actors of organised crime (US Department of State, 2015). Originally, it was exclusively terrorist groups like Hizbullah that discovered the economic benefits of drug production (heroin and cocaine) and drug trafficking in the 1990s. Groups and cells of Hizbullah also operate on the American continent, on the one hand with legal and illegal investments and on the other hand financing terrorist actions of the Hizbullah worldwide (Bell, 2011). Because South America was the favourite destination for refugees of the Lebanese Civil War in the 1990s, countries such as Argentina, Brazil and Paraguay are famous for a Lebanese diaspora that is used by the Hizbullah for organised crime and Islamist terrorism (Kittner, 2007).

Another example is the Pakistani-Indian group of organised crime called Dawood Company/D-Company that is closely affiliated with Al Qaida, the Liberation Tigers of Tamil Eelam (LTTE), Boko Haram and Lashkar-e-Tayyiba. As a hybrid actor, D-Company operates, for example, in Pakistan, India, Malaysia, Thailand, Sri Lanka, Germany, France, Great Britain and Dubai. Moreover, the Kosovo-Albanian UCK, for example, has been cooperating with the Albanian mafia since 1994 and using heroin trafficking for their fight against the Serbian government (Makarenko, 2004: 132). The Islamic Jihad Union of Uzbekistan also cooperates with the Taliban of Afghanistan and Al Qaida, another example of international cooperation in the field of drug cultivation, drug trafficking and Islamist terrorism (Goertz, 2017b). A similar cooperation, originally based on the same religious/political ideology, has supposedly existed between actors of organised crime and Al Qaida in Bosnia for years (Makarenko, 2004). This cooperation consisted of the common use of personnel resources, logistics in the area of training and smuggling routes from Afghanistan to the Balkans and Western Europe (Makarenko, 2004: 132). Transnationally organised crime as well as Jihadi organisations and groups—for example, IS and Al Qaida— command cells and groups in Western Europe, Australia, Canada and the USA in ethnical and religious milieus of the diaspora, and they are connected with conflict regions like Africa, the Middle East and Caucasus.

In North and West Africa, hybrid actors of organised crime and Islamist terrorism (Al Qaida in the Islamic Maghreb, Groupe Salafiste pour la Prédication et le Combat, GSPC) benefit from an established social and personnel infrastructure as a means for transporting drugs through the Sahel. A complex heterogeneous and cross-border network has connected state and non-state actors from Mali, Libya and Algeria since the 1990s, on all political and economic levels, for example, regional militia, Tuareg groups and Jihadists (AQIM and GSPC) (Lohmann, 2011). These organisations smuggle drugs, cigarettes, people, weapons and fuel through the Sahel. According to a current report of the United Nations Office on Drugs and Crime, approximately 25% of the cocaine that is sold in Europe comes out of West Africa. Northern Mali has developed into an important trading centre. According to the West Africa Commission on Drugs, 2014, western and northern Africa are the turnstiles for cocaine and heroin travelling to Europe from South America and Asia (WACOD, 2014).

### 3.3.2   Segmentation of the Drug Markets and Characteristics of the Actors

The drug markets are divided into segments with respect to substance and type of drugs. Cocaine and heroin dominate the international drug markets. The most prominent characteristic of the international drug market is that a tiny number of countries and regions is almost solely responsible for the production of coca and opium. Afghanistan has been the leading country for worldwide drug trafficking since the 1980s, with Myanmar another source country. In total, six countries account for 98% of the worldwide heroin production, and just three countries (Bolivia, Columbia and Peru) share the worldwide production of cocaine (UNODC, 2016a, 2016b, 2016c). Cocaine and heroin are transported many thousands of kilometres, involving dozens of actors and organisations from the point of cultivation (mainly South America and Asia) to the consumer (worldwide). The analysis of the worldwide most popular product of drug trafficking, heroin, indicates that over ten separate organisations are involved in the entire process between cultivation and sale (Paoli, Greenfield, & Reuter, 2009). Poppy and coca plants are grown almost exclusively in weak, failing or failed states, where the state actors are not capable or not willing to stop or curb their cultivation. Those involved in the production and sale of cocaine and heroin are farmers, smugglers, "high-level" dealers, "mid-level" dealers and retailers. Generally speaking, the poppies and coca plants are decentrally cultivated by individual farmers. In the case of the globally largest drug cultivation area, Afghanistan, it can be said that regional warlords—the Taliban and Al Qaida—either force the local farmers to cultivate these plants or bribe them (Mansfield, 2011).

The cultivation and sale of cannabis varies diametrically from that of cocaine and heroin because it is mostly grown in the countries of the buyers. The United Nations

Office on Drugs and Crime counts over 135 countries where cannabis is produced and sold (UNODC, 2016a, 2016b, 2016c). Synthetic drugs are produced in industrial states like Great Britain, the USA and the Netherlands, while amphetamines, for example, are produced in Myanmar.

The process of cultivating, smuggling and selling drugs requires a huge amount of heterogeneous actors. The cooperation and interaction of these actors—for example, through corruption—with the state elite in politics and the security authorities of countries like Afghanistan, North and West Africa, Tajikistan and Kyrgyzstan involved in drug trafficking creates hybrid networks of transnationally organised crime that are very hard to combat. The organisations and groups of transnationally organised crime that benefit from their regional, national, ethnic/tribal and religious/political networks are those that exist the longest, have the highest sales and are interlinked most densely on a national and international scale (Shelley, 2014: 219–221). Current empirical studies about the cultivation, the transport and the trading of drugs reveal that they are mostly dominated by (transnationally) organised crime (Reuter, 2016: 359). As a result the structure and organisation of drug trafficking varies from continent to continent, country to country, region to region. EUROPOL describes organised crime as "profit-oriented criminal activities, independent of the organisation of the syndicates, networks and groups that are involved, so that drug trafficking can be described as a prototype part of organised crime" (EUROPOL, 2013). The actors of drug trafficking usually have a national and a regional character, but they are transnationally connected, in Arab and African countries mostly ethnically and religiously, crossing the artificial borders that were created by the colonial powers.

The general picture of the organisational structures of the players in drug smuggling and trafficking is reflected by the phrase "there are no Walmarts or Starbucks in the cocaine, heroin, or cannabis markets. Retailing even the very expensive cocaine is undertaken by generally small and ephemeral enterprises" (Reuter, 2016: 359).

In conclusion, since the end of the Cold War and the disintegration of the Soviet Union, the borders between war, terrorism and organised crime have become blurred (Wilkinson, 2003). Consequently, the cultivation, the smuggling and the trade of and with drugs no longer rely on state "toleration". On the contrary, the actors essentially benefit from weak and failing states, ongoing conflicts and wars (Briscoe & Dari, 2012; Patrick, 2011). Current transnational drug trafficking is more complex, global and more hybrid. Its networks, groups and cells interact, cooperate and fuse with networks, groups, actors, tactics and means of transnational Islamist terrorism.

### 3.3.3   Afghanistan: Cooperation of Organised Crime and Jihadism in Drug Trafficking

The sheer size and illicit nature of the opium economy mean that not surprisingly, it infiltrates and seriously affects Afghanistan's economy, state, society, and politics. It generates large amounts of effective demand in the economy, provides incomes and employment including in rural areas (even though most of the final value from Afghan opium accrues outside the country), and supports the balance of payments and indirectly (through Customs duties on drug-financed imports) government revenues. The opium economy by all accounts is a massive source of corruption and undermines public institutions especially in (but not limited to) the security and justice sectors. There are worrying signs of infiltration by the drug industry into higher levels of government and into the emergent politics of the country. Thus the opium trade is widely considered to be one of the greatest threats to state-building, reconstruction, and development in Afghanistan. (Byrd & Buddenberg, 2010; UNODC, 2010)

The Afghan drug trade contributes to a vicious circle whereby the drug industry financially supports warlords and their militias, who in turn undermine the Government—which is also corrupted and captured at different levels by bribes from the drug industry. As a result the state remains ineffective and the security weak, thereby perpetuating an environment in which the drug industry can continue to thrive. (World Bank, 2005: 119)

Afghanistan is a prime example for the interconnection of drug trafficking and transnational Islamist terrorism. This fact that Afghanistan has developed to become a key player in the field of transnational trafficking has global consequences. The United Nations Office on Drugs and Crime estimated that the land suitable for cultivation of opium in Afghanistan has increased since 2015 to 200,000 ha, which implies a turnover of US$3 billion annually (UNODC Afghanistan, 2016a, 2016b, 2016c). The former Afghan minister of finance, Ashraf Ghani, states that over 60% of the gross domestic product is based on illegal trade, of which drug trafficking is the dominant portion.

More than 90% of the globally cultivated opium is cultivated in Afghanistan, and since 2005, a significant rise can be detected (UNODC, 2011). Within Afghanistan three main regions of heroin production can be detected: Badakhshan, Nangarhar and Helmand. According to the UN Office on Drugs and Crime (UNODC), each year between 2004 and 2007, significantly more opium was cultivated on a significantly larger area of land than in any year of the Taliban regime in Afghanistan (UNODC, 2008).

The history of the cultivation of opium in Afghanistan is hundreds of years old, but it is only since 2002 that Afghanistan has been responsible for the major part of opium production worldwide (Lacouture 2016). The interaction of weak to failing states, organised crime, terrorist organisations, violence and poverty, the non-existent rule of law and corruption in Afghanistan is evident. Using the province of Helmand as an example, the causal relationship between drug cultivation and drug trafficking becomes obvious: more than 62% of Western soldiers killed (mostly US and Canadian) were killed in the province of Helmand that is the stronghold of drug trafficking on the one hand and of the Taliban on the other hand (Lacouture, 2016). Up to 70% of the annual budget of the Taliban can be traced back to the cultivation of and trade with drugs (Lacouture, 2016).

In the province Badakhshan alone, the annual cultivation of opium between 2008 and 2016 grew so quickly that it doubled every year (UNODC, 2016a, 2016b, 2016c). In the province of Badghis, the annual cultivation of opium increased from 587 ha in 2008 to 2363 ha in 2012 and up to 35,244 ha in 2016. In the province of Helmand, the annual cultivation of opium rose from 26,500 ha in 2005 to over 100,000 ha in 2014 (UNODC, 2016a, 2016b, 2016c). The average amount of opium in kg per hectare increased from 18 kg in the year 2015 to 24 kg in the year 2016, an increase of over 30% (UNODC, 2016a, 2016b, 2016c).

According to various authorities of the European Union, since 2002 Afghanistan is the main supplier of heroine (EMCDDA, 2016). Heroin reaches Europe via two different transport routes: either via the historic Balkan route through Turkey or—since the 1990s—via the northern route through Afghanistan, Central Asia, Russia to Western Europe (EMCDDA, 2016). In addition to opium, Afghanistan is also the country in which the highest amount of cannabis is produced worldwide.

Afghanistan is characterised by the interaction, cooperation and fusion of state actors and non-state actors of drug trafficking. An analysis of the structure of the players of organised crime involved in the cultivation, transport and trade with opium in Afghanistan depicts a network of various local, regional, state and non-state actors who all cooperate with the Taliban and Al Qaida as of a certain level.

According to a study by the United Nations Office on Drugs and Crime (UNODC), the cultivation of and trade with drugs in Afghanistan is very closely linked to the international Hawala system (Byrd & Buddenberg, 2010; UNODC, 2010). In certain months of the year, the liquidity of the Hawala system is generated up to 100% by drug trafficking (Byrd & Buddenberg, 2010; UNODC, 2010). In southern regions like the provinces Helmand and Kandahar, the liquidity of the Hawala system is based on average to around 60% on drug trafficking, and 89–90% of the actors of Hawala in Kandahar and Helmand are involved in drug trafficking (Byrd & Buddenberg, 2010; UNODC, 2010). According to the same study, in the province of Helmand, the annual turnover based on drug cultivation and drug trade is over US$800 million and is laundered through the Hawala system. In the province of Herat, it is up to US$500 million per year (Byrd & Buddenberg, 2010; UNODC, 2010). Hawala money generated by drug trafficking forms a link between organised crime and Jihadist players in Afghanistan with the cities of Peshawar, Quetta and Karachi in Pakistan, as well as with Dubai and Iran. With regard to Afghanistan, it has to be stated that the Hawala money generated by drug trafficking alone has created a shadow economy, a parallel economy that marginalises the rule of law and legal financial transactions (Byrd & Buddenberg, 2010; UNODC, 2010).

The actors involved have adapted their tactics due to operations by special military forces and the increased threat of prosecution. Meanwhile they use conspiratorial tactics, relocating laboratories in isolated and more inaccessible areas, dividing shipments into smaller portions and spontaneously altering transport routes (UNODC, 2015). The fact remains that one could speak of the border police "turning a blind eye" and/or even active participation of certain Afghani state actors in view of the corruption, bribery of security forces, legal authorities and administration. Farther away from the influence of the capital city Kabul and the international security forces, in regions like the south and the east of Afghanistan, the cooperation between the Taliban and Al Qaida generates a new dimension of organised crime that threatens the Afghan government as well as international actors. Profits from drug trafficking and racketeering enable the Taliban, the Haqqani network and Al

Qaida to increase their level of destabilising measures such as terrorist attacks, kidnapping of politicians and attacks on international state actors.

Already in the war against the Soviet troops in the 1980s, drug trafficking created a financial basis, and the actors involved remained in control after the Soviet troop withdrawal. The interaction and cooperation of these actors quickly created a symbiosis of those involved in the cultivation, the transport and the sale of drugs. The Taliban as dominating party in this symbiosis guaranteed "security" (protection money), stopped possible rivals and their activities and "taxed" their security with approximately 20% (extortion) of the sold drugs (Peters, 2009a, 2009b: 12). After the intervention of the Western armed forces post-9/11 and the consequent fall of the Taliban government, most of the Taliban lost their positions in the Afghan political system, but in various remote, rural areas, they could retain their position and their influence in drug trafficking (Farah, 2011: 22–24).

The Taliban extort at least 10% of the opium price as protection money from every opium farmer (*ushr*) and force farmers to grow opium (Rollins, Wyler, & Rosen, 2010). On the other hand, the Taliban receive money, weapons, vehicles and other equipment from local drug lords who control the opium farmers. In addition, opium smugglers pay road tolls within Afghanistan and when crossing to neighbouring countries (Rollins et al., 2010; Townsend, 2009). Moreover, the Taliban regionally guarantee "security" for the transport of drug laboratories and chemicals for processing opium (Rollins et al., 2010). In the years 2008–2012, the Afghan government—together with international armed forces—led an opium destruction campaign. The Taliban offered local drug lords their paramilitary capabilities to stop the opium destruction campaign, using terrorist attacks and guerilla warfare (Rollins et al., 2010). Interestingly enough in the year 2000—months before 9/11—the Taliban reduced opium cultivation by 95% in comparison to the year 1999, after banning the growing of poppies (Rollins et al., 2010).

Within months of the start of the new—internationally backed—Afghan government, economical parallel structures developed in various regions and provinces of Afghanistan. Rural clan chiefs, their provincial commanders, the Taliban and Al Qaida developed a transnational hybrid drug/terrorism network that was based on a common Islamist and Jihadist ideology, overcoming regional and ethnic differences. This drug/terrorism network is a hybrid fusion of regional and international actors and benefits from common capacities and abilities in the areas of weaponry, personnel, training, transport routes and tactics.

As a consequence, the opium transported from Afghanistan over the brittle borders—both on the southern and the northern route—has been destabilising the bordering states Pakistan, Tajikistan, Uzbekistan and Turkmenistan, so that organised crime has been expanding, from top to bottom of state governments, using drug trafficking, human trafficking and arms smuggling (Cornell & Swantström, 2006). The foundations of these networks and actors are interaction and cooperation, based on ethnic and/or religious ties between Beluchis, Pashtuns, Tajiks and Uzbeks on the Afghan side of the border and Central Asia, Pakistan and Iran on the other side of the borders.

The eastern neighbour of Afghanistan, Pakistan—a nuclear power of special importance to the region—is affected by drug transports through the regions Khyber Pakhtunkhwa, Balochistan and Waziristan. As a consequence, Islamist/Jihadist parallel structures were created that already have—in part—the character of a caliphate. The Haqqani network, which is dealt with in Sect. 3.5, is an example for a hybrid actor of organised crime and Islamist terrorism.

Another neighbour of Afghanistan, Tajikistan, lies on the northern route of drug trafficking and is characterised by corruption, organised crime, state failure and civil war that is mostly financed through drug trafficking in Afghanistan (Shelley, 2014: 243).

The analysis of the cultivation of opium in Afghanistan and the development of the Taliban and Al Qaida since 2001 show that the Taliban would not have been able to exist without drug trafficking after 9/11.

The regional warlords in Afghanistan serve as intermediary between the opium farmers and the Taliban, Haqqani network and Al Qaida, creating a hybrid phenomenon that the Western coalition has been unable to control since 2001. The religious/political ideology of Jihad has been uniting dozens of different groups through its internationalisation since the 1980s. Since then the Afghan actors, with the help of Al Qaida, could contact and form ties with actors of northern and western Africa, where, for example, the Tuareg and Al Qaida in the Islamic Maghreb cooperate and control the major transport routes through the Sahel on the way to Europe. Consequently, they make use of them for trafficking drugs from Afghanistan to Europe and for further contacts and terrorist activities.

To summarise, after the Western intervention in 2001, Afghanistan quickly became one of the worldwide key players dealing with the cultivation and sale of opium. Various Afghan and international actors of organised crime and Islamist terrorism have benefitted from this, and it has enabled the high quality and quantity of many terrorist attacks against the post-Taliban government and Western actors.

## 3.4  North and West Africa: Cooperation of Organised Crime, Drug Trafficking and Trafficking of Weapons, Cigarettes and Other Goods

According to the West Africa Commission on Drugs, West and North Africa are dominated by "drug trafficking, broader organized criminal activity such as human trafficking, illicit logging, illicit capture of resources, piracy, money-laundering and terrorism" (WACOD, 2014). Thus for WACOD it seems clear that the influence of organised crime and Islamist terrorism on northern and western Africa is devastating. The menacing consequences of the cooperation between organised crime and Jihadism for North and West Africa are illustrated by the following criminal phenomena:

- Human trafficking of refugees from the Middle East through Africa to Western Europe

- Slave trade, prostitution and sex slavery in African war zones
- Money laundering by non-state actors from Western countries based on cross-border corruption of state authorities in northern and western Africa
- North and West Africa as transit regions for drug trafficking from South America to Europe and Asia to Europe
- Smuggling of cigarettes
- Gun running
- Cybercrime, with focus on identity theft
- Smuggling of stolen cars from Europe
- Piracy
- Illegal waste disposal of poisonous substances (WACOD, 2014)

These criminal phenomena have especially been developed by organised crime in North and West Africa since the beginning of the twenty-first century:

- The security authorities and other state authorities and their capabilities are weak and prone to corruption.
- The economic structures are weak and one-sided, and the laws do not adapt to globalisation and other international trends.
- Borders are poorly/not controlled.
- The cross-border connections of those ethnically and religiously related.
- Arbitrarily determined state borders from colonial times.
- Insufficiently trained border police that is prone to corruption.
- Ineffective cooperation of the security authorities of the states affected within the Economic Community of West African States (ECOWAS) (Alemia, 2013).

In a study of the West Africa Commission on Drugs, West and North Africa are "the turnstile for cocaine and heroin, that originates from South America and Asia on its way to European markets" (WACOD, 2014). Additionally, WACOD has noticed a "change of strategy of the South American drug cartels" due to the "significantly increased investigations of the US authorities" (WACOD, 2014).

The complex, cross-border network of new terrorism has enabled actors of organised crime and Islamist terrorism to cooperate since the 1990s and more intensively since the turn of the millennium. Participants include state and non-state actors from Mali, Libya and Algeria, various Tuareg groups, as well as regional and international Jihadists (Lohmann, 2011).

Actors of the Mali organisation Groupe Salafiste pour la Prédication et le Combat (GSPC) have been cooperating with Al Qaida in the Islamic Maghreb (AQIM) in West and North Africa since 2003. The amount of the illegal goods traded (drugs, cigarettes, weapons and hostages) has increased enormously in the last 10 years. Moreover, the conflicts between competing groups of organised crime and militia in north Mali and south Libya have increased. Because these actors have tight ethnical and religious ties, they could expand their influence across the borders quite easily. An alliance of Ifoghas Tuareg and Kounta Arabs repeatedly fought with Imghad Tuareg smugglers, Arab dealers from the Berabiche and smugglers of the Sahrawi.

As a result, Arab smugglers in Gao and Timbuktu formed militias to protect their smuggling operations. North African (mainly Algerian) Salafist groups steadily built up cooperation with these militias and were able to win over members of the feared Nigerian Boko Haram (ZMSBW, 2016).

### 3.4.1  Actors of Organised Crime: The Tuareg

Not only actors of organised crime—active in smuggling drugs, cigarettes, weapons and human trafficking—but also actors of international Islamist terrorism benefit from the established "social and personal infrastructure" in North Africa as a base for their operations and for access to the route through the Sahel. Hybrid networks of state and non-state actors in Mali and Libya have been cooperating with various tribes smuggling consumer goods, cigarettes, humans, weapons and fuel through the Sahel. The Tuareg play a significant part in the cooperation and interaction of the phenomena organised crime and Jihadism. They are a seminomadic Berber people with a population of 1.2–1.5 million (ZMSBW, 2016). They live in independent groups in Mali, Niger, Burkina Faso, the south of Algeria and the southwest of Libya. In Mali they represent approximately 10% of the population. It has to be said that Tuareg society is extremely heterogeneous and that the influence of the different groups varies considerably. The structure of Tuareg society is described as having horizontal and vertical castes. Besides the caste of the "noble warriors" (*imajeghen/ imushar*) and the nonnoble vassals (*imghad*), the Tuareg are subdivided into craftsmen, farmers and "slaves" (ZMSBW, 2016). The highest political category of the Tuareg is the confederation (*ettebel*) that consists of many social entities (clans). The legitimacy of the "ruling nobility" is derived from their claim to being descendants of the prophet Muhammad. But the exact significance of a clan or any other status group is regionally disputed. Thus various Tuareg groups create their own militias that often challenge each other. Attacks of "dark-skinned" groups on the Ganda Koy (Songhay)—"fair-skinned, free Tuareg"—are explained by the century-long enslavement of the Ganda Koy (ZMSBW, 2016). For this reason the Tuareg resist being subordinated to the "black" government of Mali (ZMSBW, 2016).

While the economic basis lay for centuries in the area of cattle breeding and other agricultural activities, trade and smuggling grew steadily in the last decade. This is why the Tuareg are called the "carriers of the Sahara", and consequently, they play a vital role for organised crime and Jihadism. In this role, they have smuggled humans, weapons, oil and cigarettes for the last decade. Many of their smuggling routes run through Mali and provide a livelihood for many families and clans (Fischer, 2010).

The "Mouvement National de Libération de l'Azawad", MNLA, which was founded at the end of 2011, is a Tuareg organisation, which was able to make use of highly trained and well equipped Libyan soldiers after the fall of the government of Muammar Al Gaddafi. Together with Ansar Dine, an armed group of Mali led by Iyad Al Ghali, a former high-ranking Tuareg leader, the MNLA attacked the Mali army in the north of Mali in January of 2012 in order to take over vast parts of the country. After this seizure of power and the military coup of 2012, most of the Mali civil servants fled, and the fighters of the MNLA and Ansar Dine took over two thirds of Mali within weeks. Due to internal conflicts, the Tuareg alliance MNLA fell apart, so that Ansar Dine cooperated with AQIM and the Mouvement pour l'Unicité et le Jihad en Afrique de l'Ouest (Briscoe, 2014). Some Tuareg drug traffickers cooperated with the AQIM and the MUJAO in actions in the field of organised crime.

### 3.4.2   Actors of Jihadism: Ansar Dine, Al Mourabitoun and Al Qaida in the Islamic Maghreb

The actors of transnational Islamist terrorism—in this context, for example, Al Qaida in the Islamic Maghreb, the Mouvement pour l'Unicité et le Jihad en Afrique de l'Ouest (MUJAO), Al Mourabitoun and Ansar Dine—operate in many African states and have no permanent local points of reference, and their choice of training camps is based on strategic and economical considerations.

The Salafist-Jihadist Ansar Dine fights for an Islamist state, a contemporary caliphate in the region Azawad. In summer 2012, members of Ansar Dine destroyed the mausoleum Sidi Mahmoud Ben Amar in Timbuktu that is part of the UNESCO world heritage and threatened to destroy more mausoleums. After UNESCO had put various Mali mausoleums on the UNECSO red list in June 2012, Ansar Dine continued to destroy them, for example, the mausoleums of Sidi Mahmoud, Sidi Moctar and Alpha Moya, making a mockery of UNESCO.

Since 2015, Ansar Dine have been intensifying their small war tactics against UN blue helmets and killed three men during an attack against the UN camp in Kidal in November 2015. During another attack, a few weeks later in February against the camp MINUSMA in Kidal, 6 UN soldiers were killed and 30 more injured. Afterwards Ansar Dine admitted to three more attacks: one in Tessalit in April 2016, when three French UN soldiers were killed and five more injured, and two, when four UN soldiers from Chad and seven soldiers from Mali were killed.

Al Mourabitoun is a Salafist-Jihadist organisation that emerged from a fusion of Ahmed Amers/Ahmed Al Tilemsis MUJAO and the irregular fighters of Mokhtar Belmokhtar. Like Ansar Dine, Al Mourabitoun aims at an Islamist state on the territories of Mali, Algeria, Southwest Libya and Niger.

Al Mourabitoun mostly consists of Tuaregs and other ethnic Arabs from northern Mali, mainly from Timbuktu, Kidal and Gao, but also from Algeria, Tunisia and other nations. The UN, Australia, Canada, the USA and Great Britain classify Al Mourabitoun as a terrorist organisation.[2]

On 14 May 2015, Al Mourabitoun published a radio message in which they explained their loyalty to the "Islamic State", which brought an end to their pact with Al Qaida. A few days later, Al Mourabitoun attacked a bar that was quite popular among Western foreigners in Bamako, killing five and injuring nine. Among the victims were a Frenchman and a Belgian civil servant of the EU. The terrorist attack on the Byblos Hotel in Sévaré on 11 August 2015 killed 13, among them 5 civil servants of the UN and 4 soldiers. Shortly afterwards, Al Mourabitoun admitted to being responsible for both attacks. During the hostage-taking of 170 people in the hotel Radisson Blu in Bamako on 20 November, 27 people died, and many more were injured. A coordinated terrorist attack on two hotels in Ouagadougou, the capital city of Burkina Faso on 15 January 2016, killed more than 20 people, and over 60 were injured. On 18 January 2017, a suicide bomber of Al Mourabitoun in a military camp in Gao, Mali, killed 77 people and injured over 115. That attack was the terrorist attack with the highest number of people killed by a suicide bomber in the history of Mali.

The Salafist-Jihadist "Groupe Salafiste pour la Prédication et le Combat" (GSPC) merged with Al Qaida in Islamic Maghreb (AQIM) in 2007.[3] Its political/religious agenda aims to topple the Algerian government and create a caliphate. Since its merger with Al Qaida, AQIM focused on terrorist attacks against representatives of Western companies and states (mostly from the USA and Europe) or kidnapping Westerners for ransom. The members of AQIM are mainly recruited from Algeria, from Saharan tribes—for example, the Tuareg and the Berabiche in Mali—but also from suburbs of Moroccan cities. However, the leadership positions are filled by Algerians.

On 11 April 2007, a suicide bomber of the AQIM attacked the official seat of the Algerian prime minister in Algiers, killing 33 and injuring 222. In the same year, AQIM committed two coordinated attacks with explosives on the building of the UNHCR and in the proximity of the supreme court in Algiers, killing at least 26 people, among them UN civil servants. In March 2011, the Chad government warned that the "Arabellion" in Libya would strengthen AQIM because it would gain access to military weapons.

Likewise the Algerian security authorities explained that AQIM had gained access to armour-piercing grenades from Libyan army depots. Subsequently, terror attacks on January 15 and 16 against the bar Taxi Brousse, the restaurant Cappuccino and the Splendid Hotel in Ouagadougou, Burkina Faso, killed 27 and injured over 56.

---

[2]United Nations Security Council Committee 1267. UN.org. 25 September 2014; https://www.gov.uk/government/publications/proscribed-terror-groups-or-organisations%2D%2D2

[3]Arabic تنظيم القاعدة ببلد المغرب الاسلامي.

The above-mentioned examples of Jihadist actors in North and West Africa, Ansar Dine, Al Mourabitoun and the AQIM illustrate that the following characteristics of transnational terrorism on the one hand and transnational organised crime on the other hand are quite similar:

- Decentral network or cell structure.
- The political/religious agendas of new terrorism in North and West Africa are local/regional on the one hand and international on the other hand.
- The multiple and heterogeneous financing tactics in the area of organised crime make these new actors of new terrorism very resilient.
- The multinationality of its membership complicates criminal prosecution through national and international security authorities.
- Due to their global interconnectedness, these actors are highly flexible, and thanks to their involvement in various Jihadist small wars, their level of paramilitary operations and tactics is rapidly increasing.

In the last 10 years, AQIM has proven its flexibility and adaptability in North and West Africa, rapidly adapting its reactions to regional external conditions. A crucial element of this adaptability is the ability to connect with every conflict worldwide where Muslims are involved and to recruit new members and supporters (Schweitzer & Ferber, 2005).

According to public statements of the AQIM, their attacks and assaults are directed against Westerners in northern and western Africa. The numerous terrorist attacks and assaults in the last years were carried out by only a few Jihadist actors with handguns and were logistically simple, so that their tactics of attacking Westerners or representatives of other states will be repeated in the next years and decades. Besides that, the Jihadist groups in North and West Africa possess the capabilities to carry out hit team attacks. In Mali their current strategy is to undermine the legitimacy of the Mali government and their international troops by killing and injuring them. Up till the beginning of 2017, more than 60 peacekeepers had already been killed through Jihadist attacks and assaults.

On 2 March 2017, all significant Salafist-Jihadist organisations in North and West Africa—Ansar Dine, MUJAO, Al Mourabitoun and the AQIM—entered into an alliance. This fusion of heterogeneous actors from different countries of northern and western Africa, with different ethnic backgrounds, is largely based on a common Salafist-Jihadist ideology and is a current example of a fusion of actors of new terrorism. This new alliance admitted its responsibility for a bomb attack in Gao at the beginning of 2017, where 50 people were killed.

## 3.5    The Haqqani Network as a Hybrid Actor of Organised Crime and Jihadism: New Terrorism

### 3.5.1    Structure and Characteristics

The Haqqani network is the newest hybrid actor of organised crime and Jihadism. It was founded in the 1980s by Jalaluddin Haqqani; today it is led by his sons Sirajuddin, Badruddin and Nasiruddin and their uncle Ibrahim (Dressler, 2012). The Haqqani network operates predominantly in the border areas of eastern Afghanistan and western Pakistan, in the provinces of Khost, Paktia and Paktika. According to the United Nations, the Haqqani network has also some family relationships and connections to various gulf states, Southeast Asia and South America (Dressler, 2010, 2012; Security Council Resolutions No. 1988, No. 1989 2011). The financial wealth of the Haqqani network with its multimillion dollar assets is based on both legal and illegal businesses, for example, vehicle trading, currency exchange institutes in Pakistan or building contractors in Afghanistan and Pakistan (Dressler, 2012). In addition to real estate businesses in Pakistan, import-export businesses and smuggling (e.g. timber and chromite), the Pakistani defence industry is another important branch of the Haqqani network (Peters, 2012).

With regard to Jihadism, the Haqqani network has close ties to Al Qaida, Pakistani Taliban, the Islamic Movement of Uzbekistan (IBU) and the Lashkar-e-Tayyiba in Kashmir. In 2004, Nasiruddin Haqqani travelled to Saudi Arabia together with Taliban members to collect donations for the war of the Taliban against the Western military coalition in Afghanistan (Dressler, 2012). From 2005 until 2009 Nasiruddin Haqqani travelled regularly to the United Arab Emirates and raised several hundred thousand US dollars for his network (Dressler, 2012).

His father Jalaluddin was one of the leaders of the Afghan Mujahideen fighting against Soviet troops, and consequently he was also a supporter of recruiting international Jihadists (Brown & Rassler, 2013). Abdullah Azzam and Osama bin Laden, international Jihadists right from the beginning, had a close relationship with Jalaluddin Haqqani, and it can be said that both the Haqqani network and Al Qaida came into being at the same time and have been interconnected ever since.

The strategic objective and the geographic dimension are characteristics which the Haqqani network and Al Qaida have in common. While Al Qaida's strategic objectives are on a global level, the Haqqani network focuses on Afghanistan, the border areas of Afghanistan and Pakistan as well as tribal Pashtun areas (Brown & Rassler, 2013).

Haqqani had realised the potential of global Jihad already back in the 1980s. For the *Umma*, Haqqani utilised Azzam's doctrine of an international Jihad against the Soviet troops in Afghanistan (Brown & Rassler, 2013).

The Haqqani network began to cooperate with the Taliban in 1994, when the Taliban had conquered the Afghan capital of Kabul, and Haqqani became a Taliban minister for tribal affairs. This position enabled Haqqani to expand his financial sources network in the areas of extortion and smuggling even further until the West intervened after 9/11 (Rashid, 2012). Following the intervention of Western armed forces in Afghanistan, the Haqqani network fled to the Afghan-Pakistani border areas but was soon able to reorganise its structures on Afghan territory again. When he got older, Jalaluddin Haqqani handed over responsibility for paramilitary, tactical, terrorist operations to his son Sirajuddin (Gall, 2008). According to the journalist Salaam, contemporary Afghan president Hamid Karzai supposedly offered Jalaluddin Haqqani the post as prime minister in his cabinet.

Current information sources would seem to prove that the Haqqani network assisted high-ranking leaders of Al Qaida to escape from Afghanistan to Pakistan, with Osama bin Laden among them (Bergen, 2009; Smucker, 2004). The Haqqani network concentrates its operations in North Waziristan and in the provinces of Paktia, Khost, Wardak, Logar and Ghazni with own fortified bases supposedly in Miranshah, Darpa Khel and Dande Darpa Khel (Gopal, 2009).

### 3.5.2   Terrorist Attacks, Assaults and Kidnapping for Ransom: The Perpetuation of Failing States as a Precondition for Organised Crime

The strategy of the Haqqani network can be traced back to its hybrid, dual structure that focuses on terrorist attacks, assaults and kidnappings to reach its political and economic aims: weakening the state and governmental structures of Afghanistan and its neighbouring states. For its existence and its financial profit from organised crime, the Haqqani network depends on Afghanistan's weakness. Since the beginning of the expansion of the nation-building projects by the international coalition in 2004, the Haqqani network has continuously undermined road construction in Afghanistan by terrorist attacks and assaults on the construction companies. On the one hand, their intention was to reduce the freedom of movement of the Afghan and international security forces; on the other hand, they tried to prevent any economic competition as a result of infrastructure development (Ruttig, 2009: 70–71).

Throughout the centuries, analysts of war—among them Thucydides and Hobbes—have explained that wars and armed conflicts destroy markets and regional or national economies (Peters, 2012). But the irregular, hybrid conflicts of the twentieth and twenty-first century, the so-called small wars, demonstrate that old and new actors of organised crime benefit significantly from them, while other larger parts of society suffer from the consequences of war and conflict. Consequently, these old and new actors of organised crime have a vital interest in perpetuating the state of war (Andreas, 2008; Peters, 2012). Actors of organised crime and Islamist terrorism depend on black and grey markets, and consequently they cultivate their trading by perpetuating the socio-economic conditions of war. Since the end of the Cold War, it can be assessed that civil wars and hybrid small wars last longer (Fearon, 2004; Peters, 2012). Since the end of the bipolar Cold War, small and civil wars with international warring factions support the interests of non-state actors of organised crime and terrorism (Berdal & Malone, 2000; Jarstad & Sisk, 2008; Peters, 2012). The combination of organised crime and Islamist terrorism, together with their commercial interests and common political/religious ideology, is prolonging all these conflicts and small wars significantly (Peters, 2012).

The Haqqani network, for example, was responsible for the following terrorist attacks:

- Terrorist attack on the delegation of the Norwegian foreign minister in Serena Hotel in Kabul on 14 January 2008, killing six and injuring six people (Gall, 2008)
- Kidnapping of the British journalist Sean Langan in spring 2008 (Beaumont, 2009)
- Attempted attack on the Afghan president Hamid Karzai in April 2008 (Gopal, 2009)
- Terrorist attack on the Indian embassy in Kabul on 7 July 2008, killing 58 and injuring more than 150 people (Wafa & Cowell, 2008)
- Kidnapping of the US journalist David Rohde in November 2008 (Ross, 2009)
- Terrorist attack on the CIA base Camp Chapman in the province of Khost, Afghanistan, on 30 December 2009, killing ten and injuring six people (Lamb & Amoore, 2010)
- Terrorist attack on a NATO convoy on 18 May 2010 in Kabul, killing 18 and injuring 52 people
- Terrorist attack on the Inter-Continental Hotel in Kabul on 28 June 2011, killing 21 people (Jelinek, 2011)
- Terrorist attack on the US embassy in Kabul on 12 September 2011, killing 8 and injuring 23 people (Rubin, Rivera, & Healy, 2011)
- Terrorist attack on a US forces facility in the province of Khost on 1 June 2012 (Dressler, 2012)

From 2010 until 2012, the international coalition in Afghanistan tried to weaken the Haqqani network through military offensives and drone attacks, but thanks to its financial and personnel resources, it always recovered quickly (Dressler, 2012). The complicated conditions of the terrain in the provinces of Khost, Paktika and Paktia and the excellent logistical system of the network are two major obstacles for the military offensives against the Haqqani network.

### 3.5.3  Organised Crime Activities

Jalaluddin Haqqani—son of a merchant—studied Islamic law in the Quranic school of Akora Khattak, in Afghanistan (Peters, 2012). During his war against Soviet troops in the 1980s, he was constantly supplied with weapons by the CIA and the Pakistani intelligence service ISI (Gopal, Mahsud, & Fishman, 2010: 9). Parallel to his tactical offensives or terrorist attacks, he established a close network of Quranic schools that educated the future recruits for Jihad (Peters, 2012: 15–17). Even before this he had identified and installed another effective asset for his war: the first nationwide broadcasting Jihadist radio station in Afghanistan for the indoctrination of the Afghan population (Peters, 2012: 15–17). In the late 1990s, Haqqani travelled to Saudi Arabia where he visited mosques to collect donations for his network (Peters, 2012: 21). In the 1990s Haqqani managed to control the smuggling operations in the border regions of Afghanistan, thanks to his position as a minister for tribal and border affairs of the Taliban government (Peters, 2012: 21). By that time, US and British authorities had already noticed that huge amounts of drugs were being transported from the southeast of Afghanistan to Pakistan (Peters, 2009a, 2009b). At the same time, several members of the Haqqani network were being appointed to key positions in the Afghan government which served as an additional enablement for expanding Haqqani's operations. Bakhta Jan, for example, became the leader of the Department of Border Control in the region of Paktika (Peters, 2012: 21).

After the intervention of the Western coalition forces in 2001, the Haqqani network had to flee for a few months into the Afghan-Pakistani border areas, and Haqqani became a commander of the Neo-Taliban, which led the insurgency against Western coalition forces from 2003 onwards (Peters, 2012: 22). The Haqqani network supported the families of fighters and suicide bombers who had died—suicide bombers in particular received large amounts of money—through a close network of Hawala couriers (*Hawaladars*) (Rassler & Brown, 2011: 31).

In the province of Loya Paktia, the Haqqani network has been cooperating with mullahs from various mosques in the areas of Jihadist ideology and recruitment of new Jihadists (Peters, 2012: 31). Among their Quran students, they propagate Jihad against the Western-backed Afghan government and the construction of a "new Afghanistan" since 2001 (Dressler, 2012). In 2011, 10 years after the collapse of the Taliban regime, David Rohde, a reporter from *The New York Times* who was a prisoner of the Haqqani network for 7 months, described North Waziristan as a "Taliban mini-state", where the Haqqani police patrols the streets and instructors of the Taliban indoctrinate the youth in the Quran schools and educate them paramilitarily (Rohde & Mulvihill, 2011: 227).

On district level, operative commanders of the Haqqani network receive salaries and equipment from the network but also have to generate own income through organised crime which led to the very effective idea of installing road checkpoints. At these checkpoints taxes vary from lower prices for empty trucks to high prices for trucks that transport fuel for the Afghan security authorities and Western troops (Peters, 2012; Rostum, 2009). The Haqqani network's extortion racket of large international companies and NGOs, of communication technology, construction companies and large-scale projects form an important part of the network's illegal activities (Peters, 2012: 41). The US construction company, for example, that carried out the road construction project between Gardez and Khost, financed by USAID, had to pay at least 1.5 million US dollar per year to the network (Rubin & Risen, 2011). In 2010 alone, the US Commander's Emergency Response Programme (CERP) which invested 46 million US dollars for civil-military reconstruction aid in the province of Khost supposedly had to pay 11 million US dollars for racketeering (Peters, 2012: 43).

The Haqqani network decided to let the Kandahar Taliban control drug trafficking and consequently focuses on illegal import of chemicals that are used for the processing of raw opium (hydrochloric acid and ethanoic acid) (Peters, 2012: 43).

Kidnapping for ransom (KFR) has been widespread in Afghanistan since 2005, and the official label of being "politically motivated, terrorist kidnapping" is a disguise. In fact kidnapping for ransom has become an important finance segment of organised crime in Afghanistan and Pakistan. In 2007, the Haqqani network, the Quetta Shura and other Taliban groups agreed on rules for kidnapping for ransom (Peters, 2012: 46–47). In that agreement "legitimate victims" were discussed, like politicians, civil servants of the Afghan government, members of security authorities, foreign members of NGOs, foreigners in general and members of foreign intelligence services (Peters, 2012: 47). The kidnappings of *The New York Times* journalist David Rohde, the Afghan diplomat Haji Khaliq Farahi and the US soldier Bowe Bergdahl have shown that the cooperation between the Haqqani network, Al Qaida and the Taliban works smoothly (Peters, 2012: 47–50).

The rapidly expanding trade with chromite between the Haqqani network and China, India and other countries with a high demand for chromite is another branch of industrial income for the Haqqani network (Lismore, 2011). A geological result of Afghan and US studies brought to light that Afghanistan has vast mineral resources worth around a trillion US dollars (USGS, 2007). Due to the fact that the Afghan government under President Karzai failed to set up a coordinating mining law for chromite, illegal mining by the Haqqani network is thriving in the provinces of Khost and Logar, and corrupt members of the Afghan government also benefit immensely (Peters, 2012: 59).

Instead of reducing the Afghan dependence on international cash transfers from Western democracies through chromite mining, chromite developed to a highly lucrative market for corrupt Afghan authorities, the Haqqani network and hundreds of thousands of smugglers, who sell the valuable chromite to China and India (Peters, 2012: 60).

## 3.6  Interaction and Cooperation Between the D-Company and Lashkar-e-Tayyiba

### 3.6.1  D-Company

D-Company, a syndicate owned by the Muslim Indian Dawood Ibrahim, consists of an inner network of at least 5000 members and a second broader network of at least 100,000 members (Bhonsle, 2011; Henley, 2011). Although it was founded in India, D-Company operates largely from Pakistan, although the Pakistani security authorities keep denying this (Perumal, 2013). In addition, D-Company operates in

Thailand, the United Arab Emirates, the Republic of South Africa, Saudi Arabia and Nepal (Henley, 2011; Kazim, 2010; Perumal, 2013). It cooperates with the Taliban, Al Qaida, Boko Haram and the Lashkar-e-Tayyiba (BBC, 2006a, 2006b; Rajghatta, 2010).

Since October 2003, the USA rated Dawood Ibrahim as a specially designated global terrorist.[4] In June 2006, the US government classified D-Company to be a "significant Foreign Narcotics Trafficker under the Foreign Narcotics Kingpin Designation Act".[5]

D-Company is active in the following areas of organised crime:

- Financing, drug trafficking, extortion and protection money
- Legal and illegal real estate business in almost all countries of the Middle East and Asia
- Betting
- Financing of films, among other things for money laundering
- Hawala money transfers
- International logistics and telecommunication deals
- Worldwide arms trafficking
- Slave trade and prostitution
- Contract killings (Clarke, 2011; Karaganis, 2011; Shelley, 2014)

In the terms of Islamist terrorism, D-Company took part in the attacks on 12 March 1999, when 257 people were killed and 713 injured, and in the terrorist attacks on 26 November 2008 (Mumbai attacks), when at least 175 were killed and 600 injured (Shelley, 2014). In the 1980s D-Company became a player of organised crime, and in the 1990s, it intensified its cooperation with Islamist terrorism (Shelley, 2014). The economic influence of D-Company in Pakistan is supposedly that far-reaching that it runs a shadow economy in Pakistan, invested billions of US dollars in real estate and even assisted the Pakistani central bank in a financial crisis (Meo, 2002).

In the 1980s, D-Company focused on legal investments in the film industry (Bollywood) while simultaneously starting illegal business with extortion and protection money in the same industry (Treverton, 2009). D-Company's annual sales from the Indian film industry amount up to 1.6 billion US dollars (McCarthy, 2014; Thompson, 2005).

Furthermore, D-Company is a major actor in heroin trading and earns around 500 million US dollars annually (Clarke, 2015; Cline & Shemella, 2015). While D-Company did not focus on heroin in the beginning, Dawood shifted his focus in the early 1990s to heroin and turned Karachi, Dubai and Mumbai to central hotspots of drug trafficking (Clarke, 2015; Cline & Shemella, 2015). Due to Dawood's

---

[4]US Department of the Treasury (2003). US Designates Dawood Ibrahim as Terrorist Supporter. 16 October 2003.

[5]US Department of the Treasury/Office of Foreign Assets Control (2006). An Overview of the Foreign Narcotics Kingpin Designation Act and Executive Order 12978 of 21 October 1995.

participation in the 1993 Islamist terror attacks, he had to leave India and moved to Pakistan where he intensified his cooperation with Jihadist actors and their expanding drug operations in Nigeria and Kenya (Clarke, 2015; Cline & Shemella, 2015). As part of its money laundering operation, D-Company managed to infiltrate various stock markets, for example, in India and in Pakistan (Cline & Shemella, 2015). Moreover, D-Company supposedly has similar contacts in various gulf states. After the Mumbai attacks and the move of its headquarters from Mumbai to Karachi, Pakistan, in 1993, D-Company's personnel structure was modified. As a result of the devastating terrorist attacks against Hindus, most of the Hindus who had worked for Dawood Ibrahim left his organisation and were replaced by Muslims (Lal, 2005: 298).

### 3.6.2   Lashkar-e-Tayyiba (LeT)

> The Jihad in Kashmir would soon spread to entire India. Our Mujahideen would create three Pakistans in India. We feel that Kashmir should be liberated at the earliest. Thereafter, Indian Muslims should be aroused to rise in revolt against the Indian Union so that India gets disintegrated. (Hafiz Saeed, co-founder of the LeT, in Raman, 2001: 3)

The Lashkar-e-Tayyiba (LeT)[6] is one of the largest and most active Jihadist organisations in South Asia that mostly operates in Pakistan—Muridke and Lahore (Basset, 2012: 12). LeT was founded by Hafiz Saeed, Abdullah Azzam and Zafar Iqbal in 1987, financially supported by Osama bin Laden (Atkins, 2004: 173). From the 1980s until 2002, LeT was even supported by the Pakistani government, mostly by the influential Pakistani secret service ISI. This support by ISI only ended because of the diplomatic pressure from the USA and India (Gugler, 2012). Since then the LeT is prohibited as terrorist organisation in India, Pakistan, the USA, Great Britain, Russia and Australia (Tankel, 2011). The political arm of the LeT, Jamat ud Dawah (JuD), was the last faction to be forbidden by the Pakistani government in 2015 (Times of India, 2015). A prioritised aim and part of the worldwide Jihadist agenda of the LeT is to foster the independency of the Jammu and Kashmir regions (Rabasa, Blackwill, & Chalk, 2009). In newspapers and on websites, the LeT expressed repeatedly that some of its main political goals are to destroy India, Hinduism and Judaism (Haqqani, 2005: 12–26). Consistently the LeT describes Hindus and Jews as "enemies of Islam" and India and Israel as "enemies of Pakistan" (Haqqani, 2005: 12). It interprets Jihad as a "duty of every Muslim" and the institutionalisation of a caliphate as its main religious/political goal (Tankel, 2011).

India's biggest terrorist threat can be traced back to Jihadism, operating from Pakistan and Bangladesh. LeT is the largest and most dangerous Jihadist organisation with an explicit terrorist agenda for India (Clarke, 2010).

Its origins lie in the Markaz Dawa Al Irshad (Centre for Preaching), also called MDI, which was founded in 1987 to support the Afghan international Jihad against

---

[6]Urdu لشکر طیبہ for Army of the Good, Army of the Righteous, or Army of the Pure.

the Soviet troops and to preach a fundamentalist, Jihadist version of Islam within Pakistan. The Pakistani secret service "Inter-Service Intelligence" (ISI) and the CIA supported MDI in its war against the Soviet troops, although the CIA terminated its financial and logistical support right after the withdrawal of the last Soviet troops from Afghanistan. In contrast, the Pakistani ISI continued its support for MDI in order to carry out terrorist attacks in Kashmir and India (Clarke, 2010; Raman, 2001). The founder of MDI, Hafiz Saeed, a professor for Islamic law in Pakistan, stressed the importance of a Wahhabi orthodox teaching (Shafqat, 2002). Before disputes started concerning the role of Osama bin Laden, the MDI had very close contacts to Saudi Arab mosques and Saudi Arab secret services (Clarke, 2010).

LeT was founded as a branch of MDI in the late 1980s (BBC, 2006a, 2006b). The military operations of LeT against the Soviet troops were rare and not that spectacular, but the Pakistani ISI saw LeT as a useful terrorist tool for terrorist attacks in Kashmir (Wilson, 2005).

Since the beginning of the 1990s, LeT became the terrorist tool of the MDI and became infamous for spectacular offensives against Indian armed forces and security authorities with many own losses (Clarke, 2010). In the Kargil War 1999, the LeT allied with regular Pakistani armed forces in the fight against the Indian armed forces and controlled military positions in the mountainous regions of Drass and Batalik.

Muridke, the headquarters of the LeT, is substantially based on donations from the Islamist and Wahhabi milieu in the Middle East and from Pakistani patrons. The LeT supposedly possesses over 16 Quran schools and mosques, 135 schools, many hospitals, ambulances, blood banks and hundreds of Islamist seminars in Pakistan (Clarke, 2010).

Finally, the terrorist attack on the Indian parliament at the end of 2001 led to the LeT being condemned as a terrorist organisation, as well and even by the Pakistani president Musharraf (Clarke, 2010). Until then, LeT was able to collect donations publicly in almost all shops, markets and cities in Pakistan in order to support terrorist actions in Kashmir (Clarke, 2010). In addition to that, Saeed, the founder and leader of LeT, only spent a short time in Pakistani prison custody. Saeed publicly stated that Kashmir is only the "gateway to capture India" and that the LeT would fight for territorial independence of Muslim territories in India, for example, Gujarat and Hyderabad (Clarke, 2010). Saeed described these steps only as a first phase because the final aim would be a Muslim rule over India. In addition, the LeT internationalised itself quite quickly—already before 9/11—and had close ties to international Jihadists in Bosnia, Palestine and Afghanistan (Sreedhar & Manish, 2003). As a result of this cooperation based on a common Islamist and Jihadist ideology, operational training content and logistics were shared (Clarke, 2010). The LeT also played an active role in the Chechen Jihadist fight against Russia (Clarke, 2010). In addition to India, Saeed, LeT's founder and leader, also declared Israel and the USA to be primary terrorist targets (Ismail, 2006). The arrest of an Al Qaida commander in a safe house of the LeT in Faisalabad, Pakistan, in March 2002 illustrates the close cooperation of Al Qaida and LeT (Aftergood, 2004).

LeT recruits and trains significantly more fighters than needed for its current terrorist campaigns in Kashmir which makes it less vulnerable to massive military operations, for example, air raids and drone attacks (Clarke, 2010). According to conservative estimates, the LeT has sent thousands of young Punjabi Jihadists—between 18 and 25 years of age—to the Jihad of 2004–2010 in Iraq (Clarke, 2010; Swami & Shehzad, 2004).

LeT is also well known for small war operations like hit-and-run tactics in house-to-house combat and for attacking Indian civilians, politicians and civil servants as well as police stations, hotels, airports and public transportation (Clarke, 2010; Sreedhar & Manish, 2003).

Referring to its proximity to the Taliban, the Haqqani network and the Hezbi Islami of Gulbuddin Hekmatyar are actors of new terrorism with the LeT also being active in Nuristan, a highly unstable region in northeast Afghanistan (Terrorism Focus, 2006). Alongside its activities in India and Pakistan, the LeT supposedly has cells in Great Britain, France, Australia, the USA and Italy (Clarke, 2010). On the one hand, these cells serve the financing of terrorist activities through organised crime—for example, Hawala services; on the other hand, they serve the interaction and cooperation with other international Jihadist cells and groups (Clarke, 2010).

### 3.6.3  Interaction and Cooperation

After the terrorist attacks in 1993, Dawood Ibrahim had to leave India due to the investigations against him, and consequently he shifted his organisation to Karachi, Pakistan. At the end of the 1990s, he began to build up his strategic and tactical alliance with the LeT, which had been rated as a foreign terrorist organisation (FTO) by the US government in 2001. By then D-Company began to finance and support the terrorist activities of the LeT in Kashmir (Rollins et al., 2010: 388–390; Treverton, 2009: 128–135). In addition, the LeT was supported by the D-Company in the field of recruitment and was allowed to use its smuggling routes and contact persons for its logistical preparation of terrorist attacks (Rollins et al., 2010: 388–390).

D-Company provides Jihadist organisations like LeT and Al Qaida with its know-how, its corruption-based contacts to state authorities and its logistics in the field of organised crime, for example, to transport terrorist fighters, weapons and drugs across various borders. This cooperation is particularly important for financing terrorist activities through the close Hawala net, which is provided by D-Company.

In return, D-Company benefits as well from the intensification of the interaction and cooperation with Jihadist organisations like the LeT and Al Qaida because it can use their international logistics and the international personnel structure of large Jihadist organisations—also in diaspora milieus of Western countries. The LeT has benefitted from D-Company's close Hawala net for many years, in Karachi, Pakistan, as well as in Mumbai, India, and countries of the Middle East (Clarke, 2010).

The US Drug Enforcement Administration (DEA) assessed that D-Company is assisting the LeT and that in recent years irregular fighters of the LeT have been included in drug trafficking by D-Company (Lal, 2005).

Approximately 60% of the people who died in terrorist attacks on Indian territory were killed by the LeT (Clarke, 2010: 32). The LeT also benefits from the good relations of D-Company to Saudi Arab citizens and official authorities because Saudi Arab players do have an Islamist agenda in Kashmir (Clarke, 2010: 46–47). In addition, the LeT relies on D-Company for safe houses, tap-proof telephones, weapons, explosives and further logistics on Indian territory (Clarke, 2010: 46–47).


## 3.7  Interaction, Cooperation and Fusion in the Area of Kidnapping for Ransom

Kidnapping for ransom (KFR) is a relatively new term in international affairs. In the twentieth century, organised crime in Columbia and Mexico was renowned for kidnapping for ransom. Since 11 September 2011, the use of this phenomenon has increased dramatically at the hands of Jihadist players in Iraq, Yemen, Pakistan, Afghanistan, Central Asia and northern and western Africa (i.e. Mauretania, Mali, Niger and Nigeria).

Many players involved in new terrorism now finance a high proportion of their budget with ransom money from kidnappings. Al Qaida in the Islamic Maghreb (AQIM) alone is said to have had a turnover of 89 million US dollars between 2003 and 2012 (Nünlist, 2013: 1). Al Qaida and its various offshoots (Boko Haram in Nigeria, Tehrik-e Taliban in Pakistan) and other Jihadist groups are among those players of new terrorism who use KFR as the main means of financing. Members of the Algerian Jihadist organisation Groupe Salafiste pour la Prédication et le Combat (GSPC) have cooperated since 2003 with the AQIM in West and North Africa. In Mali alone, this Jihadist alliance kidnapped more than 70 Western citizens between 2003 and 2012, ensuring that they had a significant and continuing source of income from the ransom money paid by Western governments and international companies.

The millions of US dollars extorted represent a new security challenge for Western societies, as the millions obtained are used by the players of new terrorism for recruiting new members, for the upkeep of training camps, for acquiring weapons and means of communication and for the organisation and execution of terrorist attacks (Nünlist, 2013: 2). The Sahel is a critical area for KFR, as it is here that players of new terrorism kidnap foreign employees of aid agencies, tourists, company employees, diplomats and other people so as to extort ransom from Western companies and/or states. The first international cases to come to light were in southern Algeria in 2003, when the Algerian GSPC kidnapped 32 European tourists, including 16 Germans and 4 Swiss. According to the US authorities, the government of Mali was instrumental in arranging a successful outcome between the kidnappers and the European governments by which the Mali government is said to have demanded and received at least 5 million US dollars from the German government for the 16 kidnapped Germans (Nünlist, 2013: 2).

On 16 January 2013, players of new terrorism—both Jihadi groups and groups of transnational organised crime—attacked oil production facilities in the natural gas field in In Aménas in Algeria on the border to Libya and took more than 100 international employees hostage. Before Algerian security forces stormed the oil facility, more than 39 international employees—i.e. from the USA, France, Great Britain, Japan, Norway and Romania, working for BP, the Norwegian Statoil and the Japanese JGC—were maltreated, tortured and killed.

The players of new terrorism originated from more than seven countries including Canada, Algeria, Chad, Egypt, Mauritania and Mali. The fact that the hostage-takers were able to penetrate the enclosure, despite the security measures which had been in force to Western standards for many years, was due to the cooperation of established players of organised crime, the Tuareg from northern Mali and southern Libya, and Jihadist players: Al Qaida in the Islamic Maghreb (AQIM). The mastermind behind the hostage-taking was identified as Mokhtar Belmokhtar, leader of an Al Qaida cell. Belmokhtar had already been given the names "Jihadi gangster" and "Mr. Marlboro" before the hostage-taking. These names reflected his parallel functions as leader of an Al Qaida cell and as head of a network smuggling and trading cigarettes illegally in northern and western Africa (Shelley, 2014).

After the kidnapping, international security authorities carried out an analysis of the quality of the players' equipment and planning for the kidnapping. This showed that it was representative of the cooperation of groups of transnationally organised criminals with Jihadists and also that groups such as Al Qaida had transformed in recent years to become hybrid actors, operating both in the field of transnational terrorism and transnationally organised crime.

On account of their clandestine nature, there are few reliable statistics available, but conservative estimates assume that these groups are responsible for more than 20,000 kidnappings per year worldwide (Nünlist, 2013: 3). According to US sources, in 2011 the AQIM received on average 5.4 million US dollars for every hostage released (Nünlist, 2013: 3). The so-called Islamic State supposedly extorted at least 45 million US dollars through KFR in 2013 (Adams, 2014). For years, the USA and Great Britain in particular have been trying to stop the payment of ransom money by governments or state authorities. This was supported by Resolution 2133 of the Security Council, which was passed unanimously on 17 January 2014.[7]

---

[7]"The Security Council today called upon all Member States to prevent terrorists from benefiting directly or indirectly from ransom payments or political concessions, and further, to secure the safe release of hostages. Unanimously adopting resolution 2133 (2014), the Council reaffirmed resolution 1373 (2001)—the wide-ranging text it adopted following the 11 September 2001 attacks in the United States—in particular, its decisions that all States shall prevent and suppress the financing of terrorist acts, and refrain from providing support to any entities or persons involved, including by suppressing recruitment of members of terrorist groups and eliminating the supply of weapons to them. All States should prohibit their nationals, or any persons or entities within their territories,

Just prior to this, the same strategy was adopted by the state representatives of the G8 summit: "We unequivocally reject the payment of ransom to terrorists" (Adams, 2014). However, quite a number of European countries, including France, Germany, Italy and Switzerland, are known to have repeatedly paid ransom money to Jihadi players since 2001 (Adams, 2014). For example, both Oman and Qatar act as intermediaries for European states in negotiating ransom money for kidnappings (Adams, 2014).

Paradoxically, the thriving "business" of KPR pursued by Jihadi groups and players since 11 September 2011 is a direct consequence of international measures to dry out the sources of finance available to Islamist terrorism (Mahadevan, 2013; Nünlist, 2013).

Because of the international actions to thwart its centralised sources of finance, Al Qaida transformed its financing and organisation away from its previously hierarchical form towards local, autonomous, financially independent cells (Mahadevan, 2013). For example, AQIM remodelled its financing operations, turning its attention to other sources of income such as smuggling, cocaine and arms' dealing and KFR. Between 2008 and 2014, three Al Qaida offshoots—Al Qaida in the Islamic Maghreb, Al Qaida on the Arabian peninsula and Al-Shabaab—raised at least 165 million US dollars through KFR. According to the US Treasury Department, KFR is "today's most significant source of terrorist financing" (The Week, 2014). Between 2008 and 2009, the number of known hostages taken in Afghanistan rose from 584 to 2088 and in Pakistan from 1264 to 3366 over the same period (The Week, 2014).

In the Horn of Africa, Al-Shabaab is a threat to all people from the Western world, and its influence extends as far as Kenya, Eastern Ethiopia and Djibouti (Stewart, 2014). In the summer of 2014, the Syrian Jabhat al-Nusra/Jabhat Fatah al-Sham took a group of UN peacekeeping soldiers from Fiji hostage in the Golan Heights (Stewart, 2014).

In the period 2010–2014 alone, hostage-taking of employees of international companies and tourists in northern and western Africa—mainly Europeans and Canadians—fetched at least 140 million euros, paid by German, Canadian, British, Italian, Austrian, Swedish, Spanish and other governmental institutions and companies (Briscoe, 2014; Shelley, 2014).

In Iraq, the years 2004–2010 were extremely lucrative for the players of new terrorism, due to their kidnapping of Western foreigners. Regional, Iraqi players of organised crime and international Jihadi players cooperated in kidnapping for

---

from making funds, financial assets or economic resources available for the benefit of those involved in terrorist acts. By the text adopted today, the Council called on States to cooperate closely in incidents of kidnapping and hostage-taking by terrorists, reaffirming that all States should afford one another the "greatest measure of assistance" in connection with related criminal investigations or proceedings. It also called on States to continue expert discussions on kidnapping for ransom by terrorists within the United Nations and other organizations, including the Global Counterterrorism Forum". https://www.un.org/press/en/2014/sc11262.doc.htm; 27 January 2014. Accessed: 04 March 2017.

ransom. Ransom of up to 45 million US dollars was paid for the kidnapping of Western—French, German and Italian—hostages (McGrory, 2006: 8).

Strangely enough, despite the absence of international interest, it was even more lucrative to kidnap Iraqi citizens. These kidnappings reached their zenith in 2006, when approximately 40 Iraqi citizens were kidnapped per day. With an average ransom of 10,000 US dollars, this meant 400,000 US dollars per day or a total of at least 140 million US dollars per year (Williams & Felbab-Brown, 2012).

Another group belonging to new terrorism which uses KFR is the Islamic Movement of Uzbekistan (IMU). Various analyses come to the conclusion that the IMU is responsible for up to 70% of the drug smuggling through Central Asia to Europe (Cornell, 2005; Makarenko, 2002; Williams & Felbab-Brown, 2012).

Many members of IMU fought in Afghanistan alongside the Taliban and Al Qaida against Western forces (Cornell, 2005; Williams & Felbab-Brown, 2012). The KFR practised by IMU in Central Asia was motivated by the ransom payments as well as by objectives of political terrorism (Cornell, 2005; Williams & Felbab-Brown, 2012).

The ransom money paid by state institutions could be invested in actions in the field of organised crime as well as in Jihadist activities, including for technology, weapons, equipment and recruiting highly trained personnel. To put it more drastically, international companies and European security authorities are not just the victims of these hostage-takings but also the sponsors of these crimes and their perpetrators. Thanks to KFR, the players of new terrorism can finance the escalation of their activities in the realm of organised crime in countries of the European Union and in parallel their terrorist attacks in these same countries—both with hit teams and Islamist lone wolves.

## 3.8  Summary

With the end of the Cold War, the boundaries between war, terrorism and organised crime began to crumble. Since the beginning of the twenty-first century, they gradually seem to have vanished in the small wars in the Middle East. Transnational organised crime and transnational Islamist terrorism benefit likewise from ongoing conflicts, wars, weak and failed states. As shown above, the criminal area of activity of transnational organised crime is highly heterogeneous and includes drug trafficking and human trafficking by criminal networks, child pornography, identity theft, copyright privacy, money laundering, cybercrime, looting of historical artefacts in the Middle East and kidnapping for ransom (KFR).

The empirical analysis of the interaction, cooperation and fusion of different actors of transnational organised crime and transnational Jihadism has shown that both phenomena and actors benefit from weak and failed states and conflict regions like North and West Africa, East Africa, the Middle East, the Balkans, Afghanistan, the Caucasus and others. Specifically, weak and failed states are a vital precondition for the spread and increase of the combined strength of organised crime and Islamist terrorism. In weak states, actors of organised crime and Islamist terrorism exploit the lack of governance and take over typical functions which originally had been controlled and executed exclusively by state and government authorities. Furthermore, territory without any functioning state power offers organised crime welcome opportunities for training camps, recruiting and transit areas for people and goods. It has to be stressed that organised crime and transnational Jihadism both have a destructive impact for the disintegration of political entities and the transformation of states into fragile objects by creating parallel structures, for example, on the levels of economy and security.

It could be observed that since the beginning of the twenty-first century numerous organisations, groups and cells of organised crime have gradually developed a political, religious/ideologic agenda. Thereby they have changed their formerly apolitical, criminal and primarily profit-oriented appearance in the direction of the constitutive characteristics of terrorist organisations.

Both transnational organised crime and Islamist terrorism reflect the same common trends, inasmuch as they implement the tactics and organisational principles of network structures, outsourcing and promoting autonomous cells with limited contact to the organisation's leadership, in order to avoid detection. The structure of their logistics and supply networks is in any case quite similar and often led by the same people.

Worldwide the cultivation and trafficking of drugs is one of the most lucrative sources of income of organised crime and illustrates the interaction, cooperation and fusion of actors from organised crime and Islamist terrorism. As described above, groups of transnational organised crime have been benefitting from the cultivation and trafficking of drugs since the beginning of the twenty-first century, mostly in the conflict regions of Afghanistan and its neighbouring countries, but also in North and West Africa, which helped the actors of drug trafficking to open up huge resources for the recruitment of personnel and financing of infrastructure. Due to the significant boom in the cultivation and trafficking of drugs, numerous actors of terrorism saw their chances for a sustainable financing strategy of their political/terrorist agenda. According to the *Country Reports on Terrorism 2015* of the US Department of State, more than 25 international terrorist organisations operate in the field of organised crime. The fact that a very small amount of countries and regions is responsible for nearly 100% of the production of opium centralises and strengthens organised crime and Islamist terrorism, be it in the cultivation areas of Afghanistan or the regions of the main transport routes in North and West Africa. As mentioned above, the cultivation and transport of drugs is essentially dependent on weak, failing or failed states where the governmental actors have no capabilities, will or interest to stop such illegal activities.

As the whole process of cultivating, smuggling and selling drugs involves numerous heterogeneous actors with different functions, the cooperation and interaction of these actors touches several policy fields and state functions, for example, inner and outer security, economy, agricultural policy, taxes and subsidies. Consequently, corruption in the fields of cultivating, smuggling and selling of drugs has great influence on countries like Afghanistan, Pakistan, Tajikistan and Kyrgyzstan or in North and West Africa. This cooperation with state actors creates hybrid networks which are currently and will in future be quite hard to detect or break up. The organisations and groups of transnational organised crime and the transnational Islamist terrorism which benefit from regional, national, ethnical/tribal and religious/political networks are those with the longest lifespan, the highest sales and the closest interconnectedness, both nationally and internationally.

The analysis of drug cultivation and smuggling out of Afghanistan to Western Europe shows how complex, global and hybrid these new networks, groups and cells are and how they (inter)act. As a result, the relationship of organised crime and the international terrorism in Afghanistan leads to a close network of local and regional non-state and state actors in the field of cultivation and transport of opium that all cooperate with the Taliban, the Haqqani network and Al Qaida.

Very soon after the military intervention of the Western coalition and the fall of the Taliban regime, economic and political parallel structures developed in almost all regions of Afghanistan—to a lesser extent in the capital of Kabul. Local clan chiefs, their province commanders, the Taliban, the Haqqani network and Al Qaida developed a hybrid and interwoven transnational drug/terrorism network that became a cross-border network—despite ethnical differences and different ideological Jihadi agendas. This drug/terrorism network is a hybrid fusion of regional and international actors that benefit from common capacities and capabilities in terms of weaponry, personnel, training, transport routes and tactics. Since 2004 ransom money and opium money enabled the Taliban, the Haqqani network and Al Qaida to conduct high-level destabilising actions such as terrorist attacks and assaults.

The analysis of the hybrid actors in North and West Africa, for example, Ansar Dine, Al Mourabitoun and the AQIM, has shown multiple characteristics like a decentral network or cell structure of local, regional and/or nationwide political/religious agendas, multiple and heterogeneous tactics of finance, an international membership and a fusion of organised crime and Islamist terrorism. By cooperating with international Islamist terrorists, actors of organised crime were able to benefit from a global Jihadist ideology and strategy, for example, on the level of paramilitary and tactical capabilities.

The hybrid actors in North and West Africa have proven for 10 years that they are flexible and can adapt to transforming regional and global situations. Their organisational flexibility and resilience are mainly based on the ability for recruiting from the civil population. A decisive key to gaining support from the civil population is the religious/political ideology of Islamism and Jihadism.

The analysis of the hybrid actors of D-Company, LeT and Haqqani network has shown their hybrid, dual strategy with terrorist attacks, assaults and kidnapping for ransom as the main instruments for reaching political and economic goals: weakening state and governmental structures and exploiting the resulting governance vacuums for their own agenda. In contrast to the international wars of other societies in the twentieth century, actors of new terrorism derive benefit most from conflict, small wars and the collapse of state and economic structures. As mentioned above, new terrorism is based on black and grey markets, and consequently it is the objective of new terrorist actors to protect these markets by perpetuating the socio-economic conditions of small wars. Therefore, empirical data shows that civil and small wars last longer since the end of the Cold War (Fearon, 2004; Peters, 2012).

After 9/11, LeT internationalised quite quickly and established close relations with other international Jihadists in Bosnia, Palestine and Afghanistan. In the context of this cooperation and on the basis of common Islamist and Jihadist ideology, tactical-operative contacts and logistics were exchanged. Regarding the international Jihad, LeT supposedly participated in Chechen's fight against Russia. As proof for its international activity, LeT has its own cells in Great Britain, France, Australia, the USA and Italy at its disposal. These LeT cells serve the financing of terrorist activities through organised crime, but also foster interaction and cooperation with other international Jihadist cells and groups.

To summarise the cooperation of D-Company as a worldwide established group of organised crime and the LeT as a Jihadist organisation with close ties to other international Jihadist organisations like Al Qaida, D-Company provides Jihadist organisations like LeT and Al Qaida with its know-how, its corruption-based connections to state authorities and its criminal organised logistics. This may include transporting terrorist fighters, weapons and drugs across borders or financing terrorist activities through D-Company's Hawala network. In return, D-Company benefits from its interaction and cooperation with Jihadist organisations like LeT and Al Qaida by taking advantage of the international logistics and international personnel structure of Jihadist organisations, also in the diaspora milieus of Western states.

The cooperation of Al Qaida and its branches Boko Haram in Nigeria, Tehrik-e Taliban in Pakistan and other Jihadist groups shows the new level of cooperation between actors of organised crime and international Jihadism in the twenty-first century. Kidnapping for ransom (KFR) became a vital means for its financing. The ransom money—millions of dollars—of KFR expand the threat for Western states because the actors of KFR use it to recruit new members, to finance terrorist training camps, to obtain weapons and means of communication and finally to organise terrorist attacks and assaults.

To understand the logic of terrorism and the means of combatting it, it should again be stressed that paradoxically since 9/11 the flourishing kidnapping for ransom is a causal consequence of the international "war on terror". Thanks to international operations against the centralised finance networks of Al Qaida, the latter transformed its financial structures to form a loose and intensified network of local, autonomous and financially independent cells, intensifying its activities in the area of drug trafficking, the arms trade and in particular kidnapping for ransom.

During the past 10 years, Al Qaida has proven its flexibility and adaptability to changing political and economic conditions, in Afghanistan as well as in Africa. On account of its transnational Islamist-terrorist ideology, these attributes enable Al Qaida to latch on to practically every conflict involving Muslims and to recruit new followers worldwide. Without the cooperation, interaction and partial fusion of various groups of organised crime in Afghanistan before and after 9/11, the existence of the Taliban and Al Qaida would have been endangered by the international forces. Currently, Afghanistan is well on its way to becoming what it already was for Osama bin Laden and his Al Qaida before 9/11: a safe haven to retreat to and train in (also for Western foreign fighters) and an economic (based on drug trafficking and kidnapping for ransom) and military basis for one of the most important and threatening international Jihadist organisations.

The interaction, cooperation and fusion of actors, tactics and means of Jihadism and transnational organised crime pose a substantial threat to the whole democratic, Western world but also to the human security of any conflict region worldwide. Jihadist ideology is the compelling factor behind the cooperation, interaction and partial fusion of local and regional groups and networks of organised crime with transnational, terrorist groups.

# References

Adams, P. (2014, December 12). Kidnap for ransom by extremist groups extracts high price. *BBC News*.

Aftergood, S. (2004). *Lashkar-e-Taiba*. Washington, DC: Federation of American Scientists. Retrieved May 21, 2004, from https://fas.org/irp/world/para/lashkar.htm

Alemia, E. (2013). Organized and transnational crime in West Africa. In Heinrich-Böll-Stiftung (Ed.), *Transnational organized crime: Analyses of a global challenge to democracy* (pp. 127–144). Bielefeld: Transcript.

Allum, F., & Gilmour, S. (2012). *Routledge handbook of transnational organized crime*. New York: Routledge.

Andreas, P. (2008). *Blue helmets, black markets*. Ithaca, NY: Cornell University Press.

Atkins, S. (2004). *Encyclopedia of modern worldwide extremists and extremist groups*. Westport, CT: Greenwood Press.

Basset, D. (2012). *Encyclopedia of terrorism*. Santa Barbara, CA: ABC-CLIO.

BBC. (2006a). Profile: India's fugitive gangster. Retrieved September 12, 2006, from http://news.bbc.co.uk/2/hi/south_asia/4775531.stm

BBC. (2006b). Profile: Lashkar-e-Toiba. *BBC News*. Retrieved March 17, 2006, from news.bbc.co.uk/1/hi/world/south_asia/3181925.stm

Beaumont, P. (2009, June 21). Kidnapping of British journalist Sean Langan was blamed on the network. Kidnapped US reporter makes dramatic escape from Taliban. *The Guardian*.

Bell, S. (2011, July 11). Ontario extortion racket has ties to Hezbollah. *National Post*.

Berdal, M., & Malone, D. (2000). *Greed and grievance: Economic agendas in civil wars*. Boulder, CO: Lynne Reiner.

Bergen, P. (2009, December 30). The battle for Tora Bora. *The New Republic*.

Bhonsle, R. (2011). *Countering transnational terrorism*. New Delhi: Vij Books India.

Bloom, M. (2005). *Dying to kill: The allure of suicide terror*. New York: Columbia University Press.

Bowers, C. (2009). Hawala, money laundering, and terrorism finance: Micro-lending as an end to illicit remittance. *Denver Journal of International Law and Policy, 37*(3), 379–419.

Briscoe, I. (2014). *Crime after Jihad: Armed groups, the state and illicit business in post-conflict Mali*. Den Haag: Clingendael's Conflict Research Unit.

Briscoe, I., & Dari, E. (2012). Crime and error: Why we urgently need a new approach to illicit trafficking in fragile states. *CCRU Policy Brief, 23*, 1–6. https://www.clingendael.org/sites/default/files/pdfs/20120500_cru_policy_brief_23.pdf

Brown, V., & Rassler, D. (2013). *Fountainhead of Jihad: The Haqqani network, 1973–2012*. New York: Columbia University Press.

Bybee, A. (2012). The twenty-first century expansion of the transnational drug trade in Africa. *Journal of International Affairs, 66*(1), 65–80.

Bynum, D. (2005). *Deadly connections: States that sponsor terrorism.* New York: Cambridge University Press.

Byrd, W., & Buddenberg, D. (2010). Introduction and overview. In W. Byrd & D. Buddenberg (Eds.), *Afghanistan's drug industry book: Structure, functioning, dynamics and implications for counter-narcotics policy* (pp. 1–24). United Nations – Office on Drugs and Crime. The World Bank. https://www.unodc.org/pdf/Afgh_drugindustry_Nov06.pdf

Clarke, R. (2010). *Lashkar-i-Taiba: The fallacy of subservient proxies and the future of Islamist terrorism in India.* Strategic Studies Institute/US Army War College.

Clarke, R. (2011). *Crime-terror nexus in South Asia: States, security and non-state actors.* Abingdon, OX: Routledge.

Clarke, C. (2015). *Terrorism, Inc.: The financing of terrorism, insurgency, and irregular warfare.* Santa Barbara, CA: ABO-CLIO, F. Praeger.

Cline, L., & Shemella, P. (2015). *The future of counterinsurgency: Contemporary debates in internal security strategy.* Santa Barbara, CA: ABO-CLIO-Praeger.

Collier, P., & Hoeffler, A. (1998). On economic causes of civil war. *Oxford Economic Papers, 50* (4), 563–573.

Cornell, S. (2005). Narcotics, radicalism and armed conflict in Central Asia: The Islamic movement of Uzbekistan. *Terrorism and Political Violence, 17,* 619–639.

Cornell, S., & Swantström. (2006). The Eurasian drug trade: A challenge to regional security. *Problems of Post-Communism, 53*(4), 10–28.

Director of National Intelligence. (2012). James Clapper. In U.S. Congress, Senate Select Committee on Intelligence, Current and Projected National Security Threats to the United States, 31.01.2012. Washington, DC: U.S. Government Printing Office.

Dressler, J. (2010). *The Haqqani network: From Pakistan to Afghanistan.* Washington, DC: Institute for the Study of War.

Dressler, J. (2012). *The Haqqani network, a strategic threat.* Washington, DC: Institute for the Study of War.

Drug Enforcement Administration (DEA). (2011). House Committee on Foreign Affairs, Subcommittee on Terrorism, Nonproliferation, and Trade, Narcoterrorism and the Long Reach of U.S. Law Enforcement, Part II, 17.11.2011. Washington, DC: U.S. Government Printing Office.

Duyvesteyn, I. (2004). How new is the new terrorism? *Studies in Conflict and Terrorism, 27*(5), 439–455.

EMCDDA. (2016). *European drug report 2016.* Brussels.

Esparza, G. (2003). *'La Mafia Rusa en Mexico' and organized crime and terrorist activity in Mexico, 1999–2002.* A Report prepared under an Interagency Agreement by the Federal Research Division, Library of Congress. https://www.loc.gov/rr/frd/pdf-files/OrgCrime_Mexico.pdf

European Union. (2005). *Mitteilung der Kommission an den Rat und das Europäische Parlament: "Entwicklung eines Strategiekonzepts für die Bekämpfung der organisierten Kriminalität"* [SEK 724]; June 2, 2005.

EUROPOL. (2011). *European police chiefs convention.* Luxembourg: Publications Office of the European Union.

EUROPOL. (2013). *Socta 2013 EU serious and organised crime threat assessment.* Den Haag: European Police Office.

Faith, D. (2011, Winter). The Hawala system. *Global Security Studies, 2*(1), 23–33.

Farah, D. (2011). Terrorist-criminal pipelines and criminalized states: Emerging alliances. *Prism, 2* (3), 15–32.

Farah, D. (2013). Fixers, super fixers, and shadow facilitators: How networks connect. In M. Miklaucic & J. Brewer (Eds.), *Convergence: Illicit networks and national security in the age of globalisation* (pp. 75–95). Washington, DC: National Defense University Press.

Fearon, J. (2004). Why do some civil wars last so much longer than others? *Journal of Peace Research, 41*(3), 275–231.

Fijnaut, C., & Paoli, L. (2004). *Organised crime in Europe: Patterns and policies in the European Union and beyond.* Dordrecht: Springer.

Fischer, A. (2010). *The Tuareg society within a globalized world: Saharan life in transition.* Library of Modern Middle East Studies (p. 91). London: I.B. Tauris.

Gall, C. (2008, June 17). Old-line Taliban commander is face of rising Afghan threat. *The New York Times.*

Gallagher, M. (2016). 'Criminalised' Islamic state veterans: A future major threat in organised crime development? *Perspectives on Terrorism, 10*(5). http://www.terrorismanalysts.com/pt/index.php/pot/article/view/541/html

Gopal, A. (2009). The most deadly US foe in Afghanistan. *The Christian Science Monitor.* Retrieved June 1, 2009, from https://www.csmonitor.com/World/Asia-South-Central/2009/0601/p10s01-wosc.html

Gopal, A., Mahsud, M., & Fishman, B. (2010). The South Asia channel: Inside the Haqqani network. *Foreign Policy.* Retrieved June 25, 2010, from https://foreignpolicy.com/2010/06/03/inside-the-haqqani-network/

Grabosky, P., & Stohl, M. (2010). *Crime and terrorism.* London: Sage.

Gugler, T. (2012). From Kalashnikov to Keyboard: Pakistan's Jihadiscapes and the transformation of the Lashkar-e Tayba. In R. Lohlker (Ed.), *New approaches to the analysis of Jihadism: Online and offline* (pp. 37–62). Göttingen: Vienna University Press.

Halliday, F. (1991). State and society in international relations. In M. Banks & M. Shaw (Eds.), *State and society in international relations* (pp. 191–209). London: Palgrave Macmillan.

Haqqani, H. (2005). The ideologies of South Asian Jihadi groups. *Hudson Institute, 1*, 12–26. Retrieved from https://www.hudson.org/research/9867-the-ideologies-of-south-asian-jihadi-groups

Henley, J. (2011). Who is now on the world's most wanted list? *The Guardian.* Retrieved May 4, 2011, from https://www.theguardian.com/world/2011/may/04/the-worlds-most-wanted-list

Heymann, P. (2003). *Terrorism, freedom, and security: Winning without war.* Cambridge, MA: MIT Press.

Hirschmann, K. (2016). Internationaler Terrorismus. In W. Woyke & J. Varwick (Eds.), *Handwörterbuch Internationale Politik* (pp. 228–238). Bonn: Bundeszentrale für Politische Bildung.

Horgan, J. (2009). *Walking away from terrorism: Accounts of disengagement from radical and extremist movements.* London: Routledge.

Ismail, N. (2006). The role of kinship in Indonesia's Jemmah Islamiya. *Terrorism Monitor, 4* (11) (The Jamestown Foundation). https://jamestown.org/program/the-role-of-kinship-in-indonesias-jemaah-islamiya/

Jäger, T. (2013). Transnationale Organisierte Kriminalität. *Aus Politik und Zeitgeschichte, 38–39,* 15–21.

Jarstad, A., & Sisk, T. (Eds.). (2008). *From war to democracy: Dilemmas of peacebuilding.* Cambridge: Cambridge University Press.

Jelinek, P. (2011, September 12). Haqqani group behind Afghan bombing, U.S. says. *Military Times.*

Karaganis, J. (2011). *Media piracy in emerging economies.* SSRC. http://piracy.americanassembly.org/wp-content/uploads/2011/06/MPEE-PDF1.0.4.pdf

Kazim, H. (2010, November 23). Deutschland im Visier Terrorspur führt zum Mafiapaten von Mumbai. *Der Spiegel.*

Keefe, P. (2013). The geography of badness: Mapping the hubs of the illicit global economy. In M. Kenney (Ed.), *From Pablo to Osama: Trafficking and terrorist networks, government bureaucracies, and competitive adaptation.* Pennsylvania State University Press: University Park, PA.

Kittner, C. (2007). The role of safe havens in Islamist terrorism. *Terrorism and Political Violence, 19,* 307–329.

Lacouture, M. (2016). Narco-terrorism in Afghanistan: Counternarcotics and counterinsurgency. *International Affairs Review.* Retrieved from http://www.iar-gwu.org/node/39

Lal, R. (2005, Spring). South Asian organized crime and terrorist networks. *Orbis, 49*(2), 293–304.

Lamb, C., & Amoore, M. (2010, January 10). How this suicide bomber opened a new front in Al-Qaeda's war. *The Sunday Times*.

Lismore, S. (2011). Chromite prices continue to climb on tight supply. *MineralNet.co.uk*. Retrieved May 4, 2011, from www.mineralnet.co.uk/Article/2818437/Chromite

Lohmann, A. (2011). *Who owns the Sahara? Old conflicts, new menaces: Mali and the Central Sahara between the Tuareg, Al Qaida and Organized Crime*. Abuja: Friedrich Ebert Stiftung.

Mahadevan, P. (2013). The glocalisation of Al Qaedaism. *Strategic Trends 2013* (pp. 83–101). Center for Security Studies, ETH Zurich.

Maher, S. (2016). *Salafi-Jihadism: The history of an idea*. London: C Hurst & Co.

Makarenko, T. (2002). Crime, terror, and the Central Asian drug trade. *Harvard Asia Quarterly, 6* (3), 1–24.

Makarenko, T. (2004). The crime terror continuum: Tracing the interplay between transnational organised crime and terrorism. *Global Crime, 6*(1), 129–145.

Mansfield, D. (2011). *Managing concurrent and repeated risks: Explaining the reductions in opium production in Central Helmand between 2008 and 2011*. Kabul: Afghanistan Research and Evaluation Unit.

McCarthy, N. (2014). *Bollywood: India's film industry by the numbers*. New York: Forbes.

McGrory, D. (2006, May 22). How $45M secretly bought freedom of foreign hostages. *The Times*, 8.

Meo, N. (2002, January 27). All eyes on India's most wanted. *Sunday Herald*.

Naylor, R. (2002). *Wages of crime: Black markets, illegal finance, and the underworld economy*. Ithaca, NY: Cornell University Press.

Nölke, A. (2010). Transnationale Akteure. In C. Masala, F. Sauer, & A. Wilhelm (Eds.), *Handbuch der Internationalen Politik* (pp. 395–402). Wiesbaden: VS Springer.

Nünlist, C. (2013, October). *Kidnapping for Ransom: Zur Terrorismusfinanzierung*. CSS Analysen zur Sicherheitspolitik (p. 141). Center for Security Studies (CSS), ETH Zürich.

Paoli, L., Greenfield, V., & Reuter, P. (2009). *The world heroin market: Can supply be cut?* New York: Oxford University Press.

Patrick, S. (2011). *Weak links: Fragile states, global threats and international security*. Oxford: Oxford University Press.

Perumal, S. (2013). *Daughter of the enemy: A unique historic novel*. New Delhi: Partridge Publishing.

Peters, G. (2009a). *How opium profits the Taliban*. Washington, DC: U.S. Institute of Peace.

Peters, G. (2009b). *Seeds of terror*. New York: St. Martin's Press.

Peters, G. (2012). *Haqqani network financing: The evolution of an industry*. West Point: Combating Terrorism Center.

Rabasa, A., Blackwill, R., & Chalk, P. (2009). *The lessons of Mumbai*. Occasional Paper Series. Santa Barbara, CA: The RAND Corporation.

Rajghatta, C. (2010). Dawood is a terrorist, has 'strategic alliance' with ISI, says US. *The Times of India*. Retrieved January 7, 2010, from http://timesofindia.indiatimes.com/india/Dawood-is-a-terrorist-has-strategic-alliance-with-ISI-says-US/articleshow/5418149.cms

Raman, B. (2001, January 5). Lashkar-e-Toiba: Spreading the Jehad. *The Hindu Business Line*.

Rashid, A. (2012). *Pakistan on the brink*. New York: Viking.

Rassler, D., & Brown, V. (2011). *The Haqqani Nexus and the evolution of al-Qaida*. West Point, NY: Combating Terrorism Center.

Reuter, P. (2016). Drug markets and organized crime. In M. Tony (Ed.), *The Oxford handbooks in criminology and criminal justice* (pp. 359–380). Oxford: Oxford University Press.

Rohde, D., & Mulvihill, K. (2011). *A rope and a prayer*. New York: Penguin.

Rollins, J., Wyler, L., & Rosen, S. (2010). *International terrorism and transnational crime: Security threats, U.S. policy, and considerations for congress*. Washington, DC: Congressional Research Service.

Ross, B. (2009, June 22). Taliban wanted $25 million for life of New York Times Reporter. *ABC News*. Retrieved January 15, 2019, from http://abcnews.go.com/Blotter/story?id=7895078&page=1

Rostum, A. (2009). How the U.S. funds the Taliban. *Nation*. Retrieved November 11, 2009, from http://www.thenation.com/article/how-us-funds-taliban

Roth, M., & Sever, M. (2007). The Kurdish Workers Party (PKK) as criminal syndicate: Funding terrorism through organized crime: A case study. *Studies in Conflict and Terrorism, 30*(10), 901–920.

Rubin, A., & Risen, J. (2011, May 1). Costly Afghanistan road project is marred by unsavory alliances. *New York Times*.

Rubin, A., Rivera, R., & Healy, J. (2011, September 14). U.S. blames Kabul Assault on Pakistan-based group. *The New York Times*.

Ruttig, T. (2009). Loya Paktia's insurgency. In A. Giustozzi (Ed.), *Decoding the new Taliban*. London: Hurst.

Schweitzer, Y., & Ferber, S. (2005). *Al Qaeda and the internationalization of suicide terrorism*. INSS Monographs & Memoranda 78. Tel Aviv: Institute for National Security Studies (INSS). Retrieved from http://www.inss.org.il/uploadimages/Import/(FILE)1188301256.pdf

Shafqat, S. (2002). From official Islam to Islamism: The rise of Dawat-ul-Irshad and Lashkar-e-Taiba. In C. Jaffrelot (Ed.), *Pakistan-Nationalism without a nation?* (pp. 131–149). New Delhi: Manohar Publishers and Distributors.

Shelley, L. (2014). *Dirty entanglements: Corruption, crime, and terrorism*. Cambridge: Cambridge University Press.

Smucker, P. (2004). *Al-Qaeda's great escape: The military and media on terror*. Dulles, VA: Bassey's.

Sreedhar, K., & Manish, S. (2003). *Jihadis in Jammu and Kashmir: A portrait gallery*. New Delhi: Sage.

Stewart, S. (2014). The Jihadist kidnapping threat persists. *Stratfor*. Retrieved September 25, 2014, from https://www.stratfor.com/weekly/Jihadist-kidnapping-threat-persists

Swami, P., & Shehzad, M. (2004). Lashkar raising Islamist Brigades for Iraq. *The Hindu*. Retrieved June 13, 2004, from www.hindu.com/2004/06/13/stories/2004061306050100.htm

Tankel, S. (2011). *Lashkar-e-Taiba: Past operations and future prospects*. National Security Studies Program Policy Paper. Washington, DC: New America Foundation.

Terrorism Focus. (2006, October 10). LeT recruiting Afghan refugees to support Taliban in Afghanistan. *Terrorism Focus, 3*(39) (The Jamestown Foundation).

The Times of India. (2015, January 22). Pakistan ban Jamat ud dawah and Haqqani network. *The Times of India*.

The Week. (2014). Kidnapping for Jihad. *The Week*. Retrieved September 6, 2014, from http://theweek.com/articles/444050/kidnapping-Jihad

Thompson, T. (2005, February 13). At home with India's most wanted man. *The Guardian*.

Thompson, E. (2011). *Trust is the coin of the realm lessons from the money men in Afghanistan*. Karachi: Oxford University Press Pakistan.

Townsend, J. (2009). Upcoming changes to drug-insurgency nexus in Afghanistan. *Terrorism Monitor, 7*(2) (The Jamestown Foundation). Retrieved January 23, 2009, from https://jamestown.org/program/upcoming-changes-to-the-drug-insurgency-nexus-in-afghanistan/

Treverton, G. (2009). *Film piracy, organized crime, and terrorism*. Santa Monica, CA: RAND Corporation.

United Nations Office of Drugs and Crime. (2008). *Afghanistan opium survey 2007*.

United Nations Office of Drugs and Crime. (2011). *Afghanistan cannabis survey 2011*.

United Nations Office on Drugs and Crime. (2010). *The globalization of crime: A transnational organized crime threat assessment*.

United Nations Office on Drugs and Crime. (2015). *Afghanistan: Survey*.

United Nations Office on Drugs and Crime. (2016a). *Afghanistan opium survey 2016*.

United Nations Office on Drugs and Crime. (2016b). *World drug report 2016*.

United Nations Office on Drugs and Crime. (2016c). *Afghanistan opium survey*.

US Department of Justice (DOJ). (2008a). *Overview of the law enforcement strategy to Combat International Organized Crime*, April 2008.

US Department of Justice (DOJ). (2008b, December 22). *Member of Afghan Taliban sentenced to life in prison in nation's first conviction on Narco-terror charges.*

US Department of State. (2000). *Colombian rebel connections to Mexican drug cartel.* Statement by Richard Boucher. Retrieved November 29, 2000, from http://www.fas.org/irp/news/2000/11/irp-001129-col.htm

US Department of State. (2015). *Country reports: Middle East and North Africa overview* (Chap. 2). Retrieved from http://www.state.gov/j/ct/rls/crt/2015/257517.htm

US Department of State, Office of the Coordinator for Counterterrorism. (2011). *Country reports on terrorism.* Retrieved from www.state.gov/j/ct/rls/crt/2012/

US Geological Survey. (2007). *Preliminary assessment of non-fuel mineral resources of Afghanistan 2007.* Fact Sheet 3063. Retrieved from https://pubs.usgs.gov/fs/2007/3063/fs2007-3063.pdf

US White House Strategy to combat Organised Crime. (2011). *National strategy to combat transnational organized crime*, July 2011. https://www.whitehouse.gov/sites/default/files/Strategy_to_Combat_Transnational_Organized_Crime_July_2011.pdf

Wafa, A., & Cowell, A. (2008, July 8). Suicide car blast kills 41 in Afghan Capital. *The New York Times.*

West Africa Commission on Drugs. (2014). Not just in transit: Drugs, the state and society in West Africa. Retrieved from http://cic.nyu.edu/sites/default/files/wacd_english_web_version.pdf

Wilkinson, P. (2003). Why modern terrorism? Differentiating types and distinguishing ideological motivations. In W. Kegley (Ed.), *The new global terrorism* (pp. 106–138). New York: Prentice Hall.

Williams, P., & Felbab-Brown, V. (2012). *Drug trafficking, violence and instability.* Carlisle, PA: SSI.

Wilson, J. (2005, February 24). Lashkar-e-Toiba: New threats posed by an old organization. *Terrorism Monitor, 3*(4) (The Jamestown Foundation).

World Bank International Bank for Reconstruction and Development. (2005). *World Bank country study: Afghanistan: State building, sustaining growth, and reducing poverty.* Washington, DC

Zentrum für Militärgeschichte und Sozialwissenschaften der Bundeswehr. (2016). *Mali: Wegweiser zur Geschichte.* Paderborn: Schöningh.

# Chapter 4
# New Technology in the Hands of the New Terrorism

Since the beginning of the twenty-first century, a consensus has existed in the field of socio-scientific research that the technological opportunities provided by the Internet are of vital significance for Islamist terrorism (Corman, 2011; Cornish, Lindley-French, & Yorke, 2011; Fink & Barclay, 2013). Some studies even go so far as to suggest that the existence of the Internet is a prerequisite if a terror organisation such as Al Qaida is to survive for more than 20 years, whereas from an empirical point of view, terrorist groups exist on average for less than a year (Archetti, 2015; Theohary & Rollins, 2011). It is also undisputed that without the Internet and social media, the "Islamic State" (IS) would have been unable to recruit such dramatic numbers of European and Western supporters for its Jihad in Syria and Iraq, as well as for its terror attacks in the Western world (Brooking, 2015; Goertz, 2016).

The World Wide Web is currently the most important and most frequently used communications and propaganda tool in the Islamist and Jihadist world, as it enables rapid cross-border communication and interaction and an involvement in personal fates and events at distant Jihadist hotspots. The Internet serves Islamist and Jihadist organisations, networks, groups and even individual Islamist perpetrators as a virtual university of Islamism, Salafism and Jihadism (Goertz, 2016). Islamists and Jihadists have been using the Internet intensively since the beginning of the twenty-first century—in particular over the last 10 years, in combination with the founding of social media—for the dissemination of Islamist and Jihadist propaganda and for recruiting and training new perpetrators (EUROPOL, 2009: 13–14, 20). Both large-scale Jihadist organisations such as Al Qaida and the IS and also Jihadist groups operating on a regional or national scale put social media such as Facebook and YouTube to vigorous use (Berger & Strathearn, 2013; Klausen, 2012). A study by Oxford University revealed that engineers and IT specialists are highly over-represented among Islamist and Jihadist militants worldwide (Gambetta & Hertog, 2010). A study by the UK House of Commons Select Committee on Home Affairs in 2012 found that, in absolute figures, the Internet played a far more decisive role than prisons, universities and mosques when it came to recruitment and radicalisation (UK House of Commons, Home Affairs Committee, 2012: 16). The Dutch security authorities have identified the virtual interaction between Jihadists

© Springer Nature Switzerland AG 2019
S. Goertz, A. E. Streitparth, *The New Terrorism*,
https://doi.org/10.1007/978-3-030-14592-7_4

on the Internet—in particular in the social networks—as a key radicalising factor for potential and future Islamists and Jihadists (General Intelligence and Security Service of the Netherlands, 2012). A study by the Brookings Institution found that in the year 2015 IS already had 46,000 Twitter accounts. This number has increased ever since (Berger & Morgan, 2015).

The role of Islamist imams and mullahs with no formal training in Islamic theology should be mentioned explicitly; they use the Internet and most commonly social media to propagate their radicalising Islamist concepts (Taylor & Ramsay, 2010: 106).

A conservative estimate suggests that there are over 5000 Jihadist websites worldwide (Khosrokhavar, 2009: 284). Of the so-called Media Groups, 125 alone have been identified as Jihadist networks which in turn provide websites with hundreds of links to other Jihadist websites and offers in the social networks (SITE, 2017).

The Jihadist websites serve various functions:

- Propaganda, information/disinformation, publicity
- Recruitment, motivation and radicalisation
- Instruction and training in tactical/operational (terrorist) subject matter
- Instruction and training in subject matter such as the construction of improvised explosive devices (bomb building, handling explosives)
- Financing
- Social networking
- Data mining
- Communication and organisation of tactical/operational activities (attacks, assassinations, actions)
- Psychological warfare
- Electronic attacks[1]

## 4.1   The Strategies and Tactics of Large-Scale Jihadist Organisations

By 2009, Al Qaida had already recognised the Internet as "a great medium for spreading the call of Jihad and following the news of the Mujahideen" (Islamic warriors) (Al Awlaki, 2009). In the Al Qaida training manual *Military Studies in the Jihad Against the Tyrants*, it states that one of the primary strategic objectives is "Spreading rumors and writing statements that instigate people against the enemy" (Al Qaeda, 2010). Al Qaida's "strategic 20-year plan" (2001–2021) works on the principle that there are seven steps on the road to a worldwide caliphate (Rudner, 2013). On the second step of this road, from 2003 to 2006, the Internet proved to be

---

[1]See more about the individual functions: Conway (2006), Fisher (2016), Goertz (2016), Hofman (2006), Nacos (2006), Rudner (2017), Ulph (2006), Weimann (2006, 2011).

an essential tool for Al Qaida in radicalising Islamists and Jihadists on a global scale (Springer, Regens, & Edger, 2009: 76). Numerous Jihadist mullahs and strategists referred to the Internet as the "cyber Jihad" or the "electronic Jihad", as an indispensable medium in the global struggle for the Jihad (Atayf, 2012). In the course of the fifth step of Al Qaida's "strategic 20-year plan"—from 2013 to 2016—the significance of the Internet increased considerably, in particular for mobilising the global *Umma*. Transposed to the levels of strategy and tactics, the Internet has proved to be the favourite means of communication of Al Qaida and its regional offshoots, as well as being indispensable for multiplier effects, recruiting newcomers, training, financing and tactical/operational activities (Gendron & Rudner, 2012: 25).

The influential Jihadist mullah Anwar al-Awlaki called on (potential) supporters to become "Internet Mujahideen", for example, by globally and professionally spreading Jihadist literature and accounts of Jihadist activities, which he described as "WWW Jihad" (Al Awlaki, 2009).

The findings of a Canadian court on the banning of a Jihadist website of the Global Islamic Media Front listed the following criteria for political extremism:

- Publication and dissemination of the preachings and subject matter circulated by Jihadist leaders and mullahs
- Dissemination of propaganda using various technical media
- Radicalising (potential) Jihadist terrorists
- Motivating Jihadist supporters to make financial, logistic and tactical/operational contributions
- Glorification of Jihadist "martyrs"/suicide bombers
- Sharing and spreading information about precautions to be taken to protect oneself against technical surveillance by State Intelligence Services
- Sharing and spreading of the technical know-how required for hacking into computers and networks
- Acts of technological warfare by threatening companies, groups and individuals with terrorist attacks
- Sharing and spreading tactical/operational know-how, inter alia for urban and house-to-house combat
- Sharing and spreading tactical/operational know-how for ambushes and bomb attacks
- Sharing and spreading of online magazines such as Sawt al-Jihad (Voice of Jihad), *Inspire*, *Dabiq* and *Rumiyah*
- Translation of Jihadist propaganda material into numerous languages so as to further the global *Umma* or, in other words, augmenting the target audience (in particular in Western democracies)

Accordingly, the Canadian court reasoned that Jihadist websites such as that of the Global Islamic Media Front either directly and/or indirectly foster terrorist (Jihadist) activities.[2]

---

[2]Court of Quebec, District of Montreal, Criminal and Penal Division, HM The Queen vs. Said Namouh, no. 500–73–002831-077 and 500–73–002965-081, 1.10.2009.

### 4.1.1  The Ubiquity of Mullahs of the New Jihad on the Internet

The ubiquity of Jihadist fora and Jihadist subject matter in social networks provides new terrorism, the Jihadism of the twenty-first century, with a powerful asset which for the first time in history gives the *Umma* simultaneous access to the same propaganda material on a global basis. For the very first time, a real digital link has been created between potential Islamists and Jihadists on all continents. The digital *Umma* may turn into a radicalised *Umma* because it is everlastingly bombarded—through various channels, using different methods—with homogeneous, manipulated, propaganda "information" and pictures (Kaya, 2010; Rudner, 2017).

New terrorism, or the Jihadism of the twenty-first century, is primarily based on the Internet and the technological opportunities offered by twenty-first-century media. The new generation of international Jihadists—the vast majority of which grew up and were educated in countries where the Internet was omnipresent—belong for the most part to the so-called Generation Y and Generation Z. In other words, the Internet provides them with Jihadist propaganda, recruitment, motivation and radicalisation tools in addition to communication options. The new generation of international Jihadists combines radicalisation opportunities of the real world with those of the virtual world and is open to Salafist and Jihadist narratives. The perception of new terrorism is closely associated with the new Jihadism as global Islamist terrorism. Thanks to the social networks, any (potential) Salafist or Jihadist supporter is able to find what appear to be personalised, individual Jihadist messages aiming at radicalisation. For the first time (international) Jihadists are able to obtain "information" in next to no time about the state of the *Umma* and are often manipulated—and consequently radicalised even further—by Jihadist propaganda.

As discussed in detail in Chap. 2, the essential points of Jihadist ideology are to be found both in the Quran and in the hadiths themselves and also more digestibly translated, compressed and manipulated in the Jihad interpretations of old and new mullahs. The Jihadi ideologies of the old Jihad mullahs—Hassan al-Banna, Sayyid and Muhammad Qutb as well as Mustafa Shukri—are to be found everywhere on the Internet, from their original texts to secondary texts and commentaries. On the other hand, the new Jihadist mullahs—Abdullah Yusuf Azzam, Abu Muhammad al-Maqdisi, Abu Musab al-Suri and Ayman al-Zawahiri—and their supporters make use of the media and technology options available in the twenty-first century and have realised the potential the Internet offers for their strategies. As explained in Chap. 2, Abu Muhammad al-Maqdisi already set up a key Jihadist website in 2009—Minbar al-Tawhid wa'l-Jihad—in which a Sharia Council of like-minded muftis (Islamic law teachers) provides answers to questions on the Jihad (Zelin, 2014: 335). The Jihad interpretation of Abu Musab al-Suri, one of the most important international mullahs of the new Jihad at the present time, can be found on almost all Jihadist websites (Khosrokhavar, 2009; Zelin, 2014).

At the beginning of the twentieth century, at the dawn of Islamism, the *Umma* was not de facto globally connected or interlinked. In the course of colonialisation, information was spread by Western journalists and telegraphy, but the largest part of the Muslim world was not even literate (Khosrokhavar, 2009: 195). The number of literate Muslims increased rapidly as of the 1960s (Khosrokhavar, 2009: 195), but it was not until the introduction of the Internet in the twenty-first century that the *Umma* was interlinked on a global scale, introducing a mobilisation and radicalisation potential that was completely new.

### 4.1.2   Direct and Indirect Jihadist Indoctrination: Permanent Contact with the Individual and the Supporters of Islamist and/or Jihadist Ideology

Thanks to the technical means provided by the Internet, Islamist and Jihadist ideology has been able to create a virtual cross-border Jihadist counter culture which has spread into the real world. According to Jihadist logic, this virtual Jihadist culture is an alternative counter culture to all political and social systems which are not Islamist. Therefore, the diaspora communities in Western democracies are the primary target for Jihadist propaganda activities (Rudner, 2017).

The strategic significance of the Internet for the new Jihadism is therefore particularly important as worldwide access to the Internet (theoretically) enables contact with each and every Muslim. First of all on a low threshold, cognitive level with anti-Western, anti-Israeli posts, comments and chats, then on a more militant level with posts, comments and calls for "action" and even virtual links to Jihadist content and real contacts with Jihadists, which can have a decisive impact on the radicalisation process. In short, without permanently increasing and intensifying the means of indoctrination, the influence of an extremist (in this case Islamist and/or Jihadist) ideology on individuals or groups may gradually subside. However, the millions of Islamist and Jihadist sites on the Internet in the twenty-first century make it highly improbable that Islamist/Jihadist indoctrination will diminish.

Therefore, one can differentiate between direct and indirect indoctrination with Islamist and/or Jihadist ideology. Blatantly Jihadist propaganda material such as *Inspire*, *Dabiq* and *Rumiyah* address only a small part of the umma directly, while on the indirect level, the audience for Islamist propaganda content has exponentially grown thousand-fold or even hundred thousand-fold. "Muslim identity" versus "Westernisation of the world" or "the Palestinian struggle for freedom against Israel and the USA" are topics which are shrewdly selected and guarantee Islamist and Jihadist Internet sites millions of likes. These sites are then interlinked and so a gradual transition to more intense, militant content occurs by mouse click.

The British Centre for Social Cohesion has identified three fundamental operational functions of Jihadist input on the Internet such as websites, chat rooms and social media:

- Online libraries for downloading highly extremist and radical texts, translated from Arabic
- Platform/outlet for Jihadist mullahs so that both their primary texts promoting radicalisation and their comments on daily matters involved in the way of life of "true Muslims" are accessible to all
- Fora for extremist/Jihadist discourses (Brandon, 2008, 2010)

Until his death, caused by a US drone strike in 2011, one of the most prominent Jihadist mullahs of recent times was Anwar al-Awlaki, a high-ranking Al Qaida member (Koplowitz, 2013). Al-Awlaki focused his Jihadist indoctrination and radicalisation activities with emphasis on English-speaking, educated young people—and converts—so as to achieve a "Jihadist struggle from within" from the heart of democratic society in Europe. He promulgated the "Western Jihad" of the home-grown variety (Al Awlaki, 2011). Al-Awlaki's interpretation of the Islamic theological question "Who should go on the Jihad and under what circumstances?" was that "Jihad today is obligatory for every capable Muslim" (Al Awlaki, 2009; Moon, 2010).

First investigations of radicalisation in the Western world in the category of "home-grown" revealed that both imams and mullahs without an Islamist theological education, in addition to the new Jihad mullahs (s. Chap. 2)—and the latter thanks to their omnipresence on the Internet—have a decisive influence on radicalisation processes (Springer et al., 2009). The significance of the Internet impact of Islamist and Jihadist content on radicalisation processes of the Western native Islamists and Jihadists has also been highlighted by the British MI5 (UK House of Commons, 2012).

For the easier comprehension of the scope and intensity of direct and indirect Jihadist indoctrination and the permanent contact with individuals and consequently their manipulation, Fisher uses the term "overt subculture" by which he means an alternative culture, a virtual parallel world, dominated not by the rule of law and the concept of democracy with all its civil rights such as protection of minorities but by "God's word and will" exercised by "true Muslims" (2016: 3). Lynch, Freelon and Aday (2014) use the term "Jihadist media culture" when referring to supporters of Islamist and/or Jihadist ideologies. One gains a better understanding of the idea of the permanent accessibility of (potential) supporters by taking a look at the background of theories used in relation to mass communication. Thanks to the Swarmcast principle used in social media, hierarchical mass communication as known from TV and radio broadcasts—in which the broadcasting protagonist actively sends and the receiving end user passively receives (Livingstone, 2004)—is negligible. With the Swarmcast principle there is no longer a dualistic distinction between broadcaster and receiver of subject matter and information. Information is relayed and passed on a "peer-to-peer" level.

In short, never before did a global ideology have such technological media tools at its disposal as the new Jihadism in the twenty-first century. Furthermore, the players of new terrorism, or the international Jihadism of the twenty-first century, know how to exploit the opportunities provided by the new media to recruit and radicalise generations of new Jihadists using these new technological instruments.

### 4.1.3 The Internet as a Jihadist Instrument for Propaganda, Social Networking, Communications and Tactical/ Operational Control of Terrorist Attacks and Killings

As a globally accessible, cheap, easy-to-operate and therefore highly effective means of communication, the World Wide Web is also used by Jihadists for spreading information, announcements, instructions and orders through openly accessible instant messaging services or encrypted platforms. The technical quality of Jihadist websites, blogs and fora launched since the beginning of the twenty-first century has improved rapidly, particularly in the field of encryption technology for countering reconnaissance attempts by government agencies. In recent years, online social networks have developed another virtual level of communication, which is most popular for real-time exchange and fast dissemination of information (Goertz, 2016).

Members as well as sympathisers of the Islamist and Jihadist spectrum use virtual networks in order to call for actions automatically. Calling for individual Islamist perpetrators to conduct terrorist attacks and killings in the Western world are part of the strategy of Jihadist major organisations like the "Islamic State" and Al Qaida. Accordingly, propagandistic commentaries are regularly released in response to executed strikes or killings—in the native language of the specific target audience being addressed.

Jihadist online activities can be distinguished by their operational-functional effects and the following impacts:

- Worldwide propagandistic infiltration of diaspora communities
- Gradual generation of cognitive and material support for Jihad
- Islamist theological interpretation/justification of politically motivated violence and/or terrorism
- Sharing technical instructions and operational guidelines for terrorist actions
- Soliciting direct support for or participation in preparatory activities (also in the logistics' field) for operational-tactical actions
- Indoctrination and radicalisation for terrorist attacks and killings (Phares, 2005; Taylor & Ramsay, 2010)

The spectrum of Islamist and Jihadist propaganda is exceedingly heterogeneous, polyglot and makes full use of multimedia opportunities. Boundaries between Islamist and Jihadist propaganda are blurred. Jihadist propaganda—just like all other forms of propaganda—aims at providing an idealised self-presentation in order to threaten and intimidate opponents as well as to indoctrinate, motivate and recruit sympathisers and supporters. The various media channels of the World Wide Web provide Islamists and Jihadists with numerous opportunities for multimedia dissemination of their propaganda. Relevant websites and social media profiles and accounts are linked to thousands of books, magazines, articles, essays and quotations from political-religious ideology of Islamism and Jihadism.[3] The content provided is versatile, for instance, in the form of interviews with ideologists and religious leaders, declarations of association with or dissociation from terrorist attacks or personal experience reports of "Jihad Participants" (Goertz, 2016). Visually, Jihadist propaganda covers a broad spectrum from the well-known battle and execution videos on the one hand and "proof" of functioning infrastructure, like water supply, road construction or schools on the other hand (Goertz, 2016). Propagandistic content is communicated throughout all social media networks like Facebook, YouTube, Twitter and Instagram but also via instant messaging services or in the form of videos, which are available on websites and in social networks. All content is tailored to the target audience addressed—usually young people—and presented in different technical standards and languages. Important ideologists and religious leaders of Islamist and Jihadist groups use audio, video and text messages but also videos in a report style (Goertz, 2016).

In a video post by IS' "Province Al Khair" from 22 August 2016, Islamist killings and attacks on Western targets are justified. A spokesperson of IS calls on Muslims living in Western countries to strike fear into the "non-believers" and to make their wives widows and their children orphans, as they would do with the Muslims.[4]

This video propagandistically comes along with testimonies referring to air strikes directed against IS which are supposed to have killed complete families (BfV, 2016). In answer to these air strikes, an IS spokesperson calls for terrorist attacks and killings in Western countries. Inter alia an extract from a video in which an Islamist terrorist in Würzburg (Germany) claimed responsibility for his action: on 18 July 2016 he attacked several passengers in a regional train with an axe and a knife, seriously injuring four people. Further on, the video depicts the Jihadist assault in Nice (France) as an example of a "successful operation nobody had expected". Finally the video shows different methods of how to procure or make (improvised) weapons, such as screw drivers, baseball bats and toxic liquids. It also suggests the use of vehicles, especially HGVs, as "weapons", while the IS spokesperson refers to the "successful operation" in Nice, when Mohamed Bouhlel drove his HGV into a crowd of people on the French national holiday, 14 July 2016, killing 85 pedestrians and leaving over 400 in part seriously injured (BfV, 2016). The francophone IS online magazine *Dar al-Islam* revives this incident in its tenth edition under the title "Game Over" where it states that in 2016 the "Caliphate's soldiers" have conducted terrorist attacks in the heart of Europe in a very short time and thereby avenged the many victims of bombardments in Muslim countries. As a result the IS attackers had not only caused economic losses to the tourism sector in France but had also "destroyed the French way of life" (BfV, 2016).

A German language telegram channel, which supports IS propagandistically, published the following on 22 August 2016: "Is Germany prepared for such terror?

---

[3]See, e.g. www.selefiyyah.de; www.islamfatwa.de; www.basseera.de; https://quranundhadith. wordpress.com/; www.salafipublications.com; www.salafimanjaj.com; www.diewahrereligion.de; www.islamhouse.com; www.islamland.com; www.way-to-allah.com.
[4]BfV-Newsletter No. 3/2016 – Thema 1.

What would happen, if Muslims started throwing stones from bridges as retaliation for the air strikes of the crusade coalition? Or burning houses? (. . .) It is extremely difficult for government authorities to solve such incidents, with the result that the perpetrator can repeat his actions several times, providing he isn't totally stupid. Fear among the population would increase still further, if the perpetrator filmed his action and forwarded the recording to IS media" (BfV, 2016).

Furthermore, a picture and report of an incident in Denmark in August 2016 were published, when a concrete block was thrown from a motorway bridge, hitting the car of a German family. The mother on the back seat was killed and her husband severely injured (BfV, 2016).

On 24 August 2016, IS posted an English message via social media to the "brothers and sisters living in occupied territories and in territories of unbelief", meaning Western democracies and Israel. In this, individual Jihadi perpetrators are called upon to conduct terrorist attacks, and a range of relevant methods and means is provided. For example, the use of rat poison to contaminate unpacked food such as fruit, vegetables and meat is recommended or introducing suitable poisonous substances into closed rooms through vents and air-conditioning systems (BfV, 2016). Following the terrorist logic of spreading fear, the text message advises the dissemination of false reports on poisoned fruit, vegetables or other food in order to provoke panic and economic loss. Using the same logic, it is described how fireworks can trigger off fear and mass panic at public events and highly frequented places like airports and train stations.

Jihadi fora, online chat rooms which are technically inaccessible to unauthorised visitors, are a technological substitute for avoiding visiting Islamist mosques and mosque associations which may be monitored by governmental security agencies (Berger & Stratheam, 2013; Klausen, 2012). Virtual interactions between (potential) Islamists and Jihadists create subcultural Islamist environments in a virtual world (Bertram & Ellison, 2014; Weimann, 2011), especially young people interested in Islamist and/or Jihadist ideology profit from the World Wide Web by "informing" themselves in a clandestine way in a virtual world, bypassing possible family boundaries.

In July 2014 a British adolescent was sentenced to prison for disseminating militant Islamist and Jihadist material on the Internet—although he was a participant in the British government's prevention programme "Prevent" (Whitehead, 2014).

Three underage Salafists who sympathised with IS and committed a bomb attack on a wedding party in a Sikh temple in Essen (Germany) on 16 April 2016 had known each other and radicalised in a WhatsApp group named "Adherents of the Islamic Caliphate". Their deliberations on killing "non-believers" with an explosive device were outlined in this WhatsApp group (Burger, 2016).

As the German Federal Public Prosecutor's Office stated, an underage female Islamist, Safia S., who inflicted life-threatening injuries on a federal police officer at Hannover (Germany) main railway station on 26 February 2016, was in close contact with at least one member of the "Islamic State" via chats and emails (NDR, 2016). One of Safia's comments on the Jihadist terrorist attacks of 13 November 2015 in Paris leaving 130 people dead and more than 350 injured was rated as a demonstration of sympathy with the "Islamic State" and Islamist terror by the German Federal Public Prosecutor's Office: "Yesterday was my favourite day, Allah bless our lions who were on mission in Paris yesterday" (NDR, 2016). The Prosecutor's Office assumes that Safia S. received instructions from IS middlemen for a "martyr operation" in Germany when she was in Turkey a few months before her terrorist attack. Back in Germany Safia S. kept in touch with several IS members through online chats. Shortly before her terrorist attack on the federal police officer, "Leyla", an IS member, instructed Safia how to entice a police officer "under false pretences in to a corner of the railway station, hit him with the knife, purloin the officer's pistol and shoot him" (NDR, 2016). In the same chat, Safia S. wrote: "I will surprise the unbelievers, if you know what I mean" and "I'll play with his throat" (NDR, 2016). The day before her attack on the police officer, Safia S. is said to have sent her IS contact person a video of confession (NDR, 2016).

Jihadi websites cover a broad range of relevant operational-tactical training content: flight manuals; urban warfare tactics; IT studies; introductions to biology, biochemistry and chemistry, economics and finance; production and use of explosive devices; and reconnaissance and tactics of terrorist attacks, to name but a few (EUROPOL, 2009; Lia, 2008).

It is proven that Al Qaida operators used the Internet for their communication and information sharing—for example, in the case of the terrorist attack on the editorial staff of the newspaper *Charlie Hebdo* in January 2015 or the train attack in Madrid in March 2004 (Aboudi, 2015; The Netherlands Office of the Coordinator for Counterterrorism, 2007). The terrorists who attacked *Charlie Hebdo* received their orders from top-level Al Qaida leaders, and the ones who attacked the train in Madrid in 2004 got their tactical instructions from the "Global Islamic Information Forum Website" (Aboudi, 2015; The Netherlands Office of the Coordinator for Counterterrorism, 2007).

In conclusion, numerous Jihadi actors have discovered the possibilities the Internet provides as a technical capability but also as a new dimension for propaganda, social networking, communications and tactical/operational coordination and execution of terrorist attacks. Following the netwar approach, the multiple technological capabilities of the Internet and social media have developed to a "command and control" platform[5] for Jihadism in the twenty-first century.

## 4.1.4   Training and Operational Knowledge in the Jihadi Online Magazines Inspire, Dabiq and Rumiyah

The first edition of Al Qaida's Jihadi online magazine *Inspire* focused on so-called open source Jihad, providing instructions on "How to Make a Bomb in the Kitchen

---

[5]Definition of netwar: "Lower-intensity conflict at the societal end of the spectrum in which a combatant is organised along networked lines or employs networks for operational control and other communications" (Arquilla & Ronfeldt, 1996, p. vii). For Internet as a "command and control" platform see Hannigan (2014).

of your Mom". With regard to operational security (protection against governmental monitoring activities), further advice was given on "how to use Asrar al-Mujahideen: Sending and receiving Encrypted Messages by Terrorists". *Inspire*'s third edition evaluated "technical details" of explosives for possible terrorist attacks on aircraft ("Operation Haemorrhage"), while operational instructions for "destroying buildings" and "training with the AK [Russian automatic rifle]" were covered in the fourth edition of *Inspire* by the end of 2010. Topics like "Individual Terrorism Jihad" (edition 5, spring 2011) or "Targeting Dar al-Harb" (attacking countries with no Islamic government, autumn 2011) repeatedly called for Al Qaida's strategic objective of terrorist attacks by individual perpetrators ("lone-wolf terrorism") and provided them with detailed guidance on how to use small arms and remote-controlled detonators. As early as 2010, *Inspire* seems to have provided the blueprint for the terrorist attacks of Islamist individual perpetrators with HGVs in Nice (14 July 2016) and Berlin (19 December 2016) by portraying "the idea is to use a pick-up—not to mow the grass, but the enemies of Allah". Therefore, the vehicles should be equipped with sharp blades or thick steel plates in the lower front. Edition nine, "The Convoy of Martyrs", dealt with operational-tactical techniques like information assessment or planning and preparing of terrorist attacks as well as with instructions for arson attacks in the woods and urban areas. The 11th edition from spring 2013 concentrated on acts of sabotage and causing car crashes, while edition 13 from the 24 December 2014 focused on improvised explosive devices and "lone Jihadist campaign targeting specific economic and civil aviation targets" (External Operations Reconnaissance Team 2014).

Jihadi online magazines like *Inspire* (Al Qaida), *Dabiq* (IS) and *Rumiyah* (IS) advise Islamist individual perpetrators to go for HGVs that are high, heavy and also able to speed up fast in order to cope with kerbs and obstacles. Pedestrian precincts and public ceremonies are identified as ideal targets. HGVs are estimated as the "safest and easiest weapon available against Kuffar" and one of the "most lethal methods of attack". Other potential targets could be major outdoor events, festivals, parades and markets.

In its edition of 31 May 2013, Al Qaida's online magazine *Inspire* affirmed its strategic approach of "individual Jihad", meaning individual perpetrators conducting terrorist attacks. The Islamist attacks of Boston (15 April 2013), London (22 May 2013) and Toulouse in March 2012 were praised by *Inspire* as effective examples for "individual Jihad". Basically two tactical approaches of "individual Jihad" are introduced: on the one hand low-level terrorism with thousands of little single actions (e.g. igniting cars) that all together cause great economic damage by also mobilising those Islamists who do not (yet) want to risk their lives. On the other hand, the terrorist attacks in Boston, London and France are portrayed as a tactical blueprint (BfV, 2013). Al Qaida's strategy was to address mainly Islamist individual perpetrators and small autonomous groups of the "native" extremist spectrum of people having been born and socialised in Europe.

In November 2016, IS' new online magazine *Rumiyah* covered tactical guidelines for terrorist attacks with vehicles ("Just Terror Tactics"):

**Vehicle Attacks**

*Though being an essential part of modern life, very few actually comprehend the deadly and destructive capability of the motor vehicle and its capacity of reaping large numbers of casualties if used in a premeditated manner. This was superbly demonstrated in the attack launched by the brother Mohamed Lahouaiej-Bouhlel who, while traveling at the speed of approximately 90 km per hour, plowed his 19-ton load-bearing truck into crowds celebrating Bastille Day in Nice, France, harvesting through his attack the slaughter of 86 Crusader citizens and injuring 434 more.*

*The method of such an attack is that a vehicle is plunged at a high speed into a large congregation of kufar, smashing their bodies with the vehicle's strong outer frame, while advancing forward—crushing their heads, torsos, and limbs under the vehicle's wheels and chassis—and leaving behind a trail of carnage.*

*Vehicles are like knives, as they are extremely easy to acquire. But unlike knives, which if found in one's possession can be a cause for suspicion, vehicles arouse absolutely no doubts due to their widespread use throughout the world. It is for this obvious reason that using a vehicle is one of the most comprehensive methods of attack, as it presents the opportunity for just terror for anyone possessing the ability to drive a vehicle. Likewise, it is one of the safest and easiest weapons one could employ against the kufar, while being from amongst the most lethal methods of attack and the most successful in harvesting large numbers of the kufar.*

*Acquiring a vehicle is a simple task regardless of one's location. However, the type of vehicle and its structural and technical specifications are extremely important factors for ensuring the success of the operation. Observing previous vehicle attacks, it has been shown that smaller vehicles are incapable of granting the level of carnage that is sought. Similarly, off-roaders, SUVs, and four-wheel drive vehicles lack the necessary attributes required for causing a blood bath. One of the main reasons for this is that smaller vehicles lack the weight and wheel span required for crushing many victims. Thus, smaller vehicles are least suitable for this kind of attack. Rather, the type of vehicle most appropriate for such an operation is a large load-bearing truck.*

**The Ideal Vehicle**

- *Load-bearing truck*
- *Large in size, keeping in mind its controllability*
- *Reasonably fast in speed or rate of acceleration (Note: Many European countries pre-restrict larger vehicles to specified speeds)*
- *Heavy in weight, assuring the destruction of whatever it hits*
- *Double-wheeled, giving victims less of a chance to escape being crushed by the vehicle's tires*
- *Possessing a slightly raised chassis (the under frame of the vehicle) and bumper, which allow for the mounting of sidewalks and breeching of barriers if needed*
- *If accessible, with a metal outer frame which are usually found in older cars, as the stronger outer frame allows for more damage to be caused when the vehicle is slammed into crowds, contrary to newer cars that are usually made of plastics and other weaker materials*

**Vehicles to Avoid**

- *Small cars, including larger SUVs*
- *Slower vehicles that cannot exceed 90 km per hour*
- *Load-bearing trucks with load compartments that are not fixed to the cabin, which may cause loss of control and subsequent jackknifing, especially if driven erratically*
- *Load-bearing trucks with excessively elongated trailer compartments, which can cause the driver trouble as he seeks to maneuver*

*If one has the wealth, buying a vehicle would be the easiest option. Alternatively, one could rent a vehicle or simply ask to borrow one from an acquaintance or relative who owns or has access thereto. For the one not capable of attaining a vehicle by any of these means, there is the option of hotwiring or carjacking a vehicle. This is only recommended for one possessing the know-how or having previous experience in this domain.*

**Applicable Targets**

- *Large outdoor conventions and celebrations*
- *Pedestrian-congested streets (High/Main streets)*
- *Outdoor markets*
- *Festivals*
- *Parades*
- *Political rallies*

*In general, one should consider any outdoor attraction that draws large crowds. When deciding on the target, attention should be given to that target's accessibility by the vehicle. The target should be on a road that offers the ability to accelerate to a high speed, which allows for inflicting maximum damage on those in the vehicle's path.*

*It is essential for the one seeking this method of operation to understand that it is not conditional to target gatherings restricted to government or military personnel only. All so-called "civilian" (and low-security) parades and gatherings are fair game and more devastating to Crusader nations.*

**Preparation and Planning**

- *Assessing vehicle for roadworthiness*
- *Filling vehicle with a sufficient amount of fuel*
- *Mapping out the route of the attack*
- *Surveying the route for obstacles, such as posts, signs, barriers, humps, bus stops, dumpsters, etc. which is important for sidewalk-mounted attacks, keeping in mind that more obstacles might be set up on the day of a targeted event, and doing the surveillance in an inconspicuous manner, especially if one suspects being monitored by an intelligence apparatus*
- *If accessible, a secondary weapon should be attained*

*Also, an appropriate way should be determined for announcing one's allegiance to the Khalifah of the Muslims and the goal of making Allah's word supreme, so that the motive of the attack is acknowledged. An example of such would be simply writing on dozens of sheets of paper "The Islamic State will remain!" or "I am a soldier of the Islamic State!" prior, and launching them from the vehicle's window during the execution of the attack.*

*In a bid to ensure utmost carnage upon the enemies of Allah, it is imperative that one does not exit his vehicle during the attack. Rather, he should remain inside, driving over the already harvested kufar, and continue crushing their remains until it becomes physically impossible to continue by vehicle. At this stage, one may exit the vehicle and finish his operation on foot, if he was able to obtain a secondary weapon. He could also remain in the vehicle, targeting pedestrians, the emergency services, or security forces who arrive at the scenes of just terror, until he is martyred. Having a secondary weapon, such as a gun or a knife, is also a great way to combine a vehicle attack with other forms of attacks. Depending on what is obtained, the kill count can be maximized and the level of terror resulting from the attack can be raised. This could also increase the possibility of attaining shahadah, which is the best of departures from this Dunya into the larger expanse of the Akhirah. "And hasten to forgiveness from your Lord and to a garden—the expanse of which is that of the heavens and the earth—prepared for the muttaqin" (Al 'Imran 133).*

## 4.1.5  Financing Activities on the Internet

Jihadi major organisations and affiliated regional groups engage in financing operations on the Internet, like money laundering (EUROPOL, 2009; International Monetary Fund, Legal Department, 2003; Rudner, 2013, 2017). Islamists as well as Jihadists ask for donations from individual donors, use quasi-legitimate Muslim charity organisations and interact with Islamist organisations out of the grey area between cognitive and militant Islamism (Levitt, 2004; Rudner, 2017). According to the Norwegian Defence Research Establishment Report, Zakat, the compulsory donation as one of the five pillars of Islam, is being abused for financing Islamist and Jihadi organisations by the collections of mosque communities in numerous European countries, e.g. in Great Britain, France and Germany (Barrett & Mendick, 2014; Nesser, 2004; Vidino, 2006). In turn, in the Islamic World Wahhabi and Salafist charities are known for financing Jihadi networks through private donations (Directorate for External Policies, Policy Department, 2013).

Due to the intensification of Western efforts in countering terrorist funding since 9/11, terrorist financing structures have transformed and among others concentrate on informal networks like Hawala (EUROPOL, 2009). Gemstone trading and trading with other goods are also used by Jihadi cash couriers (Bardoloi, 2004; Masciandaro, 2004). Over the last 10 years, Twitter and other social media have enabled a worldwide Jihadi crowdfunding network with a tremendous money flow (Freeman & Ruehsen, 2013; Jacobson, 2010; Seymour, 2008).

## 4.2   The Narrative of a Worldwide *Umma* of "True Muslims"

Unlike books, TV and radio broadcasting, social media are multimedia and multimodal by offering their users multiple interaction possibilities and communication channels. By addressing more channels, social media provide effective tools for propagating the Jihadi narrative of an "Islamic State". In this way sympathisers of the Islamist and Jihadi ideology receive the impression that the many thousand Jihadi social media accounts would provide more grassroot-generated and therefore more authentic information than CNN reports. The narrative of the real Jihad, the true Muslims' struggle for the "Kingdom of God on Earth", the caliphate, aims to reach as many Muslims worldwide as possible. In order to achieve this strategic end state, a first tactical objective is to enlarge and interlink the virtual *Umma* better. On a political level, the IS narrative portrays the "Islamic State" as an actor of change that finally takes sides for the Muslims who are suppressed by the West (Farwell, 2014). In the Islamist's theological view, the IS narrative refers to its adherents as "true Muslims". The underlying conviction of this narrative, that "true Muslims" are God`s instruments on earth, wins hundreds of thousands of cognitive sympathisers worldwide. Another empowering element of the IS narrative is its confidence of being victorious; in short, "God wants us to prevail". Even prior to the official proclamation of a so-called Islamic State on Syrian and Iraqi territory, in spring 2014, the narrative of the inevitable victory of "God's terrifying warriors" and the "weak unbelievers fleeing from them" spread in Twitter, Facebook and Instagram in a short time. But also pictures of these "terrifying warriors" that show them feeding little cats with milk circulate a million times in social media, which strengthens the reminiscence of Abu Huraira, a companion of Muhammad the prophet, who seems to have had a weakness for cats (Nissen, 2014). All of this enforces the cultural variety of the Jihadists and aims to create credibility, empathy and sympathy (Nissen, 2014).

From historical point of view, digital technologies like YouTube and Twitter represent technological capabilities that have the character of a game changer for extremist Jihadi mullahs and militant Jihadi actors. On the basis of digitalised information extremist, Jihadi messages are copied and linked infinitely, significantly limiting courses of action for preventive measures on the part of governmental security authorities.

Glorifying suicide attackers as "martyrs" is the most radicalising content of Jihadi propaganda on the Internet. Millions of theological Islamic explanations are linked to "martyrdom", justifying it and propagating "self-abandonment for God's struggle against the unbelievers" (EUROPOL, 2009; Roy, 2004; Vidino, 2006; Weimann, 2011). Apart from the (potentially) native Islamists and Jihadists within Western states, adolescent Muslim Internet users, e.g. in Saudi Arabia, are priority objectives for Jihadi indoctrination (Al Shehri, 2014; Musawi, 2010). New technologies on the Internet have enabled the ubiquitous range of Jihadi propaganda, and for the first time in history, it has gained worldwide coverage.

An example of extensive terrorist consequences may be the article on "Lone Jihadist Campaign" published in December 2014 in Al Qaida's online magazine

*Inspire*, where the strategy of single Islamist perpetrators conducting terrorist attacks on specific targets in Western democracies is introduced (External Operations Reconnaissance Team 2014). IS also produced a 13-minute-long propaganda video in English titled "There is No Life without Jihad", which also includes statements from native Jihadists from Great Britain and Australia (Mackey, 2014). In the video the native Jihadists accuse the Western colonial powers of being responsible for the poor economic, social and security conditions in the Near and Middle East, because the "colonial debt of the West" lies in the historic border demarcation of the area. In return, IS took a political step towards a new integrated Islamic state by removing border fences "at the old colonial border" between Syria and Iraq and by disseminating symbolic pictures of this event. When IS called its sympathisers on Twitter to wave the IS flag in public, take a video of it and post it on social media, over 20,000 IS sympathisers followed the IS hashtag #theFriday-ofSupportingISIS (Irshaid, 2014).

### 4.2.1  Online Publications and Videos: Archaic Aesthetics of Violence

With regard to online publications, the structure resembles a snowball system of Islamist and Jihadi publications as both Jihadi major organisations, IS and Al Qaida, publish their media via different media agencies on numerous platforms. They are then linked and translated by national, regional or decentralised groups, networks and single people (Goertz, 2016). Besides the English online magazine *Dabiq*, IS has established a whole network of media departments covering, for example, Al-Hayat Media Center, Al-Furqan Media, Al-L'tisam Media, Al-Ghuraba Media and Ajnad Media. IS publishes two more online magazines, the *Islamic State News* (ISN) and the *Islamic State Report* (ISR). Al Qaida already started publishing its online magazine *Inspire* back in 2010 and controls various media centres like the Al-Fajr Center, established in 2006, Al-Sahab and Al-Furqan. Especially Al-Fajr disseminates its material widely in Islamist and Jihadi fora and supports them technically in countering cyber operations from governmental authorities (Goertz, 2016).

For a long time, the most well-known media channel of the Jihadi movement was *Inspire*, Al Qaida's English language online magazine that was first launched by supporters and sympathisers in Yemen. Up till now 16 editions have been published. On the one hand and on a strategic level, *Inspire* invokes its readers continually and directly to participate in armed Jihad or prepare terrorist attacks in democratic Western countries. On the other hand and on a tactical and operational level, *Inspire* provides instructions on how to build explosives and conduct terrorist and suicidal attacks.

Not only Al Qaida but also IS has established professionally conceptualised propaganda magazines, of which the English magazine *Dabiq* is currently the most well-known one and is as easily available on the Internet as *Inspire*. The distribution of *Dabiq* has been prohibited in Germany by the Federal Ministry of the Interior. Nevertheless, the Bremen Office for the Protection of the Constitution stated in its Annual Report on the Protection of the Constitution from July 2016 that "this won't reduce the possibility of access effectively" (Senator für Inneres, Freie Hansestadt Bremen, 2016: 58).

Up till now 15 English editions of *Dabiq* have been published, while single editions and excerpts are available on the Internet in German as well. In its previous editions, *Dabiq* focused on IS strategy, its "legitimacy as a state", conflicts with other Jihadi groups and classic propaganda for the denigration of the enemy, the "unbelieving Western world". In addition, various editions of *Dabiq* menace Western, democratic countries, especially the US and European countries like Germany and France, with terrorist attacks. The Jihadi attacks in Paris on 13 November 2015, in Brussels on 22 March 2016 and in Nice on 16 July 2016 are referred to as proof that IS is capable of killing Western citizens anywhere and anytime, without the Western governmental authorities being able to prevent an attack (Senator für Inneres, Freie Hansestadt Bremen, 2016: 58).

Since 2014 even more Islamist and Jihadi online magazines have been launched, which are similar in content and structure to *Dabiq* but address other language areas, like *Dar al-Islam* for French-speaking, *Konstantiniyye* for Turkish-speaking and *Istok* for Russian-speaking target audiences (Goertz, 2016).

Starting off with the small wars in Afghanistan and Iraq, Jihadists of European origin invoke Muslims worldwide by video, audio and text messages to leave their homes and apply themselves "totally to the Jihad idea and life". For their respective target audiences, the Jihadi messages are communicated in videos accentuated by so-called Nashid (singular) or Anashid (plural), Salafist and Jihadi war hymns, which give a biased, propagandistic impression of Jihad reality (Goertz, 2016). Science and research are generally of the opinion that multimedia propaganda radicalises faster and more intensively than mere texts could do (Archetti, 2015; Lemieux & Nill, 2011).

IS online propaganda is based firstly on its official media outlets and secondly on the activities of its supporters and sympathisers. The official IS media outlets produce and disseminate online propaganda from which one can draw conclusions concerning IS communication strategy and central objectives, strategy and tactics of the organisation (Goertz, 2017). Current IS media outlets are:

- *Al-Furqan* is the main official IS media outlet and it serves as exclusive media department for the IS leadership. It acts as the exclusive media department of IS leadership. News from *Al-Furqan* often provides decisive content for the entire IS.
- *Al-Hayat Media Center* is responsible for publications in non-Arab languages. Its main target audience in lingual and contextual terms is in the Western world. Therefore design and layout of *Al-Hayat* resembles Western movie productions, computer games and high-gloss magazines.
- *Ajnad* is responsible for audio productions, for example, in the form of Islamic theological editorial contributions, Quran citations and Anashid (war songs for the glorification of the Jidahi struggle and warriors).

• *Al-Bayan Radio* is the radio propaganda component and can also be picked up on the web.
• *Al-Naba* is a weekly newspaper containing information on current events but mainly reports and graphics about tactical operations. For example, in the 40th edition of *Al-Naba*, an alleged biography of the terrorist attacker in the German city of Ansbach (the terrorist attack took place on 24 July 2016) was published on 26 July 2016 (Goertz, 2017).

On a lower level, subordinate to its media outlets, IS installed regional media offices in its IS provinces, which operate independently from each other but are still under central control of the "IS media department" (Goertz, 2017). The regional media offices are responsible for communicating local news from the provinces but occasionally there is transregional cooperation in the form of concerted actions—as for example after the terrorist attacks in Paris on 13 November 2015. In order to achieve the greatest media coverage, IS usually admits to having carried out a terrorist attack the day after it has taken place, followed by various publications of regional media offices over the next few days (Goertz, 2017). In addition to the aforementioned official media outlets and offices, IS also draws upon numerous multiplicators (supporters and sympathisers) for the production and dissemination of different Jihadi media products. These multiplicators spread IS messages and products in a kind of snowball system, translate them into other languages and partly enrich the campaign with their own content and products, which will only be tolerated if they are in line with the agenda and the narrative of IS.

Since 2014 the *Al-Hayat Media Center* (HMC) has been largely responsible for Jihadi propaganda for and the indoctrination of Western target audiences. It is well-known for its sensational high-gloss productions like the highly aestheticised features *Salil as-Sawarim IV* and *Flames of War*, not forgetting the numerous decapitation videos (Goertz, 2016). Jihadi propaganda videos like *Fisabilillah*, produced and published by the *Al-Hayat Media Center*, put forward a story with a prototypical instruction for IS propaganda's target audience: the religiously and ideologically inspired Mujahid shall bid farewell to his (peaceful) daily life and take up arms for Jihad—be it an improvised explosive device (IED), a handgun or a knife (Goertz, 2016).

Up till now *Amaq* has a special role as it only produces propaganda in favour of IS but without having been recognised officially by IS so far. *Amaq* was mentioned for the first time in August 2014 in connection with the fighting between IS and Kurdish forces for supremacy in the north Syrian town of Kobane (Goertz, 2017). *Amaq* especially disseminates quickly produced videos for mobile devices including short written messages and operation reports. To put it briefly, *Amaq* gives an official IS appearance to individually produced material like cell phone videos from supporters, sympathisers and multiplicators. In this way IS and *Amaq* generate a major impact with little effort and profit from enhanced media attention. *Amaq* does not focus on Western countries geographically or strategically but "reports" from all IS "areas of influence". However, it is conspicuous that *Amaq* has also published videos of IS terrorists who admit to carrying out terrorist attacks in Europe (Goertz, 2017).

To sum up, a nationally and regionally acting global Islamist and Jihadi network has developed which proves a high understanding for the combination of the attraction derived from the aesthetics of violence and contemporary media habits especially of the European target audience with only rudimentary Islamic theological knowledge (Zywietz, 2015). The regular use of the HD format, the composition and rhythm provide an audiovisual standard that is comparable to Western advertising industry. Islamist online propaganda is on the same qualitative technological level as Western commercial advertising spots and therefore appeals to attract the media habits of the mostly adolescent Western target audience (Fisher, 2016; Goertz, 2016; Zywietz, 2015). For the target audience born and grown up in Western countries, it is not necessary to have sophisticated Islamic theological knowledge in order to be able to sympathise with the religious and political ideology of Islamist and Jihadi videos. Many of these videos motivate aesthetically and audiovisually and cause emotional fascination (Goertz, 2016; Zywietz, 2015). Because of its modern, attractive and professional appearance, Jihadi video propaganda serves as a "starter pack" and additional information tool within the integrated approach of the Jihadi propaganda service portfolio (Rieger, Frischlich, & Bente, 2013).

As any kind of effective propaganda, Islamist and Jihadi propaganda addresses a primarily emotional level of its target audience. For this, it often uses the pop-cultural or subcultural style of rap videos, computer games and movies with specific sociolects that cover the (mostly Western) audience's entertainment habits and aesthetic sensitivity (Goertz, 2016). By displaying uncensored and inhuman brutality like beheading or burning people, many Jihadi propaganda videos appear like "Pop-Jihad". Unfortunately, adolescent prospects like this kind of archaic brutality, embedded in a modern and aesthetic framing. Be it directly or indirectly—the content of many Jihadi propaganda videos pose an archaic way of life, glorifying violence and opposing humanist norms of enlightenment and constitutional democracy (Goertz, 2017).

## 4.3  Psychological Warfare

Posts in social networks and blogs, as well as comments on pertinent Islamist, Salafist and Jihadi websites, show their timeliness and awareness concerning daily political news, political decisions by European and other Western governments and Twitter comments and statements of single Western politicians—in large quantity and surprisingly high quality (Goertz, 2017). Calls for personal or material support of Jihad fulfil an important function for Islamist and Jihadi propaganda and indoctrination, while this is backed up theologically by stating that Jihad should be a Muslim's first duty.

Jihadi actors in Syria and Iraq use several different social media, for example, Ask.fm, Facebook, Instagram, WhatsApp, PalTalk, Kik, Viber, JustPaste.it and Tumblr (Klausen, 2015). To prevent them from being detected, they use encryption software like TOR. Twitter is the most popular platform, because it was developed specifically for mobile phones and is easy to use. Content from Jihadists in the areas of operation are disseminated by website managers on Twitter and YouTube. These website managers are often young female Jihadists, partly the wives of the Jihadi insurgents (Klausen, 2015). Remarkable is also the tendency for disinformation and manipulation through Twitter information operations. TV and radio stations as well as newspapers often quote manipulated Twitter information from Islamist and Jihadi accounts. Last but not least, there are also supervisory bodies which frame the Jihadist's communication in order to provide a concerted big picture of controlled (but in part factually false) information (Fisher, 2016; Klausen, 2015).

Recipients of Jihadi psychological warfare are the Jihadist followers, Jihadi and Islamist sympathisers, "the" (perceived) enemy and journalists. Following the approach of "kill one—frighten ten thousand", Jihadi psychological warfare in social media aims to manipulate the global audience for terrorist purposes (Schmid, 2005: 138). Therefore, the Jihadi terrorist logic of spreading fear and horror tries to reach a large, worldwide audience by addressing it via Internet and especially by social media. For Jihadi psychological warfare, symbolism is a key factor. When prisoners of the "Islamic State", for example, journalists, are compelled to wear orange-coloured overalls (inspired by the prisoner's clothing in Guantanamo Bay) when being taken to their execution, the "retaliation for Guantanamo" to the world is symbolised and demonstrated.

Between 2012 and 2013, IS published relatively precise data on 10,000 operations and terrorist attacks as well as 1000 executions in Iraq. IS intended to address the Muslim world in general but also specifically the Iraqi and Syrian armed forces (Irshaid, 2014). This communication of (planned) tactical operations and operational success is a tool of psychological warfare, which aims to provoke fear and horror within the enemy's supporters. The panic escape of the modern-equipped and for years US-trained Iraqi soldiers in the battle of Mossul in summer 2014 was covered by 40,000 Tweets from IS per day (Irshaid, 2014).

The IS Twitter strategy during its spring offensive in 2014 showed several tactical principles. Irregular forces of IS used alias names, often related to their native backgrounds (e.g. *Al Amriki* and *Al Britani*), and named their Jihadi objectives and "willingness for martyrdom" in hundreds of thousands of linked videos. Pictures of their victims' mutilated bodies and detailed video footage of executions by beheading with a knife were widespread and disseminated a million times on Jihadi Twitter accounts (Klausen, 2015).

The spectrum of violence shown in IS propaganda videos covers beheading, burning to death, running over with a tank, stoning, drowning and mutilating of human bodies (ears, lips, genital area, etc.) (Goertz & Holst, 2016). In 2015 IS published video clips showing the killings of more than 1000 prisoners—mostly men—though this is just a fraction of the total executions (Goertz & Holst, 2016). During the first 18 months of its rule over significant parts of territory in Syria, IS brutally executed more than 2000 civilians, who clearly had not acted as combatants (SOHR, 2015). The show of excessive and often sadistic violence has quickly become a kind of IS trademark (Goertz & Holst, 2016). Violent acts like burning, stoning, drowning and mutilating of human bodies are not new to the history of mankind but rather a known worldwide phenomenon in different settings and variations throughout war and warlike conflicts (Eck & Hultmann, 2007). Kalyvas (1999) describes violence sociologically as a tool for (military) strategy in order to psychologically overpower an (military) adversary.

In his survey from 2015, Klausen analysed 59 Twitter accounts of international Western native Jihadists in Syria and Iraq in the period between January and March 2014. These 59 Jihadi Twitter accounts produced 154,119 tweets alone (Klausen, 2015: 5). The fact that 70% of the tweets are actually just retweets with the content (pictures, videos) from other Jihadists supports the observation of an orchestrated big picture of controlled information (Klausen, 2015). Eighty-five percent of the tweets were written in Western languages, only 9.3% in Arabic and 5.7% in a mixture of Arabic and the Western language of the native Jihadist. In the year when Klausen conducted his survey, a Twitter account had an average of 61 followers, but in contrast the 59 analysed Jihadi accounts had an average of about 900 followers (Klausen, 2015).

According to the online range of the analysed Jihadi Twitter accounts, Klausen and Zipkin differentiated the accounts into major and minor celebrities. Major celebrities (like football professionals or popular singers) have hundreds of thousands or even millions of followers and minor celebrities at least hundreds or thousands of followers. Although the average amount of followers is about 900 in the case of the analysed Twitter accounts, some individual accounts like the one of Anjem Choudary (anjemchoudary) from Great Britain has 7316 followers (Klausen, 2015: 8; Zipkin, 2014). In effect, looking at the worldwide range of Jihadi Twitter accounts, their average number of followers is equal to that of minor celebrities (Klausen, 2015; Zipkin, 2014).

A subsequent network analysis has proven that the 59 examined Jihadi Twitter accounts had strong links with Western Islamist or Jihadi organisations, for example, the British or German Salafist organisations Millatu Ibrahim and SalafiMediaUK (Klausen, 2015). Millatu Ibrahim was founded by the Austrian citizen Mohamed Mahmoud, who was formerly responsible for the Al Qaida online portal "Global Islamic Media Front". The cases of Millatu Ibrahim and SalafiMediaUK show clearly that Islamist, Salafist and Jihadi organisations exert a strong centralising influence on the content of Twitter accounts and their followers. In the case of one Jihadist, for example, his various Twitter accounts were operated by Salafist and Jihadi organisations—even after his death.

A content analysis of the 59 selected Twitter accounts is also very informative. On average four out of five tweets from war zones in Syria and Iraq had a Jihadi ideological and religious context (Klausen, 2015). Be it simply photos of a raised "Tauhid finger" or be it explicit Islamic and theological references to Quran, the Hadiths or mullahs of Jihadism (Klausen, 2015).

The content of the analysed tweets can be categorised as follows:

- Islamic and theological references, fatwas, content from Sunni, Wahhabi and Jihadi mullahs and legal scholars, Jihadi quotes and precise "Rules of Islamic Daily Life in the Caliphate"

- Reports on battles, pictures of Jihadists being killed in combat, creation of a martyr cult, connections to propaganda and recruitment of new Jihadists
- Personal communication between the owner of the Twitter account and his followers, e.g. about topics of daily life, what Jihadists eat, drink and so on
- Specific and unspecific threats against "the West" as a central part of psychological warfare (Klausen, 2015)

Islamist and Jihadi social media platforms broadly use pictures as a propaganda instrument as they transport information but also fulfil the function of symbols. The common use of Jihadi photograph "selfies" in front of dead or mutilated adversaries transports the Jihadi messages of power over life and death and the willingness of self-abandonment for Allah. The dissemination of thousands of "selfies" also indicates a change in tactics—the end of hiding the terrorist's identity behind balaclavas. Since IS got stronger in spring and summer 2014, hundreds of thousands of pictures of Jihadists circulate, showing their faces and identity (Klausen, 2015).

Photos of beheaded adversaries embody the Jihadi message of unlimited power over life or death and the worthlessness of the enemy. These messages are even outperformed by publishing pictures of Jihadists killed in combat, with a relaxed, calm and satisfied expression on their faces in death, and which are subtitled with Osama bin Laden's world-famous Jihad doctrine, "We love death more than you love life".

The wide spectrum of Jihadi photos and footage posted via Twitter and YouTube ranges from mutilated bodies to happy children wearing a suicide attacker's equipment. Especially the use of photos showing children in Jihadi contexts may cause significant psychological effects for the "far enemy", which means Western democratic societies.

In June 2014 IS Jihadists posted photos of men who had been crucified or strangled with washing lines on Twitter (Klausen, 2015). The crucified men were Syrians from Aleppo and members of the Free Syrian Army. They were militia men fighting against Assad and his regime, but they were not allied with the IS. Shortly after pictures of severed heads from Syrian Army soldiers (Assad's troops) were published on Twitter, showing them lined up on a football field and subtitling that the beheaded soldiers belonged to the 17th Division of the Syrian Army (Klausen, 2015). These tweets had a tactical function for psychological warfare.

Klausen's survey from 2015 and the survey from Carter, Maher and Neumann from 2014 have proven that hundreds of female multiplicators ("disseminators") have taken over a decisive function for Jihadi organisations in social networks.

A network analysis shows a high degree of interaction between Twitter accounts of female multiplicators and the ones of Jihadists in combat zones. The female multiplicators switched between Jihadi diction and Internet language of the "Generation Y".

The 2014 study of Carter, Maher and Neumann is based on a databank covering all information in a 12-month period from social media accounts of 190 Western native Jihadists in Syria and Iraq. Most of these 190 native Jihadists had joined one of the two Jihadi organisations of Jabhat Fatah Al Sham/Al Nusra (an Al Qaida offshoot) or IS. Carter, Maher and Neumann (2014) stress the essential function of virtual disseminators. Their popularity is due to their multiple language skills. Usually disseminators speak English and one more language, very often Arabic as well, which enhances their credibility when it comes to quotations or other use of Quran texts and interpretations. Another explanation for the disseminators' popularity is their role as a "spider" in a vast net of information. The Jihadist's tweets from Syria and Iraq are characterised by their regional limitation, while virtual multiplicators, the disseminators, have a much more comprehensive view of the small wars in the area and share this broader perspective with their followers.

Focusing on Facebook accounts that report on the small wars in Syria and Iraq from an Islamist perspective, the survey from 2014 ranked the following top ten with the most "likes":

1. Shaykh Ahmad Musa Jibril
2. Wake Up Oumma
3. Musa Cerantonio II
4. Shaam al-Ghareeba
5. Black Flags
6. Islamic News
7. We are all Islamic State of Iraq & Shaam—ISIS
8. Sheikh Sulaymaan bin Naasir al-Ulwan
9. The Victorious Party in the Land of Ash-Sham
10. Dawla Islamiya Media

It is remarkable that three of the most liked top ten accounts belong to Islamist mullahs. Consequently Carter et al. (2014) point out the great importance of so-called new clerical authorities, which means Islamist mullahs and their influence on the Islamist native subculture in Western countries. Their popularity in Facebook mirrors their Twitter profiles. For example, over 60% of the monitored Jihadists in the databank of Carter et al. (2014) are followers of Ahmad Musa Jibril. Jibril—born and living in the USA—is a US-Palestinian Islamist mullah who grew up in Saudi Arabia and was educated at the Islamic University of Medina just like his father. In 2004 he was convicted together with his father of, e.g. bank fraud, money laundering, tax evasion and illegal possession of firearms and ammunition. At the time of his arrest, Jibril maintained the Salafist website AlSalayfoon.com. Jibril neither does call for Jihad with terrorist means in public nor for Jihadi foreign fighters for Syria and/or Iraq (Carter et al., 2014). He operates indirectly by rhetorically instrumentalising topics and narratives like "the threat of the West towards true Islam" or "Western conspiracy against the Islamic world". In this respect, he derives considerable benefit from his studies of Islamic law and from being fluent in Arabic and English. And indeed, in his role as an Islamic law trained mullah, he repeatedly justifies Jihadi violence indirectly and encourages his followers to fight against the "Assad system", which in return is an indirect call for Jihad. Unlike the mullahs mentioned in Chap. 2, Jibril has not published any noteworthy Islamic theological publication. His popularity (up till now) stems exclusively from his social media accounts. His numerous followers come from the spectrum of Jihadi foreign fighters on the ground in Syria and Iraq and native Islamists and Jihadists in the Western world. Another factor increasing his popularity is his passionate rhetorical performance style in video sermons or personal addresses published and disseminated via YouTube. On the content level, he combines or rather merges Islamic theological topics with contemporary matters of interest, e.g. the "Threat of the West" or the "Piety of the true Muslim".

To sum up, the small war in Syria and Iraq is one of the first conflicts in history in which several actors communicate in real time with the outside world and influence the conflict's progress with information, disinformation and propaganda. It is important to stress that psychological warfare is effective in two respects: on the one hand, it provides online Jihadi information including contents from old but also modern and current Islamist and Jihadi mullahs, online books, excerpts and quotations or video addresses that radicalise Jihadists in combat zones on a religious and political level. On the other hand, the aforementioned Jihadists are both sender and recipient of propaganda themselves and publish eyewitness reports, pictures and footage from fighting and archaic executions of adversaries in order to demonstrate to the Western world that they are not following Western, democratic, humanist principles but exclusively their own interpretation of Jihad.

Jihadi activities in social networks like Twitter or YouTube aim to seem as if they are a bottom-up movement. However, in fact the system clearly reveals centralised information and disinformation campaigns controlled by multiplicators and disseminators, who have installed an effective Jihadi reposting mechanism (Carter et al., 2014; Klausen, 2015).

## 4.4    Recruiting by Virtual Dawa

Dawa is a key element of Islamist and Jihadi ideology and serves the recruitment, indoctrination and motivation of terrorist attackers, supporters and sympathisers. Active virtual Dawa takes place in social networks like Facebook, YouTube, Twitter and Instagram but also on websites of the respective Islamist or Jihadi organisations (Goertz, 2016). German security authorities analysed Islamist recruiting operations on the Internet and found out that since the establishment of the IS caliphate in summer 2014, more than 50% of the individuals being radicalised and deciding to join Jihadi organisations like IS or Al Qaida in Syria, Iraq, Libya and other countries did so because of online recruitment (BKA/BfV, 2016). Already back in 2007 Al-Suri, an Al Qaida leadership member, called the Internet an "activating tool to pursue Jihad and resistance in secrecy and alone [...] and to form a cell for the individual Jihad" (Lia, 2007). Seemingly authentic personal reports of Jihadis—be it in a spiritual and religious or physical and geographical dimension journey into Jihad areas —on actions, terrorist attacks and "military operations" fulfil the same important propaganda function for recruiting like instructions for ideological and tactical training (Goertz, 2016).

Personal and biographical features like "Ways to Jihad" or "Life as a Mujahid" seem apparently authentic and therefore have a high radicalisation factor and a particularly high number of likes in the social networks (Goertz, 2016).

Before 9/11 and the worldwide spread of the Internet, Islamist and Jihadi major organisations operated their recruiting, tactical operations training and ideological indoctrination primarily in camps, often located in Afghanistan or in West Pakistan. After the rapid global spread of the World Wide Web and the massive presence of Western (NATO) forces in Afghanistan, the recruitment of new Jihadists shifted to the Internet and into Jihadi online fora or social networks (General Intelligence and Security Service of the Netherlands, 2012).

Under the leadership of the USA, the military- and intelligence-led "Global War on Terror" of the international Western coalition increased the pressure on recruiting staff and infrastructure, so that Al Qaida had to transform its recruiting strategy: away from a centralised, hierarchical "recruiting pyramid" towards a decentral and loosely structured interactive system. The World Wide Web and social networks shifted the recruitment offices and processes into the virtual domain, where Jihadi "talent scouts" contacted potential Jihadists first virtually and later in the real world to radicalise them (Gendron, 2006; Rudner, 2013). Until recently Al Qaida recruited suicide attackers on the prominent online platform "Shumukh al-Islam" (Kjuka, 2013). During the first decade of the twenty-first century, the widespread availability of the Internet has enlarged the catchment area for potential Jihadis significantly: today it is almost global (Gulsby & Desa, 2014).

Since the mid-2000s a similar recruitment strategy has developed within democratic Western countries like the USA, Canada, Australia and Europe—here especially in the UK, Germany, France and Belgium (Harris-Hogan, 2012; Ilardi, 2013; Ilyas, 2013; Sydow, 2012). Virtual recruiting has a global and a local dimension by setting up small, self-sufficient and native recruiting cells in the diaspora communities, consisting of just a few Jihadis (General Intelligence and Security Service of the Netherlands, 2012; Musawi, 2010). Out of this Al-Suri developed the propaganda and recruiting doctrine for "individual Jihad" in form of terrorist attacks by Islamist single perpetrators, which was published in Al Qaida's online magazine *Inspire* (Al Suri, 2013: 24).

Good examples for the global interaction of a terrorist organisation in Somalia and worldwide Somali diaspora communities are the various Internet platforms of "Al Shabab". "Al Shabab" tries to recruit Jihadi terrorists and supporters in Western countries like Canada, the USA and European countries (Ungerleider, 2013). But also Jihadi organisations like "Jabhat Fatah Al Sham/Al Nusra" and the so-called Islamic State use the most modern Internet platforms for recruiting native Jihadis throughout the world—in Europe, North America, Australia or elsewhere (Zelin, 2013; Zelin & David, 2013). Especially British Muslims are said to have a high affinity to Jihadi online propaganda and recruiting (Nelson, 2014).

## 4.5 Summary

The technological capabilities of the twenty-first century offer various possibilities for a multidirectional exchange of Jihadi ideas, opinions, strategies and tactics. Countless social networks serve as platforms for dispute and discussion, whereby diverse kinds of information and interpretation interact and compete (Goertz, 2016). According to Islamist socialisation mechanisms and (possible) Jihadi indoctrination, it is meanwhile scientifically proven that participation in and interaction with a virtual extremist community (here, Islamist or Jihadi) on a "peer-to-peer level" represent decisive radicalisation factors and that extremist sentiments are getting "normalised" and encouraged by the phenomenon of "hyper-radicalisation" (Behrens & Goertz, 2016; Khosrokhavar, 2009; Neumann, 2016). Jihadi ideology and its mullahs and "transmitters" like IS or Al Qaida but also hundreds of thousands of supporters and sympathisers worldwide profit from the historically groundbreaking innovations the Internet, social networks and smart phones or other mobile devices provide. For "Generation Y"—an essential target audience of Islamist and Jihadi propaganda—the virtual world of the Internet is recognised as an extension of their real world (Goertz, 2016). Furthermore, by their very nature, social networks foster the formation of virtual spaces where homogeneous opinions prevail and which make dissenting opinions taboo while those with the same convictions encourage each other and increasingly radicalise their patterns of argumentation. Islamist and Jihadi ideologies profit from these "filter bubbles" inasmuch as they provide a "synchronisation and standardisation" of expressed sentiments and opinions.

Internet and telecommunications in the twenty-first century are of vital interest for new terrorism. The World Wide Web and its numerous media are currently the most important and most frequently used communication and propaganda platforms of the Islamist and Jihadist spectrum, because they allow a quick and direct cross-border communication and interaction as well as a sense of association with (seemingly authentic) personal Jihadist's fates and information about far away conflict regions. The omnipresence of Jihadi online fora and content in social networks determines the new terrorism and Jihadism in the twenty-first century. For the first time in history, Jihadism is able to provide the global *Umma* with propaganda. And again for the first time in history, a virtual and realworld bond links (potential) Islamists and Jihadists, sympathisers and supporters of all continents. Due to the continuous flow of Islamist and Jihadi propaganda, the digital *Umma* can become a radicalised *Umma*, because it is confronted with homogeneous, manipulated and propagandistic "information" through various media channels.

Current generations of international Jihadists are merging radicalisation potentials of the real and virtual world and are open to Islamist and Jihadi narratives. The phenomenon of the new terrorism is closely related to the new Jihadism as a global Islamist terrorism. On the basis of hundreds of thousands of Jihadi information sources in social networks, every (potential) Islamist and Jihadist is capable of self-radicalisation regarding (seemingly) personal, individual Jihadi narratives. All sorts of Jihadi ideology and content, Quran and Hadith quotations as well as Jihad interpretations of new and old mullahs are omnipresent on the web. Technologically, it would not have been possible before the twenty-first century to globally interlink the *Umma* (be it de facto existent or just imagined) as today. The current technological mobilisation and radicalisation capabilities are new to the world. Never before in human history did an ideology have such comparable global technological and medial capabilities as the new Jihadism in the twenty-first century. Additionally, the actors of new terrorism and international Jihadism are sophisticated in instrumentalising the technological and medial skills of their followers and supporters in order to recruit and radicalise generations of new Jihadists. The narrative of a just Jihad, the struggle of "true Muslims" for "God's empire on earth", aims to address as many Muslims worldwide as possible. According to this strategic objective, the Jihadi narrative enlarges the virtual *Umma* and interlinks it better.

On the level of psychological warfare, Jihadists use the Internet—especially social media—in the terrorist logic to provide fear and horror among a large audience. The Jihadi aesthetics of violence, the dissemination of photos showing its mutilated victims or detailed video footage of executions by beheading with a knife, are posted and shared over a million times by Jihadi accounts on Twitter and YouTube.

The small wars in Syria and Iraq are probably the first conflicts in history in which several actors communicate in real time with the outside world and influence the conflict's progress with information, disinformation and propaganda. It is important to stress that psychological warfare is effective in two respects: on the one hand, it provides online Jihadi information including contents from old but also modern and current Islamist and Jihadi mullahs, online books, excerpts and quotations or video addresses that radicalise Jihadists in combat zones on a religious and political level. On the other hand, the aforementioned Jihadists are both sender and recipient of propaganda themselves and publish eyewitness reports, pictures and footage from fighting and archaic executions of adversaries in order to demonstrate to the Western world that they are not following Western, democratic, humanist principles but exclusively their own interpretation of Jihad.

# References

Aboudi, S. (2015). Al Qaeda claims French attack, Derides Paris Rally. *Reuters*, 14.01.2015. Retrieved January 15, 2019, from http://www.reuters.com/article/2015/01/14/us-franceshootingaqapi-dUSKBN0KN0VO20150114

Al Awlaki, A. (2009). 44 Ways to support Jihad, no. 29. *Nefa Foundation*. Retrieved January 15, 2019, from http://www.anwar-alawlaki.com; www.nefafoundation.org/miscellaneous/FeaturedDocs/nefaal-Awlaki44wayssupportJihad.pdf

Al Awlaki, A. (2011). Western Jihad is here to stay. *Blogspot*. Retrieved January 15, 2019, from http://anwar-awlaki.blogspot.co.uk/2011/10/western-Jihad-is-here-to-stay.html

Al Qaeda. (2010). *Al Qaeda training manual: Military studies in the Jihad against the Tyrants*. Saffron Walden: Books Express Publishing.

Al Shehri, A. (2014). Al-Qaeda uses Twitter to Mobilize Saudi Youth. *Al-Monitor*, 09.04.2014. Retrieved January 15, 2019, from http://www.al-monitor.com/pulse/security/2014/04/al-qaeda-twitter-mobilize-saudiyouth.html

Al Suri, A. (2013). The Jihadi experiences: The strategy of deterring with terrorism. *INSPIRE*, Issue 10.

Archetti, C. (2015, February). Terrorism, communication and new media: Explaining radicalization in the digital age. *Perspectives on Terrorism*, 9(1). http://www.terrorismanalysts.com/pt/index.php/pot/article/view/401/html

Arquilla, J., & Ronfeldt, D. (1996). *The advent of Netwar*. Santa Monica, CA: RAND Corporation.

Atayf, M. (2012). Scholars speak out in favour of electronic Jihad against the enemy. *Al Arabiya News*, 30.01.2012. Retrieved January 15, 2019, from http://english.alarabiya.net/articles/2012/01/29/191307.html

Bardoloi, S. (2004). Money not always honey! *Information Management*, 20.01.2004. Retrieved January 15, 2019, from http://www.information-management.com/specialreports/20040120/7996-1.html

Barrett, D., & Mendick, R. (2014). Mainstream charities have donated thousands to Islamic group fronted by terror suspect. *Sunday Telegraph*, 02.03.2014. Retrieved January 15, 2019, from http://www.telegraph.co.uk/news/uknews/terrorism-in-the-uk/10670120/Mainstream-charities-have-donated-thousandsto-Islamic-group-fronted-by-terror-suspect.html

Behrens, C., & Goertz, S. (2016). Radikalisierungsprozesse von Islamistischen Einzeltätern und die aktuelle Analyse durch die deutschen Sicherheitsbehörden. *Kriminalistik, 11*, 686–693.

Berger, J., & Morgan, J. (2015). *The ISIS Twitter census: Defining and describing the population of ISIS supporters on Twitter*. Washington, DC: The Brookings Institution.

Berger, J., & Strathearn, B. (2013). *Who matters online: Measuring influence, evaluating content and countering violent extremism in online social networks*. London: King's College, International Centre for the Study of Radicalisation and Political Violence.

Bertram, S., & Ellison, K. (2014). Sub Saharan African terrorist groups' use of the Internet. *Journal of Terrorism Research, 5*(1), 5–26.

Brandon, J. (2008). *Virtual caliphate: Islamic extremists and their websites*. London: Centre for Social Cohesion.

Brandon, J. (2010). Terrorists targeting children via Facebook, Twitter. *Fox News*, 15.03.2010. Retrieved January 15, 2019, from www.foxnews.com/tech/2010/03/15/terrorists-targeting-children-via-facebook-twitter.html

Brooking, E. (2015). The ISIS propaganda machine is horrifying and effective: How does it work? *Council on Foreign Relations*, Retrieved August 21, 2015.

Bundesamt für Verfassungsschutz. (2013). BfV-Newsletter 1/2013, Thema 6.

Bundesamt für Verfassungsschutz. (2016). BfV-Newsletter 3/2016, Thema 1.

Bundeskriminalamt/Bundesamt für Verfassungsschutz. (2016). Analyse der Radikalisierungshintergründe und -verläufe der Personen, die aus Islamischer Motivation aus Deutschland in Richtung Syrien oder Irak ausgereist sind. Berlin.

Burger, R. (2016). Anschlag auf Sikh-Tempel: Jetzt stehen die Dschihadisten vor Gericht. *Frankfurter Allgemeine Zeitung*. 07.12.2016. Retrieved January 15, 2019, from http://www.faz.net/aktuell/politik/kampf-gegen-den-terror/prozess-beginn-um-terror-anschlag-auf-sikh-tempel-in-essen-14562221.html

Carter, J., Maher, S., & Neumann, P. (2014). *#Greenbirds: Measuring importance and influence in Syrian foreign fighter networks*. London: The International Centre for the Study of Radicalisation and Political Violence, King's College.

Conway, M. (2006, April). Terrorism and the Internet: New media – New threat? *Parliamentary Affairs, 59*(2), 283–298.

Corman, S. (2011). Understanding the role of narratives in extremist strategic communications. In L. Fenstermacher & T. Leventhal (Eds.), *Countering violent extremism: Scientific methods and strategies* (pp. 36–43). Wright-Patterson Air Force Base, OH: AF Research Laboratory.

Cornish, P., Lindley-French, J., & Yorke, C. (Eds.). (2011). *Strategic communication and national strategy: A Chatham House report*. London: Royal Institute of International Affairs.

Directorate for External Policies, Policy Department. (2013). *The involvement of Salafism/Wahhabism in the support and supply of arms to rebel groups around the world*. Brussels: European Parliament.

Eck, K., & Hultmann, L. (2007). One-sided violence against civilians in war: Insights from new fatality data. *Journal Peace Resolution, 44*, 233–246.

EUROPOL. (2009). TE-SAT 2009: EU terrorism situation and trend report. Den Haag. External Operations Reconnaissance Team (2014).

Farwell, J. (2014). The media strategy of ISIS. *Survival, 56*(6), 49–55.

Fink, N., & Barclay, J. (2013). *Mastering the narrative: Counterterrorism strategic communication and the United Nations*. Washington, DC: Center on Global Counterterrorism Cooperation.

Fisher, A. (2016). Swarmcast: How Jihadist networks maintain a persistent online presence. *Perspectives on Terrorism, 9*(3), 3–19.

Freeman, M., & Ruehsen, M. (2013). Terrorism financing methods: An overview. *Perspectives on Terrorism, 7*(4), 6–26.

Gambetta, D., & Hertog, S. (2010). *Engineers of Jihad*. Sociology working paper 2007–10. Oxford: Department of Sociology, University of Oxford.

Gendron, A. (2006). *Militant Jihadism: Radicalization, conversion, recruitment*. Trends in terrorism series (Vol. 4). Ottawa: Integrated Threat Assessment Centre.

Gendron, A., & Rudner, M. (2012). *Assessing cyber threats to Canadian infrastructure*. Canadian security intelligence service occasional paper. Ottawa: Canadian Security Intelligence Service.

General Intelligence and Security Service of the Netherlands. (2012). *Jihadism on the web: A breeding ground for Jihad in the modern age*. Zoetermeer: Algemene Inlichtingenen Veiligheidsdienst.

Goertz, S. (2016). Cyber-Jihad. *Die Kriminalpolizei*, 26–30.

Goertz, S. (2017). *Islamistischer Terrorismus*. Heidelberg: C.F.Müller.

Goertz, S., & Holst, M. (2016). Wege in den Terrorismus: Psychologische und sozialwissenschaftliche Analyseansätze von Jihadistischen Gewaltexzessen. *Die Monatsschrift für Kriminologie und Strafrechtsreform, 6*, 1–14.

Gulsby, K., & Desa, A. (2014). The new Al-Qaeda: Decentralization and recruitment. *Security and Intelligence Studies Journal, 1*(2), 53–62.

Hannigan, R. (2014). The web is a terrorist's command-and-control network of choice. *Financial Times*, 03.11.2014. Retrieved January 15, 2019, from https://www.ft.com/content/c89b6c58-6342-11e4-8a63-00144feabdc0

Harris-Hogan, S. (2012). Australian neo-Jihadist terrorism: Mapping the network and cell analysis using wiretap evidence. *Studies in Conflict and Terrorism, 35*(4), 298–314.

Hofman, B. (2006). *The use of the Internet by Islamic extremists*. CT-262-1, May 2006, Testimony presented to the house permanent select committee on intelligence, on May 4, 2006. Testimony series. Santa Monica, CA: RAND Corporation. Retrieved January 15, 2019, from https://www.rand.org/content/dam/rand/pubs/testimonies/2006/RAND_CT262-1.pdf

Ilardi, G. (2013). Interviews with Canadian radicals. *Studies in Conflict & Terrorism, 36*(9), 713–738.

Ilyas, M. (2013). Islamist groups in the UK and recruitment. *Journal of Terrorism Research, 4*(2), 37–48.

International Monetary Fund, Legal Department. (2003). *Suppressing the financing of terrorism: A handbook for legislative drafting*. Washington, DC: International Monetary Fund.

Irshaid, F. (2014). How ISIS is spreading its message online. *BBC News*, 19.06.2014. Retrieved January 15, 2019, from http://www.bbc.co.uk/news/world-middle-east-27912569

Jacobson, M. (2010). Terrorist financing and the Internet. *Studies in Conflict & Terrorism, 33*(4), 353–363.

Kalyvas, S. (1999). Wanton and senseless? The logic of massacres in Algeria. *Rationality and Society, 11*, 243–285.

Kaya, A. (2010). Individualization and institutionalization of Islam in Europe in the age of securitization. *Insight Turkey, 12*(1), 47–63.

Khosrokhavar, F. (2009). *Inside Jihadism: Understanding Jihadi movements worldwide*. London: Routledge.

Kjuka, D. (2013). Digital Jihad: Inside Al-Qaeda's social networks. *The Atlantic*, 06.03.2013. Retrieved January 15, 2019, from www.theatlantic.com/international/archive/2013/03/digital-Jihad-inside-al-qaedas-social-networks/273761/

Klausen, J. (2012). The YouTube Jihadists: A social network analysis of Al-Muhajiroun's propaganda campaign. *Perspectives on Terrorism, 6*(1), 36–53.

Klausen, J. (2015). Tweeting the Jihad: Social media networks of western foreign fighters in Syria and Iraq. *Studies in Conflict & Terrorism, 38*(1), 1–22.

Koplowitz, H. (2013). US formally admits killing Anwar Al-Awlaki, 3 other citizens, in drone strikes. *International Business Times*, 23.05.2013. Retrieved January 15, 2019, from www.ibtimes.com/us-formally-admits-killing-anwar-al-awlaki-3-other-citizens-drone-strikes-full-text-1275805

Lemieux, A., & Nill, R. (2011). The role and impact of music in promoting (and countering) violent extremism. In L. Fenstermacher & T. Leventhal (Eds.), *Countering violent extremism: Scientific methods and strategies* (pp. 143–152). Wright-Patterson Air Force Base, OH: AF Research Laboratory.

Levitt, M. (2004). *Charitable organizations and terrorist financing: A war on terror status-check.* Paper presented at the workshop "The Dimensions of Terrorist Financing," 19.03.2004. University of Pittsburgh. https://www.washingtoninstitute.org/policy-analysis/view/charitable-organizations-and-terrorist-financing-a-war-on-terror-status-che

Lia, B. (2007). Al-Suri's doctrine for decentralizing Jihadi training: Part 1. *Terrorism Monitor, 5*(1), 1–4.

Lia, B. (2008). Doctrines for Jihadi terrorist training. *Terrorism and Political Violence, 20*(4), 518–542.

Livingstone, S. (2004). The challenge of changing audiences or, what is the audience researcher to do in the age of the Internet? *European Journal of Communication, 19*(1), 75–86.

Lynch, M., Freelon, D., & Aday, S. (2014). *Syria's socially mediated civil war. Blogs and Bullets III. Peaceworks 91, January 2014.* Washington, DC: United States Institute for Peace.

Mackey, R. (2014). The case for ISIS, made in a British accent. *New York Times*, 20.06.2014. Retrieved January 15, 2019, from http://www.nytimes.com/2014/06/21/world/middleeast/the-case-for-isis-made-ina-british-accent.html

Masciandaro, D. (2004). *Global financial crime: Terrorism, money laundering and offshore centres.* Burlington, VT: Ashgate.

Moon, D. (2010). Anwar al-Awlaki: Translator of Jihad. *Asia Times*, 07.01.2010. Retrieved January 15, 2019, from http://www.atimes.com/atimes/Middle_East/LA07Ak05.html

Musawi, M. (2010). *Cheering for Osama: How Jihadists use Internet discussion forums.* London: Quilliam Foundation.

Nacos, B. (2006). Communication and recruitment of terrorists. In J. Forest (Ed.), *The making of a terrorist: Recruitment, training and root causes.* Westport, CT: Praeger Security International.

NDR. (2016). Die Geschichte der Safia S. 18.10.2016. *Norddeutscher Rundfunk.* Retrieved January 15, 2019, from http://www.ndr.de/nachrichten/niedersachsen/hannover_weser-leinegebiet/Die-Geschichte-der-Safia-S,safias102.html

Nelson, F. (2014). Terrorism in the UK: Social media is now the biggest Jihadi training camp of them all. *Daily Telegraph*, 25.04.2014. Retrieved January 15, 2019, from http://www.telegraph.co.uk/news/uknews/terrorism-in-the-uk/10786205/Terrorism-in-the-UK-Social-media-is-now-the-biggest-Jihadi-training-camp-of-them-all.html

Nesser, P. (2004). *Jihad in Europe: A survey of the motivations for Sunni Islamist terrorism in post-millennium Europe FFI report.* Oslo: Norwegian Institute for Defence Research.

Neumann, P. (2016). *Radicalized: New Jihadists and the threat to the west.* London: I.B. Tauris.

Nissen, T. (2014). Terror.com: IS's social media warfare in Syria and Iraq. Contemporary conflicts: *Military Studies, 2*(2). Copenhagen: Royal Danish Defence College.

Phares, W. (2005). *Future Jihad: Terrorist strategies against the West.* New York: Palgrave Macmillan.

Rieger, D., Frischlich, L., & Bente, G. (2013). *Propaganda 2.0: Psychological effects of right-wing and Islamic extremist Internet videos.* Köln: Wolters Kluver Luchterhand.

Roy, O. (2004). *Globalised Islam: The search for a New Ummah.* London: Hurst & Co.

Rudner, M. (2013). Al Qaeda's twenty-year strategic plan: The current phase of global terror. *Studies in Conflict & Terrorism, 36*(12), 953–980.

Rudner, M. (2017). "Electronic Jihad": The Internet as Al Qaeda's catalyst for global terror. *Studies in Conflict & Terrorism, 40*(1), 10–23.

Schmid, A. (2005). Terrorism as psychological warfare. *Democracy and Security, 1*(2), 137–146.

Senator für Inneres Freie Hansestadt Bremen. (2016). Verfassungsschutzbericht 2015. Bremen.

Seymour, B. (2008). Global money laundering. *Journal of Applied Security Research, 3*(3), 373–387.

SITE. (2017). *Media units of Jihadi groups.* Retrieved January 15, 2019, from https://ent.siteintelgroup.com/mediagroups.html

Springer, D., Regens, J., & Edger, D. (2009). *Islamic radicalism and global Jihad.* Washington, DC: Georgetown University Press.

Sydow, C. (2012). German Islamists target youth on the Internet. *Der Spiegel*, 01.11.2012. Retrieved January 15, 2019, from http://www.spiegel.de/international/germany/german-Jihadists-target-youthon-the-internet-study-finds-a-864797.html

Syrian Observatory for Human Rights (SOHR). *More than 2000 Syrian civilians executed by IS during 18 months since declaring its alleged caliphate.* 29.12.2015. Retrieved January 15, 2019, from http://www.syriahr.com/en/?p=41663

Taylor, M., & Ramsay, G. (2010). Violent radical content and the relationship between ideology and behaviour: Do counter-narratives matter? In E. Kessels (Ed.), *Countering violent extremist narratives* (pp. 94–111). Den Haag: National Coordinator for Counterterrorism.

The Netherlands Office of the Coordinator for Counterterrorism. (2007). *Jihadism and the Internet.* Den Haag: National Coordinator for Counterterrorism.

Theohary, C., & Rollins, J. (2011). *Terrorist use of the Internet: Information operations in cyberspace.* Washington, DC: Congressional Research Service Report for Congress.

U.K. House of Commons, Home Affairs Committee. (2012). *Roots of violent radicalization.* London: The Stationery Office.

Ulph, S. (2006). *The next stage in counter-terrorism: Analysing Jihadist radicalization on the web.* The Jamestown Foundation. Retrieved January 15, 2019, from www.jamestown.org/docs/JR-Slides.pdf. 23.10.2006

Ungerleider, N. (2013). How Al-Shabaab uses the Internet to recruit Americans. *Fast Company*, 26.9.2013. Retrieved January 15, 2019, from http://www.fastcompany.com/3018339/how-al-shabaab-uses-the-internet-to-recruit-americans?partnerDrss&utm_sourceDfeedburner&utm_mediumD-feed&utm_campaignDFeed%3ACfastcompany%2FheadlinesC%28FastCCompany%29

Vidino, L. (2006). *Al Qaeda in Europe: The new battleground of international Jihad.* Amherst, NY: Prometheus Books.

Weimann, G. (2006). *Terror on the Internet: The new agenda, the new challenges.* Washington, DC: United States Institute of Peace.

Weimann, G. (2011). Cyber-Fatwas and terrorism. *Studies in Conflict & Terrorism, 34*(10), 765–781.

Whitehead, T. (2014). Self styled 'father of terrorism' facing jail. *Daily Telegraph*, 05.07.2014. Retrieved January 15, 2019, from http://www.telegraph.co.uk/news/uknews/terrorism-in-the-uk/10947387/Self-styledfather-of-terrorism-facing-jail.html

Zelin, A. (2013). Foreign Jihadists in Syria: Tracking recruitment networks. *The Washington Institute for Near East Policy*, Policywatch 2186, 19.12.2013. Retrieved January 15, 2019, from https://www.washingtoninstitute.org/policy-analysis/view/foreign-jihadists-in-syria-tracking-recruitment-networks

Zelin, A. (2014). Missionare des Jihad in Libyen und Tunesien. In B. Said & H. Fouad (Eds.), *Salafismus: Auf der Suche nach dem wahren Islam* (pp. 320–349). Freiburg: Herder.

Zelin, A., & David, S. (2013). Up to 11,000 foreign fighters in Syria; Steep rise among Western Europeans. *ICSR Insight*, 17.12.2013. The Washington Institute for Near East Policy. Retrieved January 15, 2019, from https://www.washingtoninstitute.org/policy-analysis/view/up-to-11000-for eign-fighters-in-syria-steep-rise-among-western-europeans

Zipkin, N. (2014). Have 1,000 followers? You're in the 96th percentile of Twitter users. *Entrepreneur*, 19.12.2014. Retrieved 07.04.2017, from http://www.entrepreneur.com/article/230487

Zywietz, B. (2015). Islamistische Videopropaganda und die Relevanz ihrer Ästhetik. *Die Kriminalpolizei, 3*, 12–16.

# Chapter 5
# Strategy and Tactics of New Terrorism

## 5.1 Asymmetric Strategy and Tactics

The international conflict between Al Qaida and the "Islamic State" (IS), as non-state actors and government actors, like Western democracies or so-called Second and Third World countries, is characterised by the principle of asymmetry of terrorism. This asymmetry affects the interaction between international Jihadi major organisations and countries on various levels. On the one hand, for example, non-government irregular forces of major Jihadi organisations break international law by using tactical capabilities like terrorist attacks and crime against the civilian population. On the other hand, they wear no uniforms or insignia so they cannot be identified as combatants. Demilitarisation and decivilisation are constitutive elements of asymmetric conflict scenarios (Daase, 2011; Goertz, 2017a). In these asymmetric conflicts, small wars—sometimes also called "new wars" (Kaldor, 1999; Münkler, 2002)—non-state actors and irregular forces without combatant status operate beyond traditional rules of war (Goertz, 2017a), and borders between war, terrorism and crime become blurred. Seen historically and legally, so far war, civil war and terrorism have been distinguishable forms of political violence with specific rules of leadership. In contrast to this, the international Islamist new terrorism in the late twentieth and beginning twenty-first century is an expression of asymmetry of conflict because it fights against government systems by breaking international and national law (Daase, 2011).

Daase and Spencer (2010) refer to Clausewitz' categories of means, objectives and purpose when defining terrorism as a "situation, in which a non-state actor uses violence against civilians (means) in order to spread fear and horror (objectives) and force a country's government to change its policy (purpose)". Laqueur's definition of terrorism defines it as the "illegal use of violence in order to achieve political objectives by attacking innocent people" (Laqueur, 1987: 72) and "a group's use of force against a government, other ethnical groups, social classes, religions or political movements for political or religious purposes" (Laqueur, 1998: 44). Following the just-war theory, Crenshaw introduces legitimacy criteria for the use of political violence: compliance or non-compliance with international law, killing or sparing non-combatants (civilians) and engagement in a desperate or promising struggle (Crenshaw, 1983). Asymmetry is increased still further because security authorities and armed forces—especially those of Western democracies—are subject to legal, political, institutional and societal limitations (Goertz, 2017a). In cases of genocide or massive human rights abuses, Daase (2011) recognises that it is an obligation for the international community to protect the suffering civilian population—for example, in Syria and Iraq before and after the emergence of the "Islamic State". Government military and intelligence operations against terrorist organisations can "serve to limit the power and influence of terrorists, to isolate them and put them on the defensive, for example by destroying training camps and other sorts of terrorist infrastructure. This kind of physical damage can cut off terrorist groups from necessary resources and prevent them from conducting new attacks" (Daase & Spencer, 2010).

Government military and intelligence campaigns against non-state terrorist actors force the latter into permanent physical and logistical mobility, which in turn ties up their terrorist resources, and terrorist attacks therefore decrease in quality and quantity. However, governmental offensive military operations against terrorist actors may cause a cycle of violence, and a governmental overreaction with police or military forces is an intended terrorist tactical and strategic objective (Goertz, 2017a). Overreactions by government actors—for example, collateral damage—jeopardise their legitimacy in the civilian population: be it in a foreign country, where military assets are operated, or be it at home among one's own population and democratic society (Goertz, 2017a).

### 5.1.1   The "Islamic State": A Jihadi Organisation, Its Twenty-First-Century Caliphate Interpretation and Its Hybrid Strategic and Tactical Logic

Since the rapid emergence of the so-called Islamic State (IS), which culminated in the proclamation of the caliphate in Syria and Iraq in June 2014, IS was repeatedly named a "new threat", the "largest terrorist organisation ever", a "new type of terrorism" and a "worldwide terror group" (Burke, 2015; Cockburn, 2015; Weiss & Hassan, 2015). Nevertheless, all these categories only describe single aspects of IS, because it is more than a terrorist organisation. IS is an Islamist terrorist organisation operating worldwide, but it has also managed to develop worldwide credibility in the Islamist, Salafist and Jihadist spectrum with hundreds of thousands and up to millions of people in a short time. IS has achieved more than a "mere" terrorist organisation. It propagates a Salafist and Jihadist ideology, and since June 2014, it has successfully transformed this ideology into a contemporary interpretation of a caliphate. In other words, IS is not only an Islamist and Salafist ideology, but it was also successful in turning this ideology into a quasi-state structure, invading people's minds as well as their territory (Goertz & Maninger, 2016b).

In 2005 Kilcullen defined Al Qaida's worldwide Jihadi network as an insurgency and "a popular movement that seeks to overthrow the status quo through subversion, political activity, insurrection, armed conflict and terrorism" (Kilcullen, 2005: 603). Since 2014 this description is even more applicable to IS. IS is a global Jihadi popular movement, striving to weaken, undermine and overthrow secular political systems in the "Islamic world" by using the tactics of small war and terrorism. But in contrast to insurgents, who are limited to a specific territory or state, where they attack political power structures, IS is a worldwide operating Jihadi ideology, movement and terrorist organisation which attempts to influence as many states in the "Islamic world" as possible. It aims to create regional caliphate interpretations, which have already been realised in the occupied parts of Syria, Iraq and Libya.

Since the formation of a worldwide coalition and the beginning of "Operation Inherent Resolve" in September 2014, differing numbers of IS personnel strength have been discussed. While US security authorities estimated 25,000 to 35,000 irregular forces, other estimates—inter alia by the Russian FSB and Kurdish militia—indicated between 80,000 and considerably over 100,000 irregular forces (Cockburn, 2014). Bearing in mind that by the beginning of "Operation Inherent Resolve", IS controlled about one third of the territory of Syria and Iraq including a population of between 10 and 12 million people in an area of 250,000 square kilometres, the US authorities' estimate definitely seems too low (Goertz & Maninger, 2016a). In January 2015 the "International Centre for the Study of Radicalisation and Political Violence" estimated the number of "foreign" Jihadists alone to be over 20,000, so the total number of IS irregular forces would be already over 55,000 if the higher US estimate of 35,000 was added (Neumann, 2015).

Anyway, it seems more useful to categorise IS irregular forces qualitatively and—in doing so at the time of proclamation of the so-called Islamic State in June 2014—to estimate them to be at least 5000 people (Goertz & Maninger, 2016a). Furthermore police-like units, local loyal militia, recruits and logistical supporters should not be forgotten. For summer 2014 it can be assumed that there were about 60,000 to 70,000 IS forces with qualitative differences in their level of training and combat experience (Goertz & Maninger, 2016a). According to the French defence minister, during "Operation Inherent Resolve", about 22,000 IS irregular forces had been killed by February 2016 (France24, 2016). For this reason the estimate of the US government as stated above should be considered incorrect. At the end of August 2016, US commanding General MacFarland numbered the IS fighters killed during the last 12 months at 25,000 and another 20,000 during the previous 12 months. This statement—approved by the US forces—would correspond to 45,000 irregular IS forces killed up till August 2016 since the beginning of "Operation Inherent Resolve" (Batchelor, 2016). According to US military statements, about half of IS-controlled territory in Iraq and 20% in Syria were recaptured (Batchelor, 2016). When assessing the losses and damages caused to IS by "Operation Inherent Resolve", it can be stated that it is not possible to confirm the estimates of Western armed forces concerning the number of irregular IS forces. It is of more consequence to consider how many well-trained forces and leaders were killed.

A qualitative analysis of IS should reflect the causes and motivation of insurgency as well as the function of the Jihadi ideology. The question here is, in how far "Operation Inherent Resolve" and the present US strategy—based on the current counterinsurgency doctrine FM 3-24 (US-Department of the Army, 2014)—have properly identified the hybrid character of IS strategy and derived the necessary operational and tactical focus. IS is definitely more than just a terrorist organisation. Due to organisational, financial and personal inferiority, a terrorist organisation aims at destabilising a political system and at questioning the legitimacy of a government (Goertz & Maninger, 2016b). It has been empirically proven that this terrorist objective is usually regionally limited (Mockaitis, 2008; Newman, 2006; O'Neill, 2005; Shultz & Dew, 2006). In turn, IS pursues these targets only in the Western world, where it is logistically and financially inferior. In the Islamic world—up till now especially in Syria and Iraq—IS strives for the development of quasi-state and government structures and therefore established Sharia courts since 2014, police stations, orphanages and schools (Goertz & Maninger, 2016a). IS has recognised that it has to convince at least a minimum portion of the local population in the occupied territories of its "caliphate idea".

As IS is definitely inferior to the Western world when it comes to organisational, technical, personnel and financial questions, it uses asymmetric tactics and means when attacking the liberal political order of Western countries (Goertz, 2017a). It uses the logic of terrorism as a strategic means in order to spread fear of terrorist attacks among the civilian population, thereby questioning the democratic states' monopoly on the use of force and eroding the political will of post-heroic decision-makers (Goertz & Maninger, 2016b).

In Arabian and African countries like Syria, Iraq, Mali, Nigeria, Libya, Algeria and other territories, where since 2014 IS has often been equal or even superior in number to government defence and security forces, IS had the choice of fighting on the basis of conventional military principles or with asymmetric and irregular means of guerilla warfare.

In effect, this hybrid IS strategy does not only focus on weakening government actors such as Iraq or Syria with little single military and tactical operations. While IS strives for the control of territories—inter alia by operations in urban terrain and house-to-house fighting—and at the same time offers an alternative by proclaiming a Salafist and Jihadi state model of the caliphate, it goes beyond the definition of a terrorist organisation. On this insurgency level, IS strives for quasi-governmental functions as a Salafist and Jihadi caliphate state and therefore has quickly recognised that it has to win parts of the local population in the occupied territories for its Jihadi caliphate ideology and to present a functioning governmental structure as a quasi-state (Weiss & Hassan, 2015). For this reason IS installed executive institutions like militia, police forces and Sharia courts as well as social institutions like orphanages and schools (Weiss & Hassan, 2015).

Then again, in the Western world, IS is limited to the role of a "simple", "regional terrorist organisation" due to the inferiority of its organisation, financing and personnel, and therefore it tries to destabilise an existing political system and question the legitimacy of the government actors (Goertz, 2017a).

In combination with Jihadi online propaganda, the success of the incredibly rapid and numerous IS operations in 2014 led to the active IS fighters and sympathisers perceiving themselves as part of a global movement for global Jihad. When IS tore down the border ramparts of the "Sykes-Picot line" between Syria and Iraq in June 2014 after having quickly occupied large territories, this event had a worldwide symbolic Jihadi impact for the "new caliphate" as well as a tactical logistic dimension, because IS was in need of faster supply lines between Syria and Iraq (Goertz & Maninger, 2016a).

After 4 years fighting against the international coalition "Operation Inherent Resolve", the continuing existence of IS and its caliphate state depends crucially on the factor of legitimacy. On the existential level of governance, IS receives its legitimacy from its "populace" by providing quasi-governmental functions and services.

In the logic of the terrorism as a global insurgency, an analysis of IS as a phenomenon must accept that IS is more than a random terror organisation occupying territories in Syria and Iraq. Its Jihadi ideology with a globally high recruiting factor, on the one hand, and its already close operational and personal ties to Maghreb and Egypt, on the other hand, manifest the real danger of an intended IS corridor from Libya through North Sinai to Syria, Jordan and into Iraq (Goertz & Maninger, 2016a). That this corridor already exists is shown by the terrorist attacks IS conducted in Europe in 2015 and 2016. Another challenge for the Western world is IS logic of asymmetric strategy and tactics of new terrorism. The IS response to tactical and numerical weakening by "Operation Inherent Resolve" was strategic terrorist retaliation, drawing considerable public attention. According to the logic of a global insurgency, this retaliation was and is carried out on a different battleground, namely, in the Western world (Goertz & Maninger, 2016a).

To sum up, due to the factors of Jihadi ideology—struggle for the contemporary caliphate, the "ideal" Islamic State—a worldwide Islamist and theological sense of mission and high propensity to violence beyond the boundaries of the law of war, IS can be ideologically, strategically and geographically defined as a hybrid and complex global insurgency of a hitherto unknown dimension. IS is a global insurgency, a global Jihadi movement with clear political objectives: the establishment of a contemporary interpretation of a caliphate in "the Islamic world" with concurrent terrorist attacks in Western democracies.

## 5.1.2 Selected Asymmetric Tactics of New Terrorism

**Excessive, Stylised Violence and Its Media Dissemination as a Tactic of Psychological Warfare: Execution Videos**
Since the proclamation of the IS caliphate in June 2014, the public presentation of excessive and sadistic "innovative" violence quickly developed to a medially

transported trademark of IS. Most of the IS Jihadi propaganda videos show uncensored and almost inconceivable brutality. This very archaic brutality in the guise of modern aesthetics appeals to adolescent target groups (Goertz, 2017b). The spectrum of published IS violence ranges from mutilation of human bodies (e.g. ears, lips, genital area), being driven over with tanks, stoning, drowning and burning with flamethrowers or slower with methylated spirit poured over clothes to decapitation videos and deliberately dehumanising presentation of the enemy's mutilated bodies (Goertz, 2017b). This glorification of practised and published violence presents an alternative concept to Western democracies with humanist norms, against which IS fights on various terrorist levels—here on the level of psychological warfare.

The terrorist logic of spreading fear and horror among the civilian population is taken to a new and up till now unknown level, because IS lets its child soldiers execute adversaries and publishes videos worldwide from the scene. The IS video "The Nations Will Gather Against You", released on 26 August 2016, shows the execution of at least 14 Kurds and no less than five of them being executed by the children of IS fighters (Prince, 2016). The "Intelligence Group" website identified British, Tunisian, Egyptian and Uzbek citizens in the video (Prince, 2016).

Target groups for this tactic of psychological warfare are Islamists, Jihadists and sympathisers, on the one hand, and "the" (perceived) adversary, civilian population and journalists on the other hand. The excessive and stylised violence in the IS execution videos follows the principle of "kill one—frighten ten thousands" and aims to manipulate a global audience in social media terroristically. In order to reach the largest possible audience, new terrorism uses aesthetically stylised archaic violence on all online platforms, especially in social media.

In less than 24 months after the proclamation of the caliphate in June 2014, IS executed at least 4000 people and recorded the executions on video (Dearden, 2016). In 2015 alone, IS issued video clips showing the killings of more than 1000 captives (Tinnes, 2016). During the first 18 months of its occupation of Syrian territory, IS brutally executed more than 2000 Syrian civilians, who were clearly not combatants (SOHR, 2015).

On a strategic level, these Jihadi execution videos are a means of securing the attention of modern mass media in order to exploit their multiplicator function for IS propaganda news and justify the executions on a religious basis as examples for Sharia law (Goertz, 2017b). Additionally, these published execution videos demonstrate the terrorist power IS has to decide on life or brutal, slow and agonising death in order to deter and intimidate (perceived) adversaries (Goertz, 2017b). Execution videos are also intended to satisfy the IS members' and supporters' desire for revenge in terms of "retaliation".

By belonging to Jihadi organisations, developing a cognitive bond to Jihadi ideology and thereby obtaining the status of a "true Muslim", IS terrorists and supporters distance themselves politically, socially and psychologically from other groups (out-group), religions and societies (Goertz, 2017a). The belief in their own moral superiority and the struggle for the "just cause" are preconditions for the aesthetically visualised torture, mutilation and killing in execution videos as stylised acts of "justice" (defence of the caliphate). By letting the victims wear orange clothes like the prisoners in Guantanamo, the cruelties in the execution videos have a symbolic context and are presented as religiously legitimate self-defence (BfV, 2016). The result is an ideological and propagandistic dualism of "we against the others". In Arabic "the other" is a *Kafir* (singular), and "the others" are *Kuffar* (plural), which means the "infidels". By denying individualism for members of this out-group, they are "all the same". This attitude creates an anonymous distance towards the members of the out-group, which allows the Islamist terrorists a psychological and emotional retreat. Injuring, torturing and killing members of the out-group are easier for those who have no empathy for "the adversary" and "the others" (BfV, 2016).

Religious, cultural and ethnic differences increase the distance mentioned above, so that members of a different out-group are defamed as inferior creatures (Goertz, 2017a) as the Islamist abuse of Western people as *Kafir*, *Kuffar*, dogs or pigs already illustrate (BfV, 2016). Based on religious and ideological explanation patterns, the dehumanisation of "the others" plays a decisive role for the use of violence, so that the (Jihadi) individual is not held liable for his deeds, because they are committed in the name of a higher transcendental institution. Excessive and dehumanising acts of violence like killing women and children, torturing, executing and mutilating are easier to execute for the performing (Jihadi) individual, when it receives a God-given legitimacy but also the alleged certainty that the dehumanised victim is inferior because he is an "infidel" (Goertz, 2017a). Social, moral and psychological boundaries that used to contain violence are overcome (Borum, 2011).

### Large-Scale Attacks and Multiple Tactical Scenarios of International Jihadi Organisations

At the present time, and for the foreseeable future, there are two main terrorist scenarios threatening the Western world: on the one hand, the threat of large-scale attacks and multiple tactical scenarios by international Jihadi organisations, such as the "Islamic State" and Al Qaida, and on the other hand low-level attacks by Islamist lone perpetrators.

Large-scale attacks and multiple tactical scenarios by international Jihadi organisations are planned and conducted pursuant to the hierarchical top-down principle, the so-called "Mumbai/Paris/Brussels/Barcelona style" attacks. This kind of large attack is carried out by a "hit teams" with or without (para)military training and/or combat experience. Due to their simultaneous or time-lagged attacks, they pose a considerable challenge for security forces and rescue services in Western countries (Goertz, 2017c).

An analysis of the modi operandi of large-scale attacks by Jihadi organisations shows that the quality of terrorist attacks has increased and diversified since 9/11. Together with the attacks in Paris on 13 November 2015 and on 22 March 2016 in Brussels, the Jihadi attacks in Madrid on 11 March 2004 and London on 7 July 2005 belong to the category of large-scale attacks and multiple tactical scenarios. The Jihadi attack in Madrid, three days before the Spanish parliamentary election, consisted of a chain of bomb explosions in crowded commuter railway carriages. 191 people died, and 2050 were injured, 80 of them severely. After the Jihadi perpetrators had detonated ten bombs, three more explosive devices were intended to be ignited as a "second hit" in order to kill or injure rescue personnel arriving on the scene. The Jihadi attacks of Madrid can be defined as a blueprint for multiple scenarios in a European transport hub and were imitated shortly afterwards in London.

In the course of the Jihadi attacks in London on 7 July 2005, three "rucksack bombers" detonated their bombs in three underground trains almost simultaneously between 08:50 and 08:53 in the morning. About 60 minutes later, a fourth "rucksack bomber" exploded his bomb at 09:47 in a double-decker bus. The four explosions killed 56 people and injured more than 700—hundreds of them due to the kinetic energy of the detonations mutilating limbs (Goertz, 2017d).

Public transport, transport hubs and train stations are prototypical targets for terrorist attacks, because their arbitrary violence spreads fear and horror among the civilian population. For the operational and tactical planning of Islamist terrorists, simultaneous or time-lagged explosions in railway and underground trains or trams in the daily rush hour guarantee a high number of dead and injured civilians as well as possible media live coverage (Goertz, 2017d). The realisation, that every passenger on a public conveyance can become a victim of a terrorist attack, has a significant psychological impact on the civilian population (Goertz, 2017d).

In operational and tactical terms, the Jihadi attacks in Paris on 13 November 2015 even outperformed the ones in Madrid and London. They were conducted by three hit teams, each having different targets: the football stadium, a music hall and restaurants in the city centre. The French examining magistrate assessed that the quality of the IS Jihadi terrorist attack represents a leap in Islamist terrorism, while the Jihadi attackers, Jihad returnees from Syria, were far better equipped from a technical point of view than ever before. Furthermore, he described the deployment of well-trained and coordinated hit teams, who are prepared to carry out suicide attacks, as a new phenomenon (Goertz, 2017d). Choosing an international football match as a target for a terrorist attack follows the terrorist logic of broad media coverage. Millions of TV viewers worldwide would have been eyewitnesses of the suicide attacks, if the attackers had successfully entered the stadium—which they did not. Like all terrorists, Islamist terrorists try to integrate media coverage of their attacks as much as possible into their operational and tactical planning in order to profit strategically from the spread of fear and horror among the population. The series of Jihadi attacks on 13 November 2015 as one multiple large-scale attack has proven that Jihadi attackers of the new terrorism are able to conduct demanding simultaneous and coordinated attacks with terrorist means like suicide attacks, taking or shooting hostages and mass killings (Goertz, 2017d). The Jihadi attacks on 7 January 2015 ("Charlie Hebdo") and on 13 November 2015 and the attempted arrest of Jihadi suspects some hours later have shown that to some extent the terrorists have increased their combat value and tactical skills to a level comparable with military urban operations, which poses new challenges for the police in Europe (Goertz, 2017d).

EUROPOL attributes "new battle-like operation design" to Jihadi organisations like IS in Europe and furthermore their capability to conduct "a series of large-scale terrorist attacks". It also assumes that at least 5000 IS Jihadists, who have been trained in battle in Syria and Iraq, have infiltrated Europe (EUROPOL, 2016).

At the moment large crowds and major events like concerts, football matches and Christmas markets are possible targets for terrorist attacks—be it multiple large-scale attacks or low-level attacks of Islamist lone perpetrators or cells. Public transport, airports and train stations are similarly in the terrorists' focus as are representative public institutions of symbolic character like churches, synagogues, schools, public authorities and ministries or critical infrastructure of high relevance for the civilian population like energy or water supply (EUROPOL, 2015; Goertz, 2017c). Current and future modi operandi of terrorist large-scale or low-level attacks might include bomb attacks, suicide attackers, simultaneous or time-lagged attacks (e.g. double or triple), attacks with one or more vehicles, booby traps and hostage-taking.

Potential means for large-scale attacks, multiple tactical scenarios and low-level attacks of Islamist lone perpetrators or cells are explosives (e.g. self-made and consisting of aluminium powder and potassium permanganate), improvised explosive devices (IEDs) or industrial explosives. IEDs can be transported in suitcases, rucksacks and explosive vests/belts and can include nails, screws, screw nuts and splitters in order to achieve maximum dramatic human damage. Other weapons can be gas bottles, semi- or fully automatic firearms, hand grenades, side arms (e.g. knives and machetes), axes, swords or ("armoured") vehicles. While stones and heavy objects might be thrown from bridges or buildings, poisonous substances like rat poison could be inserted into unpacked food like fruit, vegetables or meat, or toxic gases like irritant gas might be brought into closed rooms through ventilation and air-conditioning systems. In short, all means and objects may be used, which might have kinetic, poisoning or any other damaging effect on people.

## 5.2   Low-Level Terrorism: Jihadist Lone Operators and Cells

The analysis of Jihadist attacks in Europe in the years 2015 to 2018 shows that they can be devided into two categories, in multiple tactical scenarios by hit teams on the one hand and in low-level terrorism, perpetrated by Jihadist lone operators and small cells. Low-level terrorism by Jihadist lone operators and cells can be defined as:

Terrorist attacks that use the simplest tactical principles and means, like weapons and everyday objects like knives and vehicles.

Concerning the question of a tactical independence or autarchy of Jihadist lone operators and cells or if they are controlled and steered tactically and logistically, it can be said that the boundaries are not clearly distinguishable.

A definition of Jihadist lone operators under scientific aspects should contain the following criteria: Jihadist lone operators operate organisationally and logistically independently of organisations, networks or groups but are inspired by their ideologies, ideas and strategies and consequently act in favour of a terrorist organisation (Behrens & Goertz, 2016: 687).

The current cases of the Jihadist lone operators Rachmat Akilow (Stockholm), Khalid Masood (London), Anis Amri (Berlin) and Safia S. (Hannover) and the attacker on a regional train close to Würzburg explain the obvious grey areas between autonomous Jihadi lone operators and their ties to the Islamist-Jihadi milieu and/or international Jihadist organisations like IS and Al Qaida.

During the Jihadist attack of a 31-year-old Tunisian Mohamed Bouhlel on 14 July 2016 in Nice on the Promenade des Anglais, the latter used a truck and firearms to kill 86 people and to injure more than 400. On the evening of 14 July, there were approximately 30,000 people present on the promenade in Nice, waiting to watch the fireworks display celebrating the national holiday. The Tunisian lone operator Mohamed Salmene Lahouaiej Bouhlel, who migrated to France in 2005, lived in Nice and had a residence permit valid until 2019. According to French security authorities, he became known as a criminal shortly before his attack and had been sentenced to a 6-month suspended sentence (Klimm, 2016). According to the French attorney general, Bouhlel had declared support for the "Islamic State" and researched propaganda material (Klimm, 2016).

During the Jihadist attack in a regional train near Würzburg, Germany, on 18 July, a supposedly underage refugee used an axe and a knife to injure five people, four of them seriously. The Jihadist lone operator attacked travellers, and according to the prosecutor, an emergency call on a mobile phone displayed the attacker shouting "Allahu akbar" (MDR, 2016). After causing an emergency brake, the train stopped before Würzburg. The attacker fled from the train and hit an uninvolved pedestrian repeatedly in the face with an axe. Police Special Forces from Southern Bavaria tracked the attacker down. When the Jihadist attacker assailed the Police Special Forces with his weapons, he was struck by two bullets (MDR, 2016). The Jihadist lone operator had travelled to Germany at the end of June 2015 as a supposed Afghan refugee passing through Hungary and Austria without documents. The police investigators doubted his name, age and his descent so that Pakistan was more likely his country of origin than Afghanistan. Furthermore, a Pakistani document was found in his room. In addition, there is a video claim of responsibility that contained various indications that the Jihadist attacker was of Pakistani descent (Diehl, 2016). Moreover, the police found a flag of the Jihadist organisation "Islamic State" in his flat, and his farewell letter to his father in the Pashto language read "and now pray for me, that I can avenge myself upon the infidels" (Diehl, 2016). In his video issued by the "Islamic State" directly after the attack, the Jihadist lone operator said "I am a soldier of the Islamic State and start a sacred operation in Germany. The times that you invaded our countries, killed our women and children are over. In the name of Allah we will attack you in every street, every village, every city and every airport. You can see that I have lived in your country and in your house. In the name of Allah I have made this plan in your house. Allah willing I will slaughter you in your own house" (Diehl, 2016). The Ministry of Interior Affairs of Bavaria confirmed the validity of this claim of responsibility via video (Die Zeit, 2016).

The Syrian refugee Mohammed Daleel was responsible for the Jihadist attack on 24 July 2015 in Ansbach, Germany. Due to entrance controls implemented at short notice by private security services at the annual music festival, the Jihadist attacker was not able to enter the open-air festival. According to German security authorities, the Jihadist attacker had been in contact with "a person from the Middle East" via mobile phone (Lohse, 2016). From the chat contact, the following passages are known:

Daleel: "Security personnel is at the entrance. I cannot enter".
Contact person: "Look for an opening".
Daleel: "I cannot find one".
Contact person: "Just enter".

The contact person also wrote: "Photograph the explosive" (Nürnberger Nachrichten, 2016). After that the improvised explosive device (IED) exploded outside a wine restaurant where 20 guests were present. The original plan was supposedly to deposit the IED in a crowd and detonate it from a safe distance (Lohse, 2016). The Jihadist chat contact supposedly instructed him to film the detonation and the impact on the crowd and to send the video to the "Islamic State" (Lohse, 2016). Three days after the attack, the Jihadist organisation "Islamic State" claimed that Daleel, the attacker, was "one of its soldiers" (Lohse, 2016). From 25 July, the federal public prosecutor's office started its investigation on the grounds of suspected membership in a terrorist organisation. According to German security authorities, Daleel had been in contact with a Saudi member of the IS who had used a Saudi telephone number but had not been on Saudi territory but on territory of the "Islamic State" (Goertz, 2017d). The Saudi embassy in Germany confirmed these details (Lohse, 2016). The question whether the Jihadist attacker was tactically in contact with the IS remains open, but it is a fact that Daleel was in contact with a contact person from the Middle East throughout the attack. According to the Ministry of Interior Affairs, the Jihadist attacker Daleel had been influenced immediately before the detonation of the IED (Lohse, 2016).

Safia S.—a 15-year-old female student who attacked a federal police officer with a knife and wounded him severely on 26 February 2016 in Hannover—is a current example of young Jihadists who are members of a European generation of native Salafists. Having grown up in liberal, democratic Europe, they were radicalised by an Islamist-Jihadist ideology that rejects all democratic principles and replaces it by a Jihadist, religious-political agenda. On the one hand, Safia S. can be classified as an Islamist lone operator; on the other hand, in the course of the legal proceedings, chat protocols showed that Safia S. had been in close contact with a member of the terrorist organisation "Islamic State". Consequently, the attack by Safia S. on a young federal police officer can be described as a hybrid form of attack by Jihadist operators.

The Jihadist attack in a church in Saint-Étienne-du-Rouvray, France, on 26 June can also be classed as low-level terrorism. Two native French Jihadists took six hostages during a church service, among them the 84-year-old catholic priest Jacques Hamel and three nuns. An 84-year-old nun managed to escape and alarmed the police who alerted the Police Special Forces: *Brigade de Recherche et d'Intervention* (BRI). Before the Police Special Forces arrived at the scene of the hostage-taking, the Jihadist attackers cut the throat of the priest in front of the altar and seriously injured an 85-year-old man with a knife. A hostage later described how the Jihadist attackers threatened the 84-year-old priest with a knife and "preached in Arabic in front of the altar" (Wiegel, 2016a, 2016b). After killing the priest, the attackers left the church and were shot in a gun fight by Police Special Forces.

Both of the Jihadist attackers had been known to the French security authorities before the attack as potential Jihadi attackers (Goertz, 2017d). The 19-year-old Adel Kermiche, the youngest of five children of a French-Algerian family, was known as having displayed behavioural problems since primary school (Duclos, 2016). At the age of 16, he quit school, and from the age of 17 on, the French security authorities observed him; among other things, he tried to travel to Jihadist territory in Syria (Duclos, 2016).

After his second attempt to travel to Syria, he was taken into custody in Turkey in May 2015. Adel Kermiche's father described him as a religious fanatic, and his sister explained that his "Jihadist brainwashing" had lasted for 2 months (Duclos, 2016). After 10 months, during which he had been in close contact with Saudi Islamists and a Jihadist from Syria, a judge released him from prison although his parents and the public prosecutor had opposed this (Goertz, 2017d). They declared that they would rather see their son in prison because they saw him as uncontrollable (Duclos, 2016). As a police measure, the Jihadist attacker, Adel Kermiche, had to wear a GPS bracelet and was only allowed to leave his parents' home between 9 and 12 o'clock.

The second Jihadist attacker, Malik Petitjean, 19 years old, a Frenchman with Algerian roots, had not been previously convicted but was added to a police card index of potential Jihadist attackers in June 2016 (Duclos, 2016). Shortly after the attack, the Jihadi organisation "Islamic State" described the two attackers as "soldiers of the Islamic State", and the Prime Minister of France explained that the attackers had acted in the name of the "Islamic State" (Der Kurier, 2016). According to the French Prime Minister, the aim of the Jihadi attackers was "a war of religions": "By attacking a priest, the Catholic Church, it is obvious what they were aiming for" (Der Kurier, 2016). The expression of the French Prime Minister, "war of religions", points out the strategic aim of the two Jihadist attackers on a church service. An 84-year-old priest and nuns in their 80s as Jihadist targets show their terrorist logic. This attack on a church service has to be rated as Jihadist symbolism with a distinct message and also encourages the threat of Jihadist copycats (Goertz, 2017d).

During the Jihadist attack in London on 22 March 2017, carried out by the lone operator Khalid Masood, 5 people were killed, and 40 were injured. This Jihadist attack was carried out on the anniversary of the terrorist attacks in Brussels 2016 and can be described as a copycat attack. The Jihadist lone operator Khalid Masood drove a rented vehicle into a crowd on Westminster bridge, shortly afterwards crashing into the fence of Westminster Palace (the British Parliament). Masood entered the precinct and killed 48-year-old police officer Keith Palmer with a knife (BBC, 2017). The parliamentary debate was interrupted for security reasons, parliament was sealed and the British Prime Minister was evacuated (BBC, 2017). One day later, the Jihadist organisation "Islamic State" declared Masood as "its soldier" (BBC, 2017). This terrorist attack was another Jihadi copycat attack of low-level terrorism with vehicles and followed the terrorist logic of attacking symbolic targets like the Palace of Westminster.

The Uzbek refugee Rachmat Akilow drove a stolen truck into a pedestrian precinct of Stockholm on 7 April killing 5 and injuring 14 people. The analysis so far shows that even a spontaneous attack—the attacker had stolen the truck without long-term planning—can produce significant terrorist damage. Akilow was identified and arrested with the help of surveillance cameras. The Jihadist lone operator from Uzbekistan had come to Sweden in October 2014, and the immigration authorities had rejected his application in June 2016 and planned to deport him in February 2017 (Die Welt, 2017b). Akilow came to the attention of the Swedish interior intelligence service in the context of the financing of terrorism. According to the Swedish police, Akilow had numerous social media contacts dealing with Salafism and Jihadism, for example, with the Islamic Movement of Uzbekistan (Tomik, 2017). On an operational level, Akilow's attack resembles the Jihadist attacks with vehicles in Nice (14 July 2016), Berlin (19 December 2016) and London (22 March 2017).

## 5.3  Summary

The analysis of the Jihadi attacks in Europe during the years 2015 to 2018 shows that the Western democracies and its security authorities need to focus on a very heterogeneous Jihadist threat. Thus—as depicted in Chap. 4—the Islamist and Jihadist content on the Internet offers thousands to hundreds of thousands of Islamists and potential Jihadists operational and tactical blueprints for new Jihadi attacks that vary from kitchen knives (Safia S. in Hannover, Germany) to vehicles (Nice, Berlin, London) to improvised explosive devices (Ansbach, Brussels) and also biological and technical warfare agents. In addition, the ubiquitous spread of operational and tactical terrorist scenarios and documentation of previous attacks on Jihadi websites and in social media enhance the threat of terrorist copycats. For example, the lone operators of Nice (2016), Berlin (2016), London (2017) and Stockholm (2017) all used the operational blueprint of Al Qaida and IS online magazines by using vehicles as kinetic means of killing and injuring hundreds of people.

The numerous Jihadist terrorist attacks in Europe between 2015 and 2018 created an extremely heterogeneous threat level with numerous possible scenarios. Currently the French Ministry of Interior Affairs counts 15,000 potential Islamist and Jihadist terrorists and/or supporters in France. Already in November 2015—6 months before the Jihadi attacks in Würzburg and Ansbach, Germany, and 13 months before the Jihadi attack of Anis Amri in Berlin—the president of the German Federal Criminal Police had to admit that the "German security services have to prioritize potential Jihadist terrorists in Germany and consequently cannot monitor all of them all the time" (Banse, Lutz, & Müller, 2015). At the time of this statement, the police estimated only 400 potential Jihadist terrorists in Germany; currently there are more than 750 (Banse et al., 2015). Five months later the president of the German intelligence service of the Interior spoke of 1100 potential Jihadist terrorists and/or supporters in Germany (N-TV, 2016). At the end of 2017, this number reached 1700 (Die Welt, 2017a). But on the operational and tactical level, the case of the 15-year-old school girl Safia S. in Hannover, Germany, shows the threat potential of just one Jihadist, using a kitchen knife to attack a police officer.

# References

Banse, D., Lutz, M., & Müller, U. (2015). Die Überwachung von Gefährdern hat große Lücken. *Die Welt*, 22.11.2015. Retrieved January 15, 2019, from https://www.welt.de/politik/deutschland/article149133020/Die-Ueberwachung-von-Gefaehrdern-hat-grosse-Luecken.html

Batchelor, T. (2016). ISIS annihilated: 45,000 Jihadis killed in war on terror (but just 3 US troops have died). *Express*, 11.08.2016. Retrieved January 15, 2019, from http://www.express.co.uk/news/world/698980/End-ISIS-45000-Jihadis-killed-Operation-Inherent-Resolve

BBC. (2017). London attack: Police appeal for information on Khalid Masood. 24.03.2017. Retrieved January 15, 2019, from http://www.bbc.com/news/uk-39377883

Behrens, C., & Goertz, S. (2016). Radikalisierungsprozesse von Islamistischen Einzeltätern und die aktuelle Analyse durch die deutschen Sicherheitsbehörden. *Kriminalistik, 11*, 686–693.

Borum, R. (2011). Radicalization into violent extremism I: A review of social science theories. *Perspectives on Radicalization and Involvement in Terrorism, 4*(4, Winter), 7–36.

Bundesamt für Verfassungsschutz. (2016). Psychologische Erklärungsansätze zum brutalen Vorgehen der Jihadisten in Syrien und im Irak. *Schlaglicht 5*. Cologne.

Burke, J. (2015). *The new threat: The past, present, and future of Islamic militancy*. New York: The New Press.

Cockburn, P. (2014). War with Isis: Islamic militants have army of 200,000, claims senior Kurdish leader. *The Independent*, 16.11.2014. Retrieved January 15, 2019, from http://www.independent.co.uk/news/world/middle-east/war-with-isis-islamic-militants-have-army-of-200000-claims-kurdish-leader-9863418.html

Cockburn, P. (2015). *The rise of the Islamic state: ISIS and the New Sunni revolution*. New York: Verso.

Crenshaw, M. (1983). *Terrorism, legitimacy, and power: The consequences of political violence*. Middletown, CT: Wesleyan University Press.

Daase, C. (2011). Neue Kriege und neue Kriegführung als Herausforderung für die Friedenspolitik. In I.-J. Werkmer & U. Kronfeld-Goharani (Eds.), *Der ambivalente Frieden: Die Friedensforschung vor neuen Herausforderungen* (pp. 21–35). Wiesbaden: VS Springer.

Daase, C., & Spencer, A. (2010). Terrorismus. In C. Masala, F. Sauer, & A. Wilhelm (Eds.), *Handbuch der internationalen Politik* (pp. 403–425). Wiesbaden: VS Springer.

Dearden, L. (2016). Isis executes more than 4,000 people in less than two years. *The Independent*, 30.4.2016. Retrieved January 15, 2019, from http://www.independent.co.uk/news/world/middle-east/isis-has-executed-more-than-4000-people-in-under-two-years-of-the-islamic-state-in-syria-a7007876.html

Der Kurier. (2016). Frankreich: Ein Attentäter trug Fußfessel. *Der Kurier*, 26.07.2016. Retrieved January 15, 2019, from https://kurier.at/politik/ausland/frankreich-geiselnahme-in-kirche-beendet/211.938.127

Die Welt. (2017a). Zahl Islamistischer Gefährder in Deutschland steigt an. *Die Welt*, 2.3.2017. Retrieved January 15, 2019, from https://www.welt.de/politik/deutschland/article162519594/Zahl-Islamistischer-Gefaehrder-in-Deutschland-steigt-an.html

Die Welt. (2017b). Terror in Stockholm. Attentäter war einer von 12,000 untergetauchten Abgewiesenen. *Die Welt*, 10.04.2017. Retrieved January 15, 2019, from https://www.welt.de/politik/ausland/article163602342/Attentaeter-war-einer-von-12-000-untergetauchten-Abgewiesenen.html

Die Zeit. (2016). Anschlag in Würzburg: Asylantrag des Täters blieb wegen Computerpanne unentdeckt. *Die Zeit*, 11.08.2016. Retrieved January 15, 2019, from http://www.zeit.de/gesell schaft/zeitgeschehen/2016-08/wuerzburg-anschlag-attentat-asylantrag-unentdeckt-computerpanne

Diehl, J. (2016). Analyse zu Bekennervideo aus Würzburg. "Märtyrer-Operation gegen Ungläubige". *Der Spiegel*, 20.07.2016. Retrieved January 15, 2019, from http://www.spiegel.de/video/bekenner-video-von-wuerzburg-wird-analysiert-video-1691300.html

Duclos, J. (2016). "Paumé", "saoulé par la France" et déterminé à rejoindre la Syrie: qui est Adel Kermiche, l'un des tueurs de Saint-Etienne-du-Rouvray? *FranceTVInfo*. Retrieved January 15, 2019, from https://www.francetvinfo.fr/faits-divers/terrorisme/saint-etienne-du-rouvray/paume-saoule-par-la-france-et-determine-a-rejoindre-la-syrie-qui-est-adel-kermiche-l-un-des-tueurs-de-saint-etienne-du-rouvray_1565211.html

EUROPOL. (2015). *Changes in modus operandi of Islamic State terrorist attacks*. Review held by experts from Member States and Europol on 29 November and 1 December 2015. Retrieved January 15, 2019, from https://www.europol.europa.eu/publications-documents/changes-in-modus-operandi-of-islamic-state-terrorist-attacks

EUROPOL. (2016). *211 terrorist attacks carried out in EU Member States in 2015, new Europol report reveals*. 20.07.2016. Retrieved January 15, 2019, from https://www.europol.europa.eu/newsroom/news/211-terrorist-attacks-carried-out-in-eu-member-states-in-2015-new-europol-report-reveals

France24. (2016). Anti-IS coalition has killed 22,000 Jihadists since mid-2014. *France24*, 21.01.2016. Retrieved January 15, 2019, from http://www.france24.com/en/20160121-anti-coalition-has-killed-22000-Jihadists-mid-2014-france

Goertz, S. (2017a). Der "Islamische Staat" und seine asymmetrische Strategie gegen westliche Demokratien. *Sicherheit und Frieden, 1*, 29–33.

Goertz, S. (2017b). Analyse der motivation und der psycho-sozialen Konstitution der Foreign Fighters des sog. Islamischen Staates. *Österreichische Militärische Zeitschrift, 3*, 348–352.

Goertz, S. (2017c). Die Gefährdungslage für Deutschland und Europa durch Islamistischen Terrorismus: Analyse der deutschen und europäischen Sicherheitsbehörden. *Kriminalistik, 4*, 10–15.

Goertz, S. (2017d). *Islamistischer Terrorismus: Analyse – Definitionen – Taktik*. Heidelberg: C.F. Müller.

Goertz, S., & Maninger, S. (2016a). Die USA im Kleinen Krieg gegen den Islamischen Staat. *Österreichische Militärische Zeitschrift, 4*, 503–508.

Goertz, S., & Maninger, S. (2016b). Der Islamische Staat als Bedrohung für Europa. *Polizei und Wissenschaft, 4*, 29–42.

Kaldor, M. (1999). *New and old wars: Organized violence in a global era*. Stanford, CA: Stanford University Press.

Kilcullen, D. (2005). Countering global insurgency. *The Journal of Strategic Studies, 28*(4), 597–617.

Klimm, L. (2016). Frankreich: Der Attentäter von Nizza – radikal, kaltblütig und labil. *Süddeutsche Zeitung* 18.07.2016. Retrieved January 15, 2019, from http://www.sueddeutsche.de/politik/frankreich-der-attentaeter-von-nizza-radikal-kaltbluetig-und-labil-1.3084147

Laqueur, W. (1987). *The age of terrorism*. Boston: Little Brown.

Laqueur, W. (1998). *Dawn of Armageddon*. New York: Oxford University Press.

Lohse, E. (2016). Würzburg und Ansbach: Attentäter hatten „seit einigen Wochen" Kontakt zum IS. *Frankfurter Allgemeine Zeitung*, 08.08.2016. Retrieved January 15, 2019, from http://www.faz.net/aktuell/politik/ausland/wuerzburg-und-ansbach-attentaeter-hatten-seit-einigen-wochen-kontakt-zum-is-14377783.html

MDR. (2016). Gewalttaten in Bayern. *MDR*. Retrieved January 15, 2019, from http://www.mdr.de/nachrichten/politik/inland/gewalt-taten-amok-terror-faq-100.html

Mockaitis, T. (2008). *The new terrorism: Myths and reality*. New York: Praeger.

Münkler, H. (2002). *Die neuen Kriege*. Reinbek: Rowohlt.

Neumann, P. (2015). Foreign fighter total in Syria/Iraq now exceeds 20,000; surpasses Afghanistan conflict in the 1980s. *ICSR Insight*, 26.01.2015. Retrieved January 15, 2019, from https://icsr.info/2015/01/26/foreign-fighter-total-syriairaq-now-exceeds-20000-surpasses-afghanistan-conflict-1980s/

Newman, E. (2006). Exploring the "root causes" of terrorism. *Studies in Conflict and Terrorism, 29*, 749–772.

N-TV. (2016). Über 1000 Gefährder in Deutschland? Verfassungsschutz: Haben IS unterschätzt. *N-TV*, 10.04.2016. Retrieved January 15, 2019, from http://www.n-tv.de/politik/Verfassungsschutz-Haben-IS-unterschaetzt-article17429121.html

Nürnberger Nachrichten. (2016). "Mach Foto von Sprengstoff". *Nürnberger Nachrichten*, 29.07.2016. Retrieved January 15, 2019, from http://www.genios.de/presse-archiv/artikel/NN/20160729/-mach-foto-von-sprengstoff/C1554C72C27F4538C1257FFE007F3A64.html

O'Neill, B. (2005). *Insurgency and terrorism: From revolution to apocalypse*. Dulles, VA: Potomac Books.

Prince, S. (2016). New ISIS video shows child soldiers executing & beheading 5 'Kurdish Fighters'. *Heavy*, 26.08.2016. Retrieved January 15, 2019, from http://heavy.com/news/2016/08/new-isis-islamic-state-amaq-news-pictures-videos-kurdish-ypg-peshmerga-execution-beheading-by-boy-child-foreign-soldiers-raqqa-syria-telegram-full-uncensored-youtube-mp4-download/

Shultz, R., & Dew, A. (2006). *Insurgents, terrorists and militias: The warriors of contemporary combat*. New York, NY: Columbia University Press.

Syrian Observatory for Human Rights (SOHR). 29.12.2015. Retrieved January 15, 2019, from http://www.syriahr.com/en/?p=41663

Tinnes, J. (2016). Counting lives lost – Monitoring camera-recorded extrajudicial executions by the "Islamic State". *Perspectives on Terrorism, 10*(1), 78–82.

Tomik, S. (2017). Wer ist der Attentäter von Stockholm? *Frankfurter Allgemeine Zeitung*, 11.04.2017. Retrieved January 15, 2019, from http://www.faz.net/aktuell/politik/ausland/rachmat-akilow-wer-ist-der-attentaeter-von-stockholm-14967761.html

US Department of the Army. (2014). FM 3-24/MCWP 3-33.5. *Insurgencies and countering insurgencies*. Washington, DC.

Weiss, M., & Hassan, H. (2015). *ISIS: Inside the army of terror*. New York: Regan Arts.

Wiegel, M. (2016a). Terror in Frankreich. Die Geburt des "Lumpenterrorismus". *Frankfurter Allgemeine Zeitung*, 13.09.2016. Retrieved January 15, 2019, from http://www.faz.net/aktuell/politik/kampf-gegen-den-terror/festnahme-eines-15-jaehrigen-terrorverdaechtigen-in-paris-14433769.html

Wiegel, M. (2016b). Wie der Mörder des Priesters die Justiz getäuscht hat. *Frankfurter Allgemeine Zeitung*, 27.07.2016. Retrieved January 15, 2019, from http://www.faz.net/aktuell/politik/kampf-gegen-den-terror/anschlag-auf-kirche-wieder-moerder-des-priesters-die-justiz-getaeuscht-hat-14359957.html

# Chapter 6
# Summary: What Is New About New Terrorism?

This book has provided an insight into what is new about the so-called new terrorism and analysed four main aspects in four main chapters:

- The ideology of Jihad
- The areas of interaction, cooperation and fusion of actors of organised crime and international Jihadism on personal, tactical and strategical levels, for example, in the cultivation of drugs, drug trafficking and kidnapping for ransom (KFR)
- The Internet and the telecommunication of the twenty-first century as a central capability of new terrorism
- Strategies and tactics of Jihadist organisations and low-level terrorism of lone operators

What is new to the ideology of Jihad: as mentioned in Chap. 2, Wahhabism, Salafism and Jihadism and their followers share a common global belief system, be it in states of the so-called Second and Third World or in Western democratic states. This special unifying bond can be traced back to the same Islamic-theological roots and their anti-modernism, their rejection of differentiation between private and public life (laicism) and between democracy and the sovereignty of the people and any man-made laws. The contemporary mullahs of the new Jihad of the twenty-first century have internationalised and globalised the theology of the Quranic Jihad and the Jihad of the old mullahs. Since the 1990s—and increasingly after 9/11 and the global war on terror by Western coalitions—the new preachers of Jihad have striven for a strategical and tactical shift in their terrorist targeting, away from the near enemy (non-Islamic regimes in the Middle East) and towards the far enemy (Western states). Abdullah Azzam, Al Maqdisi, Al Zawahiri and Al Suri are all in favour of a radicalised, worldwide Islamist *Umma* of Muslims.

On an operative level, these new preachers—above all Al Suri—are highly welcomed by Jihadists because they have added a new realpolitical level to the theological-Islamic Jihad by aiming at political and military objectives in a reasonable and effective effort/revenue ratio. This includes terrorist hit teams but also the low-level terrorism of lone operators and Jihadist cells. The mullahs of the new Jihad

© Springer Nature Switzerland AG 2019
S. Goertz, A. E. Streitparth, *The New Terrorism*,
https://doi.org/10.1007/978-3-030-14592-7_6

and new terrorism strategically propagate Jihad as a mass phenomenon and a global insurgency, based on the Islamic-theological principle of Al Wala wa-l-bara and on an Islamist, dualist world view with the dichotomy of "good versus evil" and "friend versus foe". Consequently, this decentralised and individualised new global Jihad (e.g. the terrorist attacks of Nice, Ansbach, Würzburg, Berlin, London, Stockholm and Barcelona in 2016 and 2017) is the operational component and tactical realisation of the new mullahs' theology and doctrines for the new Jihad.

The increase of Jihadist suicide attacks is another indicator of new terrorism. The analysis of the "Suicide Attack Database" in Chap. 2 has shown that Jihadist suicide attacks increased significantly after 9/11 and that Jihadist suicide attacks have become a regular operational tool of Islamist terrorism as a tactical game changer.

Referring to the aforementioned aspects of new terrorism on the level of interaction, cooperation and fusion of (regional and transnational) organised crime and international Jihadism, it can be summarised as follows: since the end of the Cold War, the boundaries between war, terrorism and organised crime have become blurred. In the small wars in the Middle East, they fell apart completely. As mentioned in Chap. 3, both transnational organised crime and international Jihadism continue to benefit from ongoing conflicts, wars and the undermining and dissolution of state structures, weak states and failed states in regions such as North and West Africa, East Africa, the Middle East, the Balkans or South and Central Asia. In these conflict regions, actors of organised crime and Islamist terrorism benefit from governance vacua and take over state functions of governance themselves. Both transnational organised crime and Islamist terrorism play a vital role in disintegration cycles which enhance state fragility by creating parallel structures, for example, on the level of economics and inner and outer security.

On the analytical level of characterising new common features, it can be observed that both phenomena—organised crime and international Jihadism—adapt to current trends by using tactics and constituting principles of network structures, outsourcing and autonomous cell structures which make it harder to detect and eliminate them. In addition, the supply chains and networks of both phenomena are quite similar, and in many cases, they are led by the same people. The analysis of drug cultivation and trafficking from Afghanistan to Western Europe has shown the complexity of these global and hybrid networks, groups and cells of the new terrorism: the analysed drug terrorism network, consisting of the Haqqani network, regional Taliban and Al Qaida, is a hybrid fusion of regional and international actors, which benefits from common capacities and capabilities in the areas of weapons, personnel, education, transport routes and tactics. Protection money and revenues from the cultivation and trafficking of opium enabled the Taliban, the Haqqani network and Al Qaida to destabilise Afghanistan and neighbouring countries through assassinations and kidnappings and by attacking international state and economical actors.

The analysis of the hybrid actors Ansar Dine, Al Mourabitoun, Al Qaida in Islamic Maghreb, the D-Company, the LeT and the Haqqani network showcases their hybrid dual strategy of terrorist attacks, assassinations and kidnapping for ransom as operational means to reach political and economic goals in order to weaken regular governmental structures and take advantage of the resulting governance vacua. The actors of new terrorism largely depend on conflicts, small wars and the collapse of state and economical structures which provide the black and grey markets needed for their business. Consequently, it is part of their strategy to maintain and even extend these black and grey markets by perpetuating the socio-economic conditions of small wars.

As analysed in Chap. 3, the interaction, cooperation and fusion of actors, tactics and means of Jihadism and organised crime are major threats to the democratic Western world and for human security in conflict regions worldwide as they perpetuate small wars, civil wars and violent conflicts and thereby cause mass migration of thousands or even millions of people. The new terrorism with its Islamist and Jihadist ideology serves as a basis for decentralised local and regional groups but also for networks of developed organised crime which cooperate, interact and merge with international terrorist groups.

Another analytical category that shows the comprehensive approach of new terrorism is the ability to effectively use the latest and most up-to-date technological innovations and the Internet; worldwide communication and a multidirectional exchange of the Jihadist ideology through new technological channels and devices have boosted their interoperability. The Jihadist ideology and its mullahs and organisations, the "Islamic State", Al Qaida, but also hundreds of thousands of individuals take advantage of the technological developments of the Internet and social networks. As shown above, thousands of Jihadist websites are promoting the Jihadism of the twenty-first century to become the new terrorism: for the first time in history, this new terrorism can radicalise and indoctrinate the Muslim *Umma* worldwide by technical means.

The hundreds of thousands to millions of websites with Islamist and Jihadist content represent a new aspect of new terrorism. Through personalised, individual Islamist, Jihadist narratives, the phenomenon of "hyper-radicalisation" can be observed (Goertz, 2017). For the first time in history, Jihadist ideology, quotations from the Quran and the Hadiths and Jihad interpretations by old and new mullahs create a ubiquitous and omnipresent mixed content on the Internet that is available to anybody free of charge. This ubiquitous dissemination of Jihadist ideology has reached a historical height and a new level of totalitarianism that enables the (imagined) *Umma* of the Muslims—de facto existent or subjectively imagined—to connect worldwide. This has already created a new potential for mobilisation and radicalisation, and it will increase further in the future. For the first time in the history of mankind, a global ideology has the technological capabilities which new terrorism possesses today.

Further features of what is new about new terrorism can be found in the analysis of the level of psychological warfare. Jihadist propaganda content is communicated with the help of the Internet—especially through social media—according to the terrorist logic of spreading fear. It is again a novelty in history that Jihadist aesthetics of violence, for example, pictures of mutilated bodies and detailed clips of executions, are shared a million times on numerous websites—without the international community or single states being able to completely contain them.

Modern technology offers international native Jihadists from Western states and a worldwide audience the opportunity to communicate in real time with Jihadists in combat from theatres of war. By doing so Jihadists are able to conduct all kinds of information, disinformation, propaganda and deception campaigns in order to influence their followers' perception of conflicts and interests on an operative and strategical level.

Regarding the change in tactical and strategical thinking of new terrorism, the Jihadist attacks in Europe between 2015 and 2017 have shown that Western democracies and their security authorities have to prepare for more heterogeneous threats. The Islamist and Jihadist content on the Internet (Chap. 4) provide thousands of Islamists and (potential) Jihadists with operational and tactical instructions for terrorist attacks. They vary from kitchen knives (Safia S. in Hannover, Germany, attacking a police officer) to vehicles (Nice, France; Berlin, Germany; London, England; Stockholm, Sweden; Barelona, Spain) to improvised explosive devices (IED) (Ansbach, Germany, and Brussels, Belgium) and also biological warfare agents (viruses, bacteria). Due to the ubiquitous dissemination of terrorist footage on Islamist and Jihadist websites and especially on social networks showing successfully accomplished terrorist attacks, there is a significant danger of Jihadist imitators (copycats). The terrorists of Nice (2016), Berlin (2016), London (2017), Stockholm (2017) and Barcelona (2017) all carried out blueprints for terrorist attacks which they found on Jihadist online platforms of Al Qaida and the "Islamic State" (IS), namely, using vehicles as weapons to kill and wound hundreds of people.

What is also new about new terrorism is the quality and quantity of so-called low-level terrorism, as can be seen in the attacks in Europe in the years 2015 to 2018 (attacks with vehicles, knives and improvised explosive devices). Also new is the quantity of potential Jihadist terrorists: the French Ministry of Interior Affairs currently names 15,000 potential French Jihadist terrorists, and the German Ministry of Interior Affairs estimates the number to be around 1600 in Germany. However, these numbers do not include undetected cases. The mere observation of thousands of potential Jihadist terrorists would overstrain the means of European security authorities.

Jihadism in the form of new terrorism constitutes the largest militant, anti-Western, anti-democratic movement worldwide of the present day and in the future. The problem is that this new terrorism is more than a major terrorist organisation with limited political agendas as was the case with the terrorist organisations, groups and cells of the twentieth century. The Jihadism of the new terrorism is backed by a massive supporter movement on every continent, with an average of ten times the number of active Jihadists.

Chapters 2 to 4 show that, although its followers are separated geographically by large distances and social differences (education, job possibilities, life expectancy), new Jihadist terrorism has managed to create two streams which work in close cooperation, thanks to their common ideological bond. To do this, they took advantage of the small wars in Afghanistan, Iraq and Syria at the beginning of the twenty-first century and the game-changing new technologies of the Internet and telecommunication. Due to different economic and social backgrounds of the two Jihadist movements in the so-called Second and Third World on the one hand and the First World on the other hand, the respective radicalisation processes in weak and failing states are different to those in Western democracies. As analysed in Chaps. 2 to 4, various factors—for example, the small wars in the Middle East and the so-called Arabellion or Arab Spring in the Middle East and North Africa—resulted in Salafist and Jihadist narratives, based on the historically new means of communication and the Internet, making a global *Umma* of Muslims and the realisation of a Muslim goal that is more than 1000 years old appear tangible. A contemporary caliphate would be the realisation of a Quranic state model of Mohammed and his followers that is more than 1300 years old. The implication of this narrative for an Islamic State in the twenty-first century should not be underestimated for the Jihadist ideology and its worldwide Salafist and Jihadist milieus.

To repeat, the new terrorism is more than tactical-operative terrorism, a means of terrorist organisations. The new terrorism has become a global ideology, with millions of links on Salafist and Jihadist websites. The Jihadist online magazines *Inspire* (Al Qaida), *Dabiq* ("Islamic State") and *Rumiyah* ("Islamic State") as well as the existence of hundreds of thousands of Salafist and Jihadist accounts in social media are further indicators for the new terrorism in the twenty-first century.

As explained in Chap. 2, the preachers of new terrorism have developed the concept of Jihad further, transforming it to comply with modernism or postmodernism and modifying Jihad on the levels of theology, strategy, doctrine and tactics. Low-level terrorism is an operative-tactical means of new terrorism that possesses a historically unsurpassed potential to radicalise the Salafist/Jihadist ideology. A further indicator for new terrorism is the sheer size, the numbers of potential Jihadist terrorists and supporters that threaten security worldwide.

The international Jihad of the twenty-first century has many more followers than the Jihadists of the Afghan War (1980 to 1088). The share of foreign fighters in the Afghan Jihad of the 1980s was never higher than 5% (Burke, 2015: 40). But already in 2014, more than 20,000 international Jihadists (foreign fighters)—later more than 30,000—joined the IS in Syria and Iraq. The Jihad against the Soviet troops in Afghanistan was to 95% an Afghan Jihad, consequently never a truly international Jihad. But, as shown in Chap. 5, the IS possessed up to 60,000 fighters in 2014 and 2015 (with differences concerning the level of education and war experience) (Neumann, 2015). In other words, we can say that more than 20,000 international Jihadists (foreign fighters) of 50,000 to 60,000 irregular fighters of the IS represented approximately 33% or more in total, which is an indicator for a truly international Jihad, a Jihad of the twenty-first century.

Next to the new quantitative level of the new terrorism is the qualitative level: first of all, the combat experience of the fighters of IS and Al Qaida is based on years of small war activities (since 2001 in Afghanistan, since 2003 in Iraq, since 2010 in Syria) which implies a tactical knowledge of house-to-house fighting, attack, defence and terrorist tactics like ambushes and IEDs, which have reached a historically high level.

Secondly, the new Jihadists can pass on actual combat experience and knowledge to hundreds of thousands of potential Jihadi terrorists, both directly, on social media and thousands of websites. The resulting Jihadi potential poses a serious threat to the inner security of democratic states. In addition to the operative-tactical level, there is the ideological, psychological and theological level of new terrorism, of a new Jihadi *Umma* that is globally connected. New technologies like the Internet create an abundance of new possibilities and means for Salafists and Jihadists, as supporters and sympathisers.

Contemporary reports on the Afghan Jihad of the 1980s hardly mentioned the international Jihadists (5% in the Afghan Jihad). But the high number of international Jihadists of the "Islamic State" will have a significant snowball effect on future generations of Jihadists and Jihadi supporters. The following number illustrates the extent of the threat, which the new terrorism poses to human security worldwide: in the 10 years from 2001 to 2011, more than 250,000 people were killed worldwide in conflicts related to the new terrorism (Burke, 2015: 502–505).

An additional new feature is the connection of new terrorism to the so-called Arabellion or Arab Spring in numerous countries, for example, Egypt, Algeria, Iraq, Syria, Yemen, Jordan, Libya, Tunisia, Mauretania, Oman and Saudi Arabia (Cavatorta & Merone, 2016; Lynch, 2016). The so-called Arabellion or Arab Spring caused various small wars which led to huge Jihadi movements and a Jihadi participation in those small wars.[1] Connected with the so-called Arabellion is the refugee crisis which started in 2015, causing hundreds of thousands of people to flee to Western Europe. Many Jihadi attacks in Europe from 2015 to 2018 were perpetrated and/or supported by Salafists and Jihadi terrorists who came to Europe posing as refugees. Despite the fact that the "Islamic State" has lost up to 95% of its territory, its legacy of a contemporary caliphate will last for many years. Its Salafist/Jihadist ideology cannot be defeated by military means.

This analysis has examined the new terrorism on the levels of ideology, cooperation of actors of organised crime and international terrorism and technology (foremost the Internet) and on the level of strategy and tactics. In the future, political science as well as international relations, law and Middle East regional studies will have to examine this phenomenon on various levels. Furthermore, it will be the responsibility of the security authorities to identify and analyse the interaction and connection of numerous levels of the new terrorism as a matter of priority. To ward off the terrorist threat, this first step should be followed by a second, involving counter terrorist strategies and tactics and requiring Western democracies to sensitise and rethink their security architecture.

# References

Anderson, L. (2011, May/June). Demystifying the Arab Spring: Parsing the differences between Tunisia, Egypt, and Libya. *Foreign Affairs, 90*(3), 2–7.

Beinin, J., & Vairel, F. (2011). *Social movements, mobilization, and contestation in the Middle East and North Africa*. Stanford, CA: Stanford University Press.

---

[1]More elaboration on the Arab Spring, see Anderson (2011), Beinin and Vairel (2011), Brownlee, Masoud, and Reynolds (2013), Lutterbeck (2013), Tausch (2013).

Brownlee, J., Masoud, T., & Reynolds, A. (2013). *The Arab Spring: The politics of transformation in North Africa and the Middle East*. Oxford: Oxford University Press.

Burke, J. (2015). *The new threat: The past, present, and future of Islamic militancy*. London: Vintage.

Cavatorta, F., & Merone, F. (2016). *Salafism after the Arab awakening*. London: Hurst.

Goertz, S. (2017). *Islamistischer terrorismus: Analyse – Definitionen – Taktik*. Heidelberg: C.F. Müller.

Lutterbeck, D. (2013). Arab uprisings, armed forces, and civil-military relations. *Armed Forces & Society, 39*(1), 28–52.

Lynch, M. (2016). *The New Arab Wars. Uprising and anarchy in the Middle East*. New York: Public Affairs.

Neumann, P. (2015). Foreign fighter total in Syria/Iraq now exceeds 20,000; surpasses Afghanistan conflict in the 1980s. *ICSR Insight*, 26.01.2015. Retrieved January 15, 2019, from http://icsr.info/2015/01/foreign-fighter-total-syriairaq-now-exceeds-20000-surpasses-afghanistan-conflict-1980s/

Tausch, A. (Fall 2013). A look at international survey data about Arab opinion. *Middle East Review of International Affairs, 17*(3), 57–74.

CPSIA information can be obtained
at www.ICGtesting.com
Printed in the USA
LVHW032123130519
617655LV00008B/179/P